The History
of Rockville Centre

PRESTON R. BASSETT

AND

ARTHUR L. HODGES

Salisbury Printers, Uniondale, New York

1969

Preface

AT THE TIME OF PLANNING for the 75th anniversary of the incorporation of the Village of Rockville Centre, it was suggested that a history of the Village would be a most appropriate contribution to the occasion. Strangely enough no history of the Village had ever been written, and all that existed were a few scattered articles and the reminiscences of some of the old timers. The standard histories of Long Island give Rockville Centre scant mention, in a few paragraphs only. This is due not only to lack of information but also to the fact that its incorporation was of comparatively late date.

Arthur Hodges, our present Village historian, gladly took up the project and asked me, since I had been his predecessor in that office, if I would collaborate with him. This I was pleased to do, and it has been a happy arrangement, as our interests in the background of the Village are, fortunately, complementary. My interest started with the geology of the South Shore and its effect on the early history of the region, from the Indians to the old mill operators and the earliest settlers. Arthur Hodges, on the other hand, as editor of *The Nassau Daily Review* for many years, has had first-hand knowledge of the growth of the Village, the development of its government, and its outstanding public services. He has also known personally most of the men who have played important parts in the last half-century of the Village.

We hope that our joint effort will have filled the need for a history of the region which is comprehensive in both place and time. The story covers the Mill River area rather than just the Village. In time, it covers over 300 years instead of just the 75 years since the incorporation that we are celebrating.

PRESTON R. BASSETT

Table of Contents

Illustrations

Acknowledgments

THIS HISTORY OF ROCKVILLE CENTRE is a story of the evolution of the village and development of its environs since the white man first came to the area more than 325 years ago.

We have tried to report the significant highlights and romantic aspects of three centuries in a manner that will hold the reader's attention without getting him bogged down in endless details and dates that are available in public records but are of little general interest. Inevitably we have missed some episodes that could appropriately have been included, as many have participated in the progress that has been made since 1643.

There have been two principal sources of information for the authors in compiling this history—the bound files of old newspapers published in the area and the minutes of the Rockville Centre Village Board since the village was incorporated in 1893.

James E. Stiles, the late publisher of the *Nassau Daily Review-Star*, acquired bound files of several old weekly newspapers, published respectively in Hempstead, Freeport and Rockville Centre, as he was assembling the weekly newspapers that were merged to form the *Nassau Daily Review*. He placed a high value on these old files, appreciating their historic importance, so that eventually they were given, in excellent condition, to the Nassau County Museum by the *Long Island Press* after it had acquired the *Nassau Daily Review-Star* and merged the two newspapers.

More than twenty years ago Mr. Bassett spent many Saturdays in the library of the *Review-Star* pouring over these old files. Arthur Hodges, as editor of the *Review-Star*, referred to them regularly over a quarter of a century.

The authors are indebted to many individuals and organizations for additional information of value. We have the records and minutes of churches, various organizations and special items of historical value made available as we were preparing this history.

We wish to acknowledge our appreciation for the many old pictures sent to us by individuals, including Former Village President Edwin G. Wright, the families of several former mayors and village presidents and photographs of former officers of the Bank of Rockville Centre, the first bank on the South Shore, loaned to us by W. Vance Kniffin of Chemical Bank New York Trust Company. Mr. William K. Harrison, librarian of the Rockville Centre Public library, was keenly interested and helped us in many ways.

We are also indebted to Rockville Centre village officials and employees who co-operated in helping us assemble data of an essential nature. Mayor John A. Anderson and members of the Village Board showed their keen interest in the project by placing an advance order for 500 copies of the history to help finance its publication. We are grateful to all of the several hundred individuals who also placed advance orders for the history. This gave it the aspect of a civic project in which many could participate to advantage.

We could never have accomplished this without the enthusiasm and sustained interest of Former Village Trustee Charles V. Day, who as chairman of Rockville Centre's 75th Anniversary Committee, handled the advance sale and collaborated in many details involved in planning the publication and distribution of the history.

We were fortunate also in having as printers and publishers Mr. and Mrs. Bernard Belinky, of Salisbury Printers, well known to both of the authors, who took a keen personal interest in helping us plan an attractive format for presenting our story.

ARTHUR L. HODGES

The History
of Rockville Centre

CHAPTER I

The Indians

THE WHITE MAN'S HISTORY of the region between the Hempstead Plains and the Rockaways, which includes what is now Rockville Centre, started very suddenly during the last few months of the year 1643. It was at that time that the peaceful tribe of the Rockaway Indians received their first formal calls from white men. Quite by coincidence there were two separate expeditions that visited the Rockaway Indians within a few months of each other. The first was a small group of Dutchmen led by DeVries, whom Governor Kieft of New Amsterdam had sent out to make an agreement with them for peaceful coexistence and mutual protection. DeVries was pleasantly surprised not only to be admitted to the Indian village, but to be welcomed and entertained by the Sachem Tackapousha.

As the only existing account that has come down to us of the village of the Rockaway Indians is in DeVries' report, we quote:

> At evening we arrived at Rechqua Akie where we found the chief, who had one eye, with two or three hundred Indians and about thirty houses. They led us into his house and treated us as to what they had as oysters and fish that they catch there.

The houses mentioned were undoubtedly the typical 'long houses' which the Indians of this region constructed of bowed saplings sheathed with bark. They looked like Quonset huts. However, they were made long enough so that each house could accommodate from ten to twenty persons. A fair estimate, therefore, of the village population, counting squaws and children, would be about 500 total.

In December 1643, only a few months after DeVries' successful visit, a second group appeared at the Rockaway village to see

Tackapousha. These men were Englishmen who had come over to Long Island from Stamford, Connecticut. Their mission was quite different from that of DeVries. They were scouting for a new place to settle and had authority to purchase suitable land if they could find it. Their story is one of restlessness. The story starts in 1630 when, in one of the many ships that followed the Mayflower to Massachusetts, the Reverend Richard Denton and his flock arrived from England and settled in Watertown near Boston. By 1634, however, Denton and his followers left Watertown and pushed down into the Connecticut wilds, settling the town of Wethersfield. There they stayed until 1641 when, once again, they moved on to found Stamford, Connecticut. The best explanation of the Reverend Denton's restlessness is a comment by Cotton Mather that he was a very independent man and could brook no interference or controversy.

No sooner had they built their Stamford homes than, gazing at the rolling hills across Long Island Sound, they thought "the grass looked greener" on the other side, so it was in 1643 that Denton dispatched Robert Fordham and John Carman to look the country over and to negotiate with the Indians. They sailed across Long Island Sound, landing in one of the pleasant North Shore bays, most likely the present Hempstead Harbor. From there they started on foot through the thickly wooded Roslyn hills. On inquiry of some of the scattered Manhasset or Matinecock Indians, who occupied that region, they were told to proceed south across the Island, and that they would find the Sachem Tackapousha at his village in Rockaway. Undoubtedly the North Shore Indians were rather anxious to pass these unwelcome visitors on to their South Shore neighbors.

So Fordham and Carman proceeded southward through the rugged forested hills until they came to the region which is now Mineola. Here both the hills and the woods stopped abruptly and they gazed in awe across a vast level grassy plain. Never in all their travels through New England had they seen anything like this: a readymade pasture for grazing sheep and cattle.

Little did they realize that they were standing on the terminal moraine of the great ice sheet that at one time covered all of the northern part of America, including all of New England. The great meadow which stretched out before them was the out-wash plain formed when the glacier melted. The water from the melting ice formed countless rivulets which flowed toward the ocean. These streams carried large quantities of sand from the moraine and spread it evenly over all of what is known as the Shore Shore. The streams were not swift enough to carry stones or boulders, hence there are no rocks to be found on the south shore.

Fordham and Carman crossed the four miles of grassy plains hoping to find water. Just as they came to the southern border they found it. Two small streams, less than a mile apart, joined together just at the edge of the south woods and, as one larger stream, flowed southward into a long swamp and disappeared into the thick south woods. This would be an ideal location for their new village. It had extensive pasture, good water, and isolation from other settlements. Even the Indians did not live on the plains but preferred to live near the shores.

With this town spot in mind, which was soon to become Hempstead, they hurried on through the south woods following the Indian trail which skirted the edge of the long swamp, probably about where Peninsula Boulevard now runs. The long swamp is now the Hempstead Lake Reservoir. After traveling about three miles down the swamp trail, they came to the Indian village right in the vicinity that 200 years later, became Rockville Centre. They found Tackapousha and must have spent several days there as Tackapousha called in the chiefs of the nearby tribes, the Marsapeagues and the Merricokes to negotiate with the Englishmen. Tackapousha appears to have been the head chief of all three tribes.

On Dec. 13, 1643 Tackapousha and six other chiefs signed a deed which reads in part as follows:

> Be it known by all men by these presents that we the Indyans of Marsapeague Merricoke and Rokaway . . . have sold unto Robert ffordham and John Carman, Englishmen, all that half part of the Great Plains, lying toward the south side of Long Island, to be measured by a straight line from our present town plott Nortward, and from the North End of the line, to run with a right line East and West to the uttermost limits of itt (the Great Plain), and from both ends to run down with a straight line to the South Sea; with all the woodlands, meadows, marshes, pastures and appurtenances thereunto belonging, to have and to hold to them and their heirs and assigns forever. . . .

This was indeed a large tract of land. It encompassed all the southern half of what is now Nassau County. Unfortunately we have no record of what Fordham and Carman originally agreed to pay for it. There is reason to believe, however, that the pay was quite inadequate because, a dozen years later, Governor Nichols of New York wrote to the magistrates of the Town of Hempstead, suggesting that they "pay Tackapousha further gratuities for payment of lands which he said were bought too cheap. It would be best you pay more and prevent trouble and settle it once for all." The magistrates apparently took the governor's advice, for the records show that in 1657 seven of the magistrates met with Tackapousha and his chiefs and renegotiated. The Indians were hard to please but Mr. Gildersleeve, one of the magistrates, reported that the payment which was finally agreed on, consisted of: "sum great cattle, and sume small cattle, and sume wampum and sume hatchets, sume knives, sume trading cloth and I think they had some powder and led and they went away for anything I know very well satisfied." The total value was about 42 pounds.

Tackapousha was evidently finally satisfied, as some years later he paid another visit with twenty of his Indians to Governor Nichols and told him that he had no particular business except to declare his friendship and to say he was glad to see all things well. He even presented the governor with a large string of white wampum.

At no time did the Hempstead fathers ever attempt to dispossess the Indians from their village. In fact they protected them and even allotted them land on which to raise their corn and beans. For almost fifty years the Indians remained the only inhabitants of the Rockaway Peninsula, for it was not until 1690 that David Cornell built the first house in that region. Hempstead men, however, were allocated land on the peninsula for pasturage or raising crops, though they did not live there. They did fence their land and this caused trouble. The Indians did not understand fences. They considered that they had hunting rights anywhere at any time, so they climbed the fences and with their dogs did much damage to both crops and cattle. In the old Hempstead Town records there are many entries such as these:

> It is ordered that ... yf any Cowes or Horss shall be destroyed by ye Indians or their dogs the whole shall pay for their loss . . . But first they are to try to get recompence from the Indians. Nov. 18, 1659.

It is ordered that Noe Person . . . shall give ore Selle any Kinde of Dooges to the Indians upon the Forfittuer of Fiffty Gillders. Nov. 25, 1661.

A warning note from Peter Stuyvesant to the Magistrates of Hempstead, written in Sept. 1660, gives the Indians' point of view on this problem. He states that Tackapousha has complained to him that "certain inhabitants of Heemsted do enter upon his grounds and make fenses upon his plantings and threaten to burn his houses." Then Stuyvesant adds: "If you do not desist in eight days you must come in with the Sachem and explain to us the reason for your proceedings."

It is commendable that, in spite of the basic misunderstandings as to property rights and the confusion between hunting rights and trespassing, there was no open violence between the settlers and the Indians. The inevitable outcome was, in a way, sadder than a burst of violence—it was slow decimation. Perhaps the best picture that we have as to what was happening to the Long Island Indians was given us by a contemporary eye witness, no less an authority than Daniel Denton, son of the founder of Hempstead.

In 1670 Daniel Denton published in London a little pamphlet entitled "Brief Description of New York formerly called New Netherland." It was the first publication in English to give details of Long Island. In it he states as follows:

To say something of the Indians, there is now but few on the Island, and those few no way hurtful but rather serviceable to the English, and it is to be admired, how strangely they have decreast by the Hand of God, since the English first settling of those parts; for since my time, where there were six towns, they are reduced to two small villages, and it hath been generally observed, that where the English come to settle, a Divine Hand makes way for them, by removing or cutting off the Indians either by Wars one with the other, or by some raging mortal Disease.

It was, in fact, small pox and measles, diseases unknown to the Indians until they were inadvertently brought into the New World by the European settlers. Both diseases had a high rate of mortality among the Indians and caused their numbers to dwindle rapidly. Undoubtedly Rockaway Village was one of the two remaining villages mentioned by Denton. But even that was slowly disappearing, since by 1685 the records note that there are now only ten Indian families in Rockaway Village.

The last of the Indians apparently moved over onto Barnum's

Island and the site of the once prosperous Indian village in Rockville Centre was lost, almost without trace. Its exact location is unknown. There being no stones in the area, the Indians had neither stone hearths nor stone foundations to mark the ancient site. There was one deposit, however, that indicated the location of their prosperous days. This was the great heaps of shells which accumulated where the Indians for many years had discarded them both from their kitchens and from their main industry of wampum making. These large shell deposits were still so conspicuous many years later that, when the village of Rockville Centre started to grow, the street which ran near them was named Shellbank Avenue, a name which it still retains today.

In addition to the shell banks another very significant indication of the importance of this area as an Indian settlement is the number of unusual artifacts that were found in the region about a hundred years ago. Three large copper axes were dug up in Rockville Centre and two were dug up in East Rockaway. Then, in 1862, on the eastern edge of Rockville Centre there was discovered at a depth of three feet a ring of twenty-three flint spear heads, set upright. In the center of this circle were four jasper axe heads and two copper axe heads. This most unusual cache must have had some tribal or religious significance. Some of these axes measured 7 inches by 4 inches, big pieces of copper even by today's standards. But there was no copper within hundreds of miles of Long Island. The axes must have come from the Lake Superior region, a thousand miles away. Algonkin Indians inhabited that region, so it is most likely that there existed trade between the western Algonkins of Lake Superior and the eastern Algonkins of Long Island. Rockaway wampum must have been traded for Lake Superior copper.

Recent studies of the Long Island Indians bring out the fact that their settlements extended over a much longer time than used to be supposed. Excavations on the north shore have exposed artifacts that are several thousand years old and it is estimated that even the Rockaway Village was occupied by the Indians for many centuries. This is not surprising as it is evident that the site was probably the most desirable along the entire south side of the Island. For a distance of a hundred miles from Coney

Island to Southampton the shore is bordered by a continuous series of salt marshes, bays, and barrier bars such as Fire Island. Throughout almost this entire distance it was necessary to use a boat or canoe to cross the bays or thread the tidal streams in order to reach the ocean beach.

There was one small section in this whole length, however, where solid land extended across the marshes and bays directly to the ocean shore. This was the Rockaway Peninsula, the cherished land of the Rockaway Indians. And so, because of its central location, they chose the base of this peninsula for their village. The trail south led directly to the ocean beach where they could gather shells, the trail north ran by the long swamp up to the Hempstead Plains where they could hunt small game; and between the village and the Plains were the South Woods where they hunted big game. East and west of the village were Rockaway Bay and Jamaica Bay where they gathered oysters and clams and caught the fish that DeVries mentions. The location was indeed central for all their needs.

Even their name is derived from a description of their territory —Reckouackie. The Algonkin word 'Reckou' meant 'sandy' and the word 'Acke' meant 'place'. The first white men had considerable trouble both in spelling and in pronouncing this name. DeVries, in his first report, called it Rechqua Akie. The first attempt by the English spelled it Reckouwhackie. After a variety of simplifications, it appears in the old records as Rocoway or Rokaway, but by 1675 the name had been completely anglicized to Rockaway. And so 'the sandy place' became Rockaway, although there is not a rock to be found on the whole peninsula.

The Hempstead settlers seldom mentioned the Indian Village in their records. They referred to the whole peninusla as the Rockaways. By 1665, however, they became more specific and used the terms Nere Rocoway and Far Rocoway. The names were loosely used and merely indicated the distance from Hempstead. Near Rockaway included all the territory that now makes up the villages of Rockville Centre, Oceanside, East Rockaway, and Lynbrook. Far Rockaway included the rest of the peninsula toward the ocean.

The old Sand Hole Church as it appeared in 1874. (From the Brainard Collection at the Nassau County Museum.)

CHAPTER II

How Rockville Centre Got Its Name

At the end of the 17th century, as the last of the Indians retired to Barnum's Island, there were no residents left in Near Rockaway. The Hempstead farmers used the land only for pasturing cattle and growing hay. But this situation did not last long for in 1710 a hardy pioneer by the name of Michael DeMott obtained permission to build a mill 3½ miles south of Hempstead on the stream which flowed through the Long Swamp. This took considerable courage as the 3½ miles intervening were heavily wooded and wolves still roamed in them. But DeMott picked his mill site and started work on the dam, which act fixed the location of Rockville Centre, even though 140 years would intervene before the village was established.

The dam is the one just north of the Long Island railroad tracks as the line enters Rockville Centre. The pond is now called Smith's Pond, but it was Michael DeMott who picked the site. Nothing is known as to how DeMott built the mill dam but there is a piece of local folk lore which is very significant. At the eastern end of the dam, just north of Merrick Road, there is an old cemetery and the site of an old church. The original church structure was built in 1790 and was called the Sandhole church. There was allegedly an extensive sand hole near the church but even in 1790 no one could remember how it got there. It seems most probable that it was from this excavation that DeMott obtained the fill for his dam. Such an early date is corroborated by an entry in the old Hempstead Town Records dated 1725. It is a report on the viewing of a route for a new road on the west side of the swamp from the Plains to the Rockaways. It states in part as follows:

so in Jan. 1725 we viewed and do judge the road necessary,—beginning at ye edge of ye plains, through a lane past John Dorlon's land and from thence . . . down ye course of ye path formerly made by Joseph Langdon to ye brook called Deep River, then over said River to a red oak sapling near the Sand Hoole, the road to go between the Sand Hoole and ye old mill pond . . .

In the intervening 250 years the sand hole has completely filled in and disappeared, the church is gone, and there is nothing left now but the cemetery and the name.

In 1730 Anthony DeMott took over the operation of the mill and continued as the miller for fifty years, until 1780. During this period the Near Rockaway territory was settled by a few scattered farmsteads. When the Revolutionary War started, these settlers, quite out of touch with the rebellious colonists, wanted nothing more than to be let alone. They were for the status quo, which of course made them Tories. As they were uncooperative and were interfering with the local activities of the patriots, they were proving to be a nuisance and George Washington ordered the arrest of some of the leaders.

To escape capture, a group of those who were sought, hid out in the swamp above Anthony DeMott's mill pond. It was said that DeMott signaled to them when there was danger by hanging a sheet from the window of the mill, warning them to stay out of sight.

One Saturday in June 1776, to quote from Onderdonck's "Revolutionary Incidents":—"a party of Whig soldiers went to Hempstead Swamp at the head of DeMott's mill pond to take up some Tories who were hiding there . . . A party of nine of them in two sedge boats were concealed in the swamp at the head of the mill pond. Stephen Rider climbed an oak tree to reconnoiter, when a ball whistled by his head. He saw the smoke whence it came and, a loaded gun being handed to him, he fired and the ball passed through the body of George Smith."

The Tories then surrendered. George Smith was treated by Dr. Searing. The wound was in his shoulder and was not fatal but the skirmish had drawn the first blood spilled on Long Island in the Revolutionary War. Kenneth Roberts, in his novel "Oliver Wiswell," builds this episode into an exciting tale. The site of this skirmish was about where Peninsula Boulevard curves around the Tanglewood Swamp just north of Smith's Pond.

Soon after this episode, however, the British gained control of Long Island and British troops were quartered in Hempstead. During their occupancy two of His Majesty's military surveyors, George Taylor and Andrew Skinner, made an excellent map of the area. It was the first accurate map of the region and shows much of interest. A copy of this map, dated 1781, is in the library of the New York Historical Society.

This map shows four mill ponds on the stream from Hempstead to Rockaway Bay. Two were near Hempstead, about where Southern State Parkway now crosses the Hempstead Reservoir. The third one was Anthony DeMott's in what is now Rockville Centre, and the fourth was a tide mill located in East Rockaway where the stream reached tide water. Two roads are shown running south from Hempstead, one either side of the Long Swamp. They pass through heavily wooded land with no houses except the mills themselves. In those days the road down the west side was called Long Lane, and the one down the east side was called Swamp Road. As time went on and there was more travel on these roads, Long Lane became Ocean Avenue, and the Swamp Road became Old Mill Road.

These roads joined just below DeMott's mill dam and continued down the Rockaway Peninsula to Far Rockaway. Even though the DeMott mill and the tide mill at East Rockaway had both been operating for over fifty years when this map was made, they had not attracted many settlers to the Near Rockaway region. The map shows only about four houses in the area which is now Rockville Centre, about six in Oceanside, thirteen around Pearsall's Corners, now Lynbrook, and a row of four or five houses on the water front of East Rockaway. The total number of residents was less than half of the number that had lived in the Rockaway Indian Village a hundred and forty years earlier.

There were, however, scattered through the Far Rockaway country another twenty farm houses, so that altogether there were enough inhabitants to become interested in establishing a local church. It was too difficult to drive the family four miles through the deep woods along muddy roads to attend the Hempstead churches. So, a few years after the end of the Revolutionary

War, when life was again normal, the Near Rockaway folks decided to build their own church. It was to be nonsectarian so that any group might worship there. They chose a site near the Sand Hole, just east of the old DeMott mill pond. It was about the center of the scattered community, equidistant from Pearsall's Corners, East Rockaway, and Oceanside.

The land was donated by Isaac Denton. The local farmers contributed the materials, and they themselves erected the structure in 1790. It was small, measuring about 20 feet by 30 feet. A single door in front opened directly into the church which had rough movable benches and a gallery across the end over the door. At the farther end was a high pulpit. It was estimated to have cost less than $1,000. Although it was built for use by any denomination, preachers were very scarce and it was used mainly, from the first, by Methodist circuit riders. Within a few years it was considered to be a Methodist church and became the fourth one established on Long Island. The first three, at Newtown, Searingtown, and Commack, had all been founded only a few years earlier, between 1785 and 1789.

The first rider appointed to the Long Island circuit was the Reverend Ezekial Cooper. In one of his reports he comments:

> The people of Searingtown are somewhat more wealthy and intelligent than those of Near Rockaway but are destitute of the knowledge of Christ.

An idea of the rugged life led by these circuit riders can be gained from the following quotation from the diary of the Reverend Mitchel Bull:

> Sunday, May 10, 1806, stopped at David DeMott's house, preach at Near Rockaway 10:30 AM, preach at Lester Raynor's (Freeport) 3 PM. Mon. May 11, preach at Elijah Chichester's, Amityville. May 12, preach at William Allaby's, Babylon. May 13, preach at Widow Week's. May 14, rest and visit.

Such was the religious life of the South Shore. The little Sandhole Church served the community for twenty-seven years before it burned down in 1817. It was replaced by a larger structure which served several more generations until it burned and was replaced again with a third structure which stood until 1914 when it also was destroyed by fire. By that time, however, its usefulness had long since gone. Both Rockville Centre and Pearsall's Corners had grown to the point where each wanted its own Methodist church.

In 1870 it was decided to establish two new churches, St. Mark's in Rockville Centre and St. James' at Pearsall's. The Sandhole Church was to be used only for burial services or special occasions. So it fell into disuse and was practically abandoned after a century's service to the community.

In 1780 Anthony DeMott retired as the miller after fifty years of faithful service, and Israel Smith became the new owner and operator. Israel's greatgrandfather, John Rock Smith, had been one of the original Hempstead settlers who had come over with the Reverend Richard Denton from Stamford. Israel was 51 years old when he started to run the mill so he was very happy to take on his 15 year old son, Mordecai as his apprentice, to assist him in the strenuous activity. Mordecai was a bright, industrious, and pious youth. He learned to be a good miller while in his early twenties. He was also a regular attendant at the Sandhole Church, and his interest grew until he was soon pinch-hitting as preacher when the circuit rider didn't appear. By 1825 he was called the Reverend Mordecai Rock Smith.

Israel lived until 1806. He was 77 years of age when he died, Mordecai had been running the mill for some years but in 1806, after his father's death, he became the owner. The mill pond was no longer called DeMott's Pond but became known as Smith Pond, a name it still holds today. Mordecai became the leading citizen of the community. He filled many offices: was justice of the peace, as well as being the preacher and the miller. He had also added wool carding and fulling machines to his grist mill, and in his later years he even ran a country store adjacent to his mill. His activities became the center of the community.

It could not yet be called a village, and news or excitement was rare in its placid existence. It was seldom mentioned in the records or news of Hempstead. The old New England expression of "going to mill or to meeting" applied very well as there was nowhere else to go.

There were, however, during these quiet years, a few events worth recording. The year 1816 was one of extreme hardship for the farmers. Frost and snow continued all through the spring and cold weather lasted right through the summer. Few crops ripened, so there was almost no grist to be ground at the mill. It came to be known as "the year without a summer."

In the fall of 1821 a hurricane hit Long Island. The tide rose 13 feet in one hour. Along the south shore between Coney Island and Fire Island Inlet, nine Long Island sailing vessels were destroyed with a loss of 21 lives. One of the ships was the schooner Glorian, manned by 'Uncle Josie' Robinson, which foundered off Rockaway Beach. It was carrying cordwood to New York City. Uncle Josie placed a piece of cordwood under each arm and managed to ride in through the surf, and lived to tell the tale. He was the hero of the day.

In the unusually cold winter of 1836–1837 there were, however, two tragic shipwrecks on the Rockaway shore that occurred within seven weeks of each other. The casualties totaled 188. Both were American ships bringing immigrants from England to New York, The ship 'Bristol' was wrecked on Nov. 20, 1836, The barque 'Mexico' on Jan. 3, 1837.

A Currier & Ives Print of the Wreck of the "Mexico" at Point Lookout in 1837. This was said to be the first shipwreck print ever published by Currier & Ives.

There have been numerous accounts of these disasters, but the following quotations are from a little known publication which was written shortly after their occurrence and published in 1840 by S. A. Howland. It is entitled "Recent Shipwrecks and Other Disasters at Sea." Under the section on 'Shipwreck of the Bristol' it states:

> The ship Bristol sailed from Liverpool Oct. 15, having on board a crew of sixteen men, including officers, and about one hundred passengers, chiefly emigrants. She had a fair passage across the Atlantic, and was off Sandy Hook at 9 o'clock on Saturday night, Nov. 20, with her lanterns out as a signal for a pilot; at which time the gale had just commenced. No pilots, however, were out, and the ship was obliged to stand off. About 4 o'clock on Sunday morning she struck on Far Rockaway, and at daylight, though within half a mile of shore, owing to the heavy sea, no relief could be afforded to the distressed passengers and crew, who were clinging to the shrouds and other parts of the rigging; during the day many lost their hold and were drowned. About 11 o'clock at night, the sea somewhat abating, some boats went to her relief, and succeeded in taking off the captain, a portion of the crew, and some of the passengers. The captain was the last to leave. All were rescued who were still clinging to the wreck when the boats reached it, but during the night the ship went to pieces, and the next morning her stern-post was all that remained.
>
> Here was a ship within five miles of her port, and making every exertion to procure a pilot, and yet no pilot was to be had; and the gale subsequently coming on, caught her so much in-shore that it was impossible to claw off, and the fatal result was the destruction of the vessel, and the sacrifice of many human beings.

On October 23d, 1836, only a week after the Bristol had sailed from Liverpool, the barque Mexico set sail from the same port. It, however, had an ill-starred trip right from the start. It ran into storms, head winds and high seas which prolonged the voyage to 69 days, or twice the time it had taken the Bristol. The delay had caused provisions to run low so the 112 passengers were on short rations. They arrived finally at Sandy Hook on the night of Dec. 31st, and early the next morning signaled for a pilot. The weather, however, had become extremely cold and a northwest gale with heavy snow sprang up. No pilot made an appearance.

> The Barque was blown out to sea. Six of the crew were badly frost-bitten, the captain, mate and two seamen were all that were left to hand and reef the sails.

For three days the ship was buffeted until on January 2nd, having been driven eastward along the coast, it grounded off the beach about opposite Christian Hook. As the hulk pounded on the beach it finally filled with water and the captain ordered all passengers on deck and cut away the foremast. Waves were breaking over the ice-covered deck, and the half-starved, half-frozen passengers huddled together, clinging to each other, in sight and hearing of the people on shore who were powerless to give aid. During that terrible day and night one hundred and eight persons froze to death. More than half of them were women and children.

The next morning Raynor R. Smith, the famous wrecking master and his crew of life savers dragged a boat two miles across the ice and frozen marshland to the beach and launched it in the surf whose fury had somewhat lessened. They just managed to save the captain and seven men who still survived and were clinging to the bowsprit. However, the sea was too rough to make more than the one trip.

The succeeding day sixty of the frozen bodies were gathered from the beach and piled like cordwood on sleds. They were carried to the barn of John Lott where they were laid in rows for identification. The following description is quoted from a letter written by a New York gentleman who visited the barn the following day.

> In half an hour we came to Lott's Tavern some four or five miles from the beach where the ship lay,—I went out to the barn. The doors were open and such a scene as presented to my view I never could have contemplated. Sixty bodies of all ages were lying before me on the floor, all frozen, and as solid as marble. Some with their hands clenched as if for warmth, and almost everyone with an arm crooked as it would be in clinging to the rigging.
>
> There were scattered about among the number five or six beautiful little girls, their cheeks and lips as red as roses, with their calm blue eyes open as though they were about to speak. On the arms of some were the impressions of the rope which they had clung to,—the mark of the twist deeply sunk into the flesh. There were a brother and sister locked in each other's arms. One little girl was raised on tiptoe and had frozen just in that position. It was an awful sight. And to observe the stout rugged sailors who could endure so much hardship,—here they lay, masses of ice.

The shocked inhabitants of the Rockaways immediately made plans for the burial of the unidentified bodies from both of the disasters. A lot 35 feet by 161 feet was set aside in the Sandhole cemetery. It was called the 'Mariners' Lot.' A long common grave was prepared and 139 bodies, the victims of both disasters, were buried in two extended rows. It was then decided to mark the site with a suitable monument. The funds were raised in several different ways. The nucleus of the fund consisted of all the money that had been found on the bodies of the victims. This was supplemented by contributions from the residents of the Rockaways. All of Queens County was then solicited. One distinguished citizen of Hempstead offered to make a liberal contribution if he were permitted to compose a verse which would be carved on the monument. The committee approved and the following verse, still readable on the monument, has brought considerable notoriety to the cemetery.

> In this grave from the wide ocean dost sleep
> The bodies of those that had crossed the deep
> And instead of being landed safe on the shore
> On a cold frosty night they all were no more.

As soon as the twelve-foot marble shaft had been dedicated on October 26, 1840, the 'verse' became a subject of controversy and ridicule. Letters to the press and editorials called it the worst piece of doggerel that had ever been perpetrated. It was urged that the Southside people should remove it as it would be considered an indication of "the ignorance and want of literature of the people among whom it stands in marble reproach."

An editorial in the Brooklyn Daily Eagle states:

> As the epitaph was perhaps the only literary attempt of the author, he doubtless thought it was a masterpiece and the committee were too delicate to refuse it . . . But may some friendly hand remove that epitaph and save his memory from heavy damages!

Fortunately the slender monument still stands intact, the tallest stone in the cemetery and the 'verse' is treasured as an unsophisticated quaint piece of folk lore.

Hardly had the monument to the shipwreck victims been erected than another exciting event hit the community: a flood. It was early spring in the year 1839. The winter had been severe and snow lay deep on the Hempstead Plains. The first week of March brought a sudden thaw, ice dammed the head of Mill River, the ground was frozen, so water accumulated in Hempstead. By March 6th Front Street was under four to six feet of water, stores and homes were flooded. At about noon the ice jam broke and the torrent started down Mill River Valley.

At this time two more mills had been established on Mill River, one by David DeMott at the foot of what is now DeMott Avenue, and the other by Leonard Cornell at what is now Lakeview Avenue. This made a total of six mills on the River, so the situation was alarming. Some unknown hero on horseback raced down the Old Mill Road to spread the alarm.

Mordecai immediately rushed out and opened his flood gates and emptied his mill pond before the torrent arrived. This quick action saved his dam from being washed out. Daniel Tredwell, in his "Reminiscences" states: "When the water broke through the blockade, it rushed down with great fury and carried away all the mill dams on the stream, except Mordecai Smith's."

In 1842 the peculiar wave of Millerism reached even to this isolated region. There was, during that summer, a large encampment of Millerites in the woods between Hempstead and Rockville Centre. They were the followers of William Miller who had announced that the world would come to an end in April 1843 with the second coming of Christ, and that it would be wise for each person to prepare himself for the event. Tents were pitched around the grounds and meetings were held quite like the camp meetings of the Methodists. A small but loyal group became so convinced that, when the fatal day approached in April 1843, they assembled in a barn on the northern edge of Rockville Centre. They were arrayed in ascension robes on the night before the coming of Christ and the world's end. Daniel Tredwell states:

> They spent their last night on earth in praying and singing, and not until the dawn of day did it dawn upon these misguided idiots of the ridiculous spectacle they made in returning to their homes in their most absurd trousseau. Some felt the disgrace keenly. These remained in the barn all day and left under the cover of darkness.

In 1848 Robert Pettit opened a general store on the point of land between the two roads now known as Merrick Road and Lincoln Avenue. The building was a small wooden structure which faced to the west. A wide low porch with one step extended across the front. Behind the store was a large barn which he used for storage.

There were, at this time, thirteen homesteads, each with its own farm, in the area now Rockville Centre, but Pettit was counting on the trade of the entire Rockaway area. He carried farm tools, hardware, boots and shoes, and the staple groceries.

To establish his store as the real center of the area, he quite logically figured that if he could get permission to open a Post Office, he would be filling a most important need in the isolated community. So he applied to Washington and was told he must select a name for the Post Office. Pettit wished to honor the Reverend Mordecai Rock Smith, the outstanding citizen of the community, but this caused unexpected complications. The story of what transpired has since been told with many variations. The most authentic is probably the statement of George D. A. Combes, the first Village Historian of Rockville Centre. He states as follows:

> When the post-office was first established it had to be named. The names of Smithfield, Smithville, Smithtown, and Smithburg were, in turn, suggested and, in turn, rejected by the Federal postal authorities as being already in use, after which the name of Rockville was suggested, 'Rock' being the middle name of the man who was to be honored. This is one of the distinguishing names used by the various families of Smiths on Long Island. Even as early as 1650 these distinctive names were necessary in order to keep the various families separate. But the name Rockville fared no better than the others, as it also was already in use. In final desperation the word 'Centre' was added and, with this addition, the name Rockville Centre was finally accepted by the Postoffice Department.

The following note is appended to the above statement:

> I had this story from my grandmother, Susan Davison Combes, who was a sister-in-law of Robert Pettit, the first postmaster.

There should be added to the above story an explanation as to how the designation 'Rock' came into use. Among the first settlers of Stamford there were several Smiths. It is said that among them one, John Smith, built his house against a huge rock which he used as the back of his fireplace. He came to be known as John Smith Rock or John Rock Smith even before he came from Stamford to Hempstead with Denton's original flock. He brought the name 'Rock' along with him. There is a deed on record, of 1667, stating that John Smith Rock purchased a parcel of meadow land on the north side of a neck called Rockaway.

His descendents were prolific. Mordecai was of the fourth generation, but even at that time there were so many 'Rock Smiths' in the area that they had to be subdivided. The branch of the family that settled around Raynorstown (now Freeport), became known as the 'Raynor Rock Smiths.' It was, in fact, the Raynor Rock Smiths, father and six sons, who were the famous life savers of the South Shore and who were the heroes in rescuing the survivors of the wrecks of the 'Bristol' and the 'Mexico.'

However, Mordecai was the one whom Pettit wished to honor when he selected the name of 'Rockville.' It is surprising that 'Rock' could once again find its way into the naming of this rockless region. First it was the anglicized name of the Algonkin word for 'sandy,' and secondly it was the name of a large unknown rock somewhere in Connecticut.

The archives of the Post Office Department in Washington record the date of the establishment of the Rockville Centre Post Office as January 27, 1849. The Hempstead Inquirer first published the name 'Rockville Centre' in its issue of Feb. 17, 1849 when it announced the new post office. The new name was greeted with little fanfare. Rarely was it mentioned in the Hempstead Inquirer during the next few years except for the annual listing of letters uncalled for, an occasional obituary, or an auction notice such as follows:

> Auction—will be sold at public auction on Wed. Dec. 8, 1852 at 10 AM the movable property of the subscriber, viz, 1 horse, 3 cows, 1 pig, farm wagon, buggy, harness, poultry, hay, oats, potatoes, fence posts, rails, grindstone and house furnishings.
>
> William Pettit, Rockville Centre.

But new projects were stirring which foreshadowed change. Perhaps the most important was the visit of William McAlpine who arrived in the fall of 1851 to take some measurements on the flow of water in the Mill River. This was a much more significant visit than the inhabitants realized. McAlpine was an expert engineer sent out by the Brooklyn Water Works Company to investigate and report on the flow of all the streams of the south shore, from Jamaica to Rockville Centre.

Brooklyn was growing fast and its local well capacity could not keep up with the demands for water. The situation was serious and it was realized that something must be done. The only hinterland to which Brooklyn could turn was Queens County with its many clear streams. So McAlpine was employed to develop a plan and report to the Brooklyn Board of Water Supply. He made measurements on six streams east of Jamaica and found that the largest one was the Mill River which had a flow of 9.9 million gallons a day, even in the dry autumn months. The total flow of all six streams was over 19 million gallons a day, so he proposed that an aqueduct be constructed from Rockville Centre to Richmond Hill, and that the water from all six streams flow into it to be carried to the foot of Richmond Hill where it would then be pumped up to a reservoir on the top of the hill, for distribution to the city of Brooklyn.

His general plan was accepted, and the first piece of real estate purchased by the Brooklyn Water Supply Company was Leonard Cornell's mill pond. The pond was enlarged, a new and more substantial dam was constructed, and it was renamed Hempstead Pond. This is the picturesque pond just north of Lakeview Avenue. The new Peninsula Boulevard now runs along its eastern shore where the Old Mill Road used to be.

Smith's mill pond, being below the level of the aqueduct, was at first of no interest to the water company, but two years later, in 1853, in their continued search for more water, they decided to acquire Smith's pond and put in a pumping station to pump its water up into the aqueduct. Fortunately Mordecai did not live to see this final ending of his mill, for he died in 1852, having run the mill for over sixty years. His son, Parmenas Smith, who had been operating the mill in Mordecai's last years, sold the property to Brooklyn for $11,500.

Mordecai Smith was buried in the Sandhole cemetery. His gravestone is marked simply—"In memory of Mordecai Smith who died October 21, 1852, aged 87 years, 2 months." His memory was honored on Saturday, June 15, 1968, when a bronze plaque was unveiled at his grave with appropriate ceremony.

During the 1840s a new type of road was becoming popular in New York State. It was called a Plank Road. These roads were built by private Companies who collected tolls for their use. The fact that the heavy plank construction greatly diminished the problems of sand, mud, and dust, as the farmers hauled their market wagons to the city markets, made them glad to pay the tolls. It saved them many hours.

In 1852 a group of south shore residents, including Tredwell Davis of Rockville Centre, organized a company called The Merrick and Jamaica Plank Road Company. Their purpose was to make available a good road directly from the south shore farms into the city without the necessity of traveling up to Hempstead in order to use the old Hempstead Turnpike. Bids were opened in June 1852 and soon thereafter work was started on what is now Merrick Road.

So in the first years of the 1850s the quiet little settlement suddenly found itself with a new name, a post office, a new plank road with access direct to the city, and the great activity of the Brooklyn Water Supply Company constructing reservoirs and aqueducts in its midst. A group of farsighted citizens saw great possibilities in the future of the area. In 1854 they organized a small real estate company. As might be expected, Robert Pettit was one of the founders. Their first act was to purchase the Mordecai Smith farm on the edge of the old Smith mill pond which Brooklyn had taken over. They then filed with the Queens County clerk a map of Rockville Centre, showing the old farm broken up into building lots.

The following advertisement was then published in the Queens County papers:

> The subscribers, having purchased the farm of the late Reverend Mordecai Smith on the Merrick and Jamaica Plank Roads, nine miles from Jamaica and three miles from Hempstead Village, offer for sale a large number of building lots 50 feet front and 200 feet deep. The site is one unsurpassed within the state for salubrity of climate and beauty of location. It lies on a natural terrace, commanding an extensive view of the country and the lake lately purchased by the city of Brooklyn as a reservoir for their waterworks. The Rockaway Bay, renowned for its abundance of game and shellfish of all kinds, lies within less than a mile from the village. The property is partially improved, a post officebeing already established and stages pass three or four times to and from the city of New York. Gentlemen wishing a country seat will find it to their advantage to secure lots in said village.
>
>   John P. Rhodes, President
>   Robert Pettit, Treasurer and
>   Julius Auerback, Secretary.

It should be noted that the three or four stages that pass to and from the city were not daily but weekly. A stage went into the city one day and out again the next day.

The Smith farm was laid out to include three streets. The street nearest the pond was named Banks Avenue, the second or middle street was named Center Avenue, and the easternmost street was called Village Avenue. The lots sold well so John P. Rhodes soon acquired the farm of Israel Wright just north of the Smith farm, and divided this also into lots. The two farms together consisted of 100 acres.

Among the earliest purchasers in this new locality were sea captains, both active and retired. One told another of the attractive neighborhood, near enough to smell the ocean and accessible to the great port of New York. Three sea captains from Maine built houses on three corners of a street that crossed Village Avenue at its northern end, and so named it Maine Avenue.

In 1859 a very detailed map of Queens County was published. It was the first map which carried the name of Rockville Centre. On this map the old area which had been known as Near Rockaway is shown as four separate settlements. 'Rockville Centre' is the central one; 'Pearsall's Corners,' now Lynbrook, lies to the east; 'Christian Hook,' now Oceanside, lies to the southwest, and the name of 'Near Rockaway' clings to the little community, now East Rockaway, to the south. Each of these villages consisted of 60 or more houses which, with another 50 houses scattered between them, made a total of about 300 houses in the area.

The entire south shore was growing rapidly. Villages were prospering from Jamaica out to Babylon. It was, in fact, growing much more rapidly than the central part of the Island. But during the 1840s the Long Island Railroad had laid its tracks all the way from Brooklyn to Greenport through the center of the Island, quite inconvenient for the south shore towns. The Southsiders were becoming restless and asked the officials for branch lines to serve their needs. The railroad officials, having a monopoly, were very autocratic and answered that if they wanted to use the railroad they must truck their own freight and stage their passengers up to the main line.

By 1860 the indignant Southsiders had organized to build their

own railroad and would have done so immediately had not the
Civil War, with its financial upsets, come along at just that time.
As soon as the war was over, the project was picked up and pushed
to completion rapidly so that by 1867 there was train service on
the South Shore Railroad from Freeport into Brooklyn.

Another significant event occurred while the railroad was
being constructed. John H. Reed, on June 16, 1865, published in
Rockville Centre the first issue of a newspaper which he called
'The Picket.' The establishment of both a railroad and a newspaper for the community amounted to a Declaration of Indepen-
dence. For over 200 years the Rockaway country had been totally
dependent on its mother village, Hempstead, for its contact with
the world. Now it was on its own. Hempstead, which had been
called 'the 'Town Spot' and 'the 'Hub,' was now just another
neighbor. Rockville Centre joined the Greater New York community on equal terms with many other towns.

CHAPTER III

The Hempstead Reservoir

Bᴇꜰᴏʀᴇ turning to the affairs of the now well established village, the story of the upper reaches of the Old Mill River Valley should be told, as this valley forms an important boundary of the present village of Rockville Centre. When the Brooklyn Water Supply Co. had decided on the project of converting Cornell's and Smith's mill ponds into reservoirs and connecting them to the new aqueduct, everyone thought that the plans were final. So in 1850 an enterprising young man, by the name of William F. Oliver, obtained the rights to build a new mill about a mile above Cornell's Pond.

At this site, Oliver built an unusually large mill three stories high which he advertised as "the Largest Mill on Long Island." In fact, he was a great believer in advertising and the Hempstead Inquirer carried frequent, conspicuous, and informative ads of his activities as a miller for the next 25 years. To quote just one, of August 22nd, 1863, it reads:–

> EAGLE MILLS—Flour from red and white wheat, Rye flour, Graham flour, midlings, fine white meal, yellow meal, Oat meal, corn meal, cracked corn, ground meal, oil meal, oats, rye, wheat, bran, and every variety of mill stuff furnished with dispatch to any part of the village free of expense.
>
> William F. Oliver

Oliver ran his mill until about 1873, at which time the Brooklyn Water Supply Co. still looking for more area in which to impound water for the increasing needs of the city, decided to buy the the entire Mill River Valley all the way up to Hempstead. In this valley they planned to construct a large storage reservoir almost

William F. Oliver's Eagle Mills which stood on the East bank of Mill River opposite end of Eagle Avenue, Lakeview. There was a road across the dam to the mills. (From a contemporary painting by J. Evers of Hempstead, 1865, now owned by Miss O. Langdon, a descendant of William F. Oliver.)

three miles in length. This great engineering project, when finished, completely flooded two mill sites. One was Oliver's mill and the other was a small mill at the foot of DeMott Avenue that had once been operated by Isaac DeMott. The mill sites were forgotten and lost at the bottom of Hempstead Lake for over eighty years.

Then in 1947 Hempstead Lake was temporarily drained so that the causeway for the Southern State Parkway could be constructed across it. (Originally the Southern State Parkway ran around the Southern tip of the lake in a long loop.) The 1947 draining of the lake provided a most unexpected opportunity for the writer (Preston R. Bassett) to attempt to locate the site of Oliver's mill. In the village of Lakeview, on the western side, is a street called Eagle Avenue which runs directly toward the lake. Figuring that Eagle Avenue might well have some past connection with the Eagle Mill I explored the muddy lake bottom in a line extending out from the end of Eagle Avenue. Near the eastern shore there was a rather extensive mound in the lake bottom and digging quickly produced the sought-for-evidence. Among broken bricks there were fragments of red ware, stone ware, and blue Staffordshire pottery; pieces of Sandwich glass, of patterns dating to the 1850's, hand-wrought nails, odd bits of iron and pewter, fragments of pre-Civil War whiskey bottles, and even the bowl and several pieces of the stem of an old clay pipe. There were the butt ends of some heavy planks, probably the walls of the mill sluice-way. So this was all that was left of Oliver's Eagle Mill.

Encouraged by this find, I explored the little settlement of Lakeview in hopes of finding an old resident with a long memory. And there he was. Thomas Rhodes, aged 86 in 1947, who had been born on Eagle Avenue. His memory was remarkable.

Mr. Rhodes remembered the exciting year 1873 when the Brooklyn Water Works started the construction of the Hempstead Storage Reservoir. Groups of workers with oxen and horses were cutting down all the trees and clearing out all the muck and swamp undergrowth. Then in 1874 they tore down Oliver's Mill and on one week-end several steam shovels moved in and scooped away the entire mill dam, including that part of Eagle Avenue. It was a sad occasion, as this was the last of the mills on the old Mill

River, and for the first time in 200 years the steady-flowing stream was not turning a mill wheel.

Davison's Mill down at East Rockaway, at the mouth of the river, was still operating, but that was a tide mill, and not dependent on the flow of the river, so it continued to operate for another generation, until the Twentieth Century made it obsolete. In recent years the old Davison Mill was moved to the grounds of the East Rockaway Village Hall on Atlantic Avenue, where it is now preserved and has been turned into a museum by the Old Grist Mill Society of East Rockaway.

Construction of the Hempstead Storage Reservoir made it necessary to relocate Mill Road, as part of the old route would be flooded when the reservoir filled up. An item in the South Side Observer of April 11, 1873, describes one result of these changes, which were made through the woods that still flourished on both sides of the Mill River Valley:

> An old citizen who used to be well acquainted with the old Mill Road, knowing every inch from Hempstead to Rockville Centre, found himself bewildered the other night. The changes made by the Brooklyn Water Board are so complete that after wandering for some time and finding no familiar spot he was obliged to ask where he was. He thinks modern improvements are a humbug.

This bewildered old citizen, probably the last man who ever got lost between Hempstead and Rockville Centre, wasn't too far wrong. The Hempstead Storage Reservoir almost turned out to be a "humbug."

There was a sharp difference of opinion among the engineers as to its feasibility. William McAlpine, who, 22 years earlier, had laid out the successful aqueduct and pond system, said that dams on the South Shore streams should not be more than eight feet high, or about the height of the old mill dams. But an arbitrary group in the Brooklyn Water Board said the higher the dam the more water you could impound, so they proposed a 22 foot dam which would form a reservoir over two miles long and 20 feet deep, capable of impounding one billion gallons of water. The idea was to fill it during the wet season and then use it during the dry season. Actually the Hempstead Lake is nearly three miles long and was once locally referred to as the "Three Mile Lake."

To appreciate what happened, we must have a basic understanding of Long Island's south shore geology. When the great continental ice sheet started to melt, about 11,000 years ago, its southern edge lay along the line of hills that marks the northern boundary of Hempstead Plains. The streams from the melting glacier carried great quantities of sand and gravel out onto the slope toward the sea, and built the vast outwash plains that make up the broad, flat south shore. These flooding streams formed numerous parallel, shallow valleys across the outwash plains. When the ice had retreated from Long Island the streams ceased to flow, but the shallow valleys remained as fossil valleys, since they have neither eroded nor filled in during the past 10,000 years.

Rainfall, however, sinking onto this pervious sand, built up a vast underground reservoir of water, which is the reason why it is possible to drill a good well at any point on the entire south shore. The water table, which is the top of this underground reservoir, is so near the ground level that these shallow glacial valleys actually dip down into it. So the water oozes up through the valley bottoms and forms swamps, and the swamps drain down the valleys to form the "christal streams" of Daniel Denton. The mill dams and the aqueduct ponds did not noticeably retard this stream flow, but a 22 foot dam would collect water until it was over 20 feet higher than the water table. This pressure of water would reverse the flow, and the water would seep down in to the pervious sands, instead of rising and collecting. In other words, the water would seep out as fast as it ran in, and as a consequence, the reservoir would never be filled to such a height. Even if a rainy day raised its level temporarily, the surplus could not be stored, but would sink into the sand again within a week.

So warned McAlpine and his associates, but the Brooklyn Water Board disagreed, and a contract was let to Kingsley and Keeney to start on the great project. After several years of work and an expenditure of $1,400,000, work was stopped and some tests were made. When the gates were closed, the reservoir started to fill at the expected rate of about 6,000,000 gallons a day, but as the water got deeper the flow decreased alarmingly. After the reservoir was about half full, the next four feet of depth reduced the influx to one seventh. It was apparent that the reservoir could

Mordecai Smith property on Smith's Pond about where Bee Bus Company headquarters now stands. House in foreground is believed to be birthplace of Mordecai Smith. He probably lived in two story white house in background at right, while the building at the left was the barn on the property. Photograph was taken in the days of the glass plate, and the specks showing throughout the picture are on the original in the Brainard Collection at the Nassau County Museum.

never be filled, so they had to compromise by using it at only one-half to one-third of its estimated capacity. McAlpine was right; water would flow out as easily as in, through the sandy bottom of Mill River Valley.

The local people were, however, quite oblivious to Brooklyn's troubles. Whereas there was litigation and hard feelings back in Brooklyn, the south shore citizens had acquired a beautiful lake; migrating ducks by the thousands made it a major stop on their seasonal flights, bridle paths around the shores made wonderful riding. When Brooklyn was finally tied in with New York's Catskill water supply, the Long Island supply became only supplementary. In 1925 the Hempstead Reservoir became Hempstead Lake Park, a splendid open space, a nature preserve with recreational facilities and picturesque roads and trails. No one knows or cares that the lake is only half as deep as it was planned to be. It is beautiful and one of Nassau County's great assets, the finest gift that Brooklyn has contributed to its neighbor, and a most fitting way to preserve permanently the historic old Mill River valley.

In 1967, during another dry spell, the lake again was lowered to a level where the site of the old Isaac DeMott mill could be explored. The newly formed Rockville Centre Historical Society organized a dig and were fortunate in finding one of the original millstones as well as many other artifacts. This millstone was exhibited in 1968 at the Rockville Centre Historic Exhibit in celebration of the 75th anniversary of the incorporation of the Village.

Rockville Centre had other gains through the impact of the building of the reservoir and aqueduct, pond system and pumping stations. Many years later Sunrise Highway was built along the right of way of the old aqueduct or conduit, as it was subsequently called. While the reservoir was under construction young William H. Kingsley of the firm of Kingsley and Keeney met and married one of Mordecai Smith's descendants, presumably a grand-daughter. In later years the Kingsleys became important in Brooklyn, leaders in many civic projects and reputedly at one time part owners of the Brooklyn Eagle. Judge Maurice J. Moore, who served Rockville Centre as police justice for nearly 30 years, as a

Brooklyn attorney used to handle legal matters for the Kingsley family and he reports that they were always proud of their relationship to Mordecai Smith, and probably the most prosperous branch of the family.

Another well known family came to Rockville Centre as a result of Brooklyn's search for water. The late Andrew Edwards, who spent virtually his entire career with the Bank of Rockville Centre, eventually serving as a director and Secretary-Treasurer, was the son of a man who came to Rockville Centre as engineer of the pumping station at Smith's Pond. Andrew Edwards married the daughter of John T. Davison, so important in the early history of the village.

As Brooklyn continued to need more and more water it contracted for another reservoir in the next valley beyond the Mill River Valley, eventually, of course, having ponds at Baldwin, Freeport, Merrick and other south shore villages as far east as Massapequa.

The reservoir to be constructed beyond the Hempstead Reservoir was to have been filled by the next stream over, known as Parsonage Creek. The Brooklyn Water Board gave the contract to a man named Freel who constructed a reservoir immediately east of Long Beach road, south of Seaman avenue and extending all the way down to the Long Island Rail Road. But this reservoir, instead of filling only half full, never had any appreciable amount of water at all. It became known as "Freel's Folly," although old residents of Rockville Centre recall it as the "Dry Reservoir."

When the reservoir failed to hold water the City of Brooklyn refused to pay Freel for his work, said to have cost in the neighborhood of $2,000,000. Freel took the case to court and proved that he had followed the specifications given him by the Brooklyn Water Board. The court held that Freel was entitled to his money. The Brooklyn Water Board had been wrong before and it had still ordered a deep reservoir despite its experience with the Hempstead Reservoir.

The Dry Reservoir remained a wide open space in Rockville Centre all through the 1920's. Enough water gathered in small ponds and puddles to provide good ice skating in Winter. In Summer the boys used to play ball out there and children and adults loved to roam around the area with their dogs. In the 1920's it was used for a brief time as a landing field for small planes.

The City of Brooklyn disposed of the property when it was found that it would never serve the purpose for which it was built. No doubt there were many owners over the years. There was a story in the 1920's that Edwin W. "Daddy" Browning, wealthy New York real estate man who became famous through his marriage to a teen age girl, "Peaches" Browning, owned it at one time. A later owner was Robert West, prominent Rockville Centre resident, whose home stood about where Temple B'Nai Sholom now stands at Hempstead and Lakeview Avenues. Old friends recall that Mr. West was often teased about his purchase of a "white elephant."

The Dry Reservoir, however, covered many acres of land that became more valuable every year. Eventually it became known as Greystone, a real estate development which today must encompass hundreds of homes, so the last owner of the acreage must have found it a very profitable investment.

CHAPTER IV

The Picket

Rᴏᴄᴋᴠɪʟʟᴇ Cᴇɴᴛʀᴇ's ꜰɪʀꜱᴛ ɴᴇᴡꜱᴘᴀᴘᴇʀ was established in 1865 when John H. Reed, a Brooklyn printer, brought out "The Picket," a four-page weekly newspaper. In the first issue, published Friday, June 16, 1865, the editor and proprietor inserted this succinct announcement:

> To the readers of the Picket: We have at last begun to issue the Picket, though somewhat later than anticipated.

The Picket was not only Rockville Centre's first newspaper, it was the first newspaper on the South Shore in any village between Babylon and Far Rockaway, then called Rockaway. Under different names and eventually as Long Island's first daily newspaper outside of Greater New York, this publication was to serve Rockville Centre and the South Shore continuously for 88 years, ending with the final suspension of the Nassau Daily Review-Star in July, 1953.

The name of the Picket suggests the war psychology that existed at the time although the Civil War ended a few weeks before the first issue of the Picket came off the press. Beneath the one-column masthead listing John H. Reed as editor and proprietor was the legend, "An Independent Union Newspaper." This did not refer to a labor union, but proclaimed that the Picket was a staunch supporter of the United States, or Federal Union, and identified with the Union party. Subsequent issues in listing candidates for local offices showed that there was a Union Party, at least locally, in addition to the national Republican and Democratic parties.

Beneath the name of the paper on its front page was the motto, or slogan, "Our Liberties We Prize, and Our Rights We Will Maintain."

John H. Reed appears to have had a good basic education. The scanty news items that appeared in the Picket were well written, grammatically correct, and with a selection of words and a dignity superior to what might be found in many weekly newspapers a century later. John H. Reed was also a public-spirited, religious man who immediately entered into the life of the area. Several years later he was serving as Superintendent of the Sunday School of the Christian Hook Methodist Church and sponsored a Sunday School picnic in a "park" at Islip, for which the South Side Rail Road ran a special train. Hundreds attended, not only from Rockville Centre and Oceanside, but villages all along the line as the guest speaker was Horace Greeley, famous editor of the New York Tribune and later Democratic candidate for President. The date of this picnic arranged by the editor of the Picket was September 2, 1869.

When the Picket was established there was neither a church nor a public school within the present village limits of Rockville Centre. There were probably less than 100 houses in the village itself, centered around Village Avenue and Merrick Road, although in those days Merrick Road through Rockville Centre was called Jamaica Avenue, as it was a section of the Jamaica Plank Road. The Jamaica Plank Road was a toll road, maintained poorly by the corporation which owned it. It was not even planked all the way, but planking had been laid down in the places susceptible of developing the deepest mud in wet weather and after the Spring thaw. The poor condition of the plank road was a favorite subject of "letters to the editor" from the time the Picket began publication and for many years afterwards.

If all the farm houses within the area that now constitutes Rockville Centre were counted as part of the village as of 1865 the number would have been greatly increased because there were farms along Merrick Road, Hempstead and Village Avenues and on the South Side of the village as well.

By 1865 Rockville Centre, nevertheless, had achieved substantial commercial development, apparently in anticipation of completion of the South Side Rail Road. During this period articles on Long Island in the New York newspapers always cited Rockville Centre as the coming village on the South Shore.

The largest regular advertisements in early issues of the Picket were inserted by Weyant and Company, which more than a year prior to the establishment of the Picket had purchased and enlarged the store of Robert Pettit and Sons, located at the Southeast corner of Village Avenue and Merrick Road. The principals of Weyant and Company at this time were F. H. Weyant, J. S. Terry and E. H. Vandewater, local family names that continued in Rockville Centre until this generation. Weyant and Company ran a general store which they advertised as an "Assortment Emporium" offering groceries, millinery, dry goods, clothing, farming utensils, etc.

Other advertisements in the Picket showed that Rockville Centre had a blacksmith shop, a furniture store which also sold coffins, an ice cream parlor and a store, or barn, where Carman and Denton sold fish guano. Charles H. Dorlon was proprietor of the local hotel, called "Rockville Centre House," while Charles H. Losea advertised his local industry as "carriage maker."

The largest advertisement in early issues of the Picket, however, was inserted by William F. Oliver, who had a grist mill on the East Side of Mill River, now Hempstead Lake, and a feed and grain store on Main Street, Hempstead. The advertisements stated that this mill had been in operation since 1850.

There were commuters in the Rockville Centre area even then. A regular notice appearing in the Picket stated that the Rockaway and Hempstead stage "leaves Near Rockaway at 6:25 a.m., arriving in time for the 7:24 train leaving for New York. Returning stage leaves Hempstead upon the arrival of the train which leaves James Slip at 4:30 p.m."

Hempstead had train service several years before the South Shore villages and stages connections between them and Hempstead made it practical for the first time for South Shore residents to go to New York and Brooklyn daily for business.

The first Long Island commuters were not City people who moved to the "country" for the sake of their children, but ambi-

tious natives who wanted to take advantage of the superior economic and professional opportunities afforded by the City. Some
of the early natives did commute at considerable hardship and
some who got a foothold in the City moved there until development of rail service made it practical for them to move back to
their native villages.

By 1865 old farms in the vicinity of Rockville Centre were
already being subdivided and sold in anticipation of the completion
of the railroad. An article appearing about this time in the New
York Evening Post speaks of Rockville Centre as being second
only to Jamaica in population along the route of the proposed
South Side Rail Road and states that cleared land near the stations
can be bought as low as $100 an acre. Rockville Centre land was
already selling higher than this, nevertheless. Current advertisements offered lots within 10 minutes walk of the proposed station,
50 x 200 feet, at $200 to $500, except that the same-priced lots
on Washington Avenue were only 50x150 feet. It is likely that
purchasers in those days usually bought several lots, because the
well-to-do families kept their own cow and a carriage horse or
"buggy horse." Some of them undoubtedly raised pigs and
chickens, too, all of which required more than a single lot. Many
present residents of Rockville Centre can recall large old homes
that once stood throughout the village on plots of an acre or even
larger.

The New York Evening Post in the article just mentioned was
not particularly complimentary about the South Shore, about to
be opened for development by the completion of the South Side
Rail Road. After referring to Rockville Centre as a coming community it proceeded to say that few Southsiders could read and
that the natives existed by primitive farming and fishing. These
comments appeared in a newspaper owned by a Long Island
resident. The New York Evening Post was the property of
William Cullen Bryant, better known as the poet who wrote
"The Death of the Flowers" and "Thanatopsis." Bryant even
then had a country home at Roslyn, "Cedarmere," still occupied
by his descendants, but he was not actually a commuter. He had
a New York home and it is unlikely he had ever visited Rockville
Centre, Oceanside, Freeport or Baldwin.

While it is well known that illiteracy was much more prevalent 100 years ago than it is today and that living standards were generally lower, except for good home cooking, not all of the Southsiders were fishermen, farmers or illiterate. Many of the leaders whose names will appear in this history represented families that had already lived in this area 100 to 200 years and had prospered in business, and in the professions as lawyers, doctors and bankers.

In the September 20, 1862, issue of the Hempstead Inquirer, already about 30 years old, there appeared the following "Social Item."

> Fair and Festival—The ladies of the Rockville Centre Church will hold a fair and festival in the grove of Mr. Hewlett Abrams near the schoolhouse on Wednesday, September 29, for the sale of useful and fancy articles. Dinner and tea provided, price 25 cents. The proceeds are to be applied to the building of a new personage.

Neither the church nor the schoolhouse involved in this event actually were in Rockville Centre. The church was the Old Sand Hole Methodist Church, which stood at the end of the cemetery on Long Lane, later named Ocean Avenue, just North of the Jamaica Plank Road, later called Merrick Road. The schoolhouse where the fair and festival was held was farther North in what would now be Lakeview.

The Hempstead Inquirer also reported a few months later that a public meeting was held at the home of Stephen Langdon on February 14, 1863, for the purpose of giving a name to the place on the road leading from William Rhodes to Joseph Langdon's. Stephen Langdon, the host, was appointed chairman and William L. Rhodes secretary. The following resolution was adopted:

> Resolved, That the place be hereafter known as and called 'Woodfield.' Be it also resolved that the proceedings of this meeting be published in the Hempstead Inquirer.

This was the origin of Woodfield Road, which carries the same name 100 years later.

While the largest mill in the area in 1865 was William F. Oliver's Eagle Mill, Rockville Centre residents had a nearer mill to patronize. In the early 1866 issues of the Picket there was a small advertisement which read,

> Windmill—Get Your Grain ground while the wind blows. Clinton F. Combes, the subscriber, having purchased the windmill property lately owned by Mordecai A. Smith, announces that he is prepared to grind the peoples grain at the usual rates.

This Mordecai Smith was the nephew of the pastor-miller Mordecai Smith who is regarded as the father of Rockville Centre. The Reverend Mordecai Smith died in 1852, while the nephew lived until 1865.

An item in the Picket of November 24, 1865, state that Mordecai A. Smith had left Rockville Centre several weeks before to visit relatives in New Brunswick, but got only as far as Brooklyn where he was taken ill and subsequently died of "consumption," or tuberculosis.

Earlier that year Mordecai had sought the Democratic nomination for Superintendent of the Poor of Queens County, but the nomination was given to William Curtis at the party convention in Hempstead. Mordecai ran anyway as an independent, but was not elected. It may have been his disgust at this setback which led him to decide to go away on a visit just before his final illness overtook him.

During the Winter advertising in the Picket got an impetus when several enterprising local residents offered cordwood for sale, while John Paff noted that he had arranged his saloon to accommodate ladies, as he also served meals. "His oyster stews are delicious," commented the Picket.

The Picket in an issue of December, 1866, announced that a meeting would be held at Near Rockaway to discuss steps to get a post office for that village. When Near Rockaway ultimately was granted a post office the name was changed to East Rockaway. Thus the term "Near Rockaway," which had once encompassed a wide area including Rockville Centre, passed into history.

Both New York and Long Island papers devoted much space during 1867 to the forthcoming opening of the South Side Rail Road. The New York World declared it would open up a section of Long Island that is "both healthful and beautiful.

In July the Picket reported that the railroad would be finished to Rockville Centre in August, but August passed without any trains reaching Rockville Centre unless they were work trains. In its September 6, 1867, issue the Picket exulted, "At last after many delays the long expected railroad has been laid to and through Rockville Centre.

The first trains actually passed over the new line Monday, September 23, 1867, and while a big celebration was held at Freeport Rockville Centre seems to have taken the event in its stride without much ado.

The Long Island City Star, however, took occasion to pay a tribute to John H. Reed for his foresight in opening a newspaper along the right of way, at Rockville Centre. He showed rare courage, said the Star, and its success "demonstrates the clear foresight he possessed in starting it." It also stated that the Picket's printing and publishing office was nearly opposite We-yant's store, which as has been noted, stood at the Southeast corner of Village Avenue and Merrick Road.

Immediately after the trains started running the Picket announced that the mail left the Rockville Centre Post Office at 1:30 and 4:40 p.m. daily. It noted that the steam trains drawing the cars stopped at the edge of Brooklyn while horses, or mules, drew them through the populous streets to the East River.

The Picket soon began publishing a railroad time table which indicated the trains ran as far as Babylon when the line was first open. It would soon be extended all the way to Patchogue, passing some stations with names that are no longer in use. It took these early trains, making all stops, about an hour and a half to travel the 27 miles between Jamaica and Babylon. Apparently South Shore commuters even in those early days heard the familiar cry, "Change at Jamaica."

In 1868, the year after the railroad was opened, an advertisement in the Picket showed that commutation between Rockville Centre and New York cost $65 a year. The rate was $30 for two months, or $45 for six months, which shows the savings involved in an annual ticket for those who could afford it. The cost of commuting from Pearsall's Corner, or Lynbrook as it subsequently became, was the same as commuting from Rockville Centre, although the rates were lower at stations nearer the City and higher at stations East of Rockville Centre.

It was announced in March, 1868, that John H. Reed, editor of the Picket, had been appointed postmaster to succeed F. H. Weyant, of Weyant's store, "who is about to remove from this place."

A previous announcement had reported dissolution of the Weyant, Terry, Vandewater partnership and formation of a new partnership consisting of F. H. Weyant, Cornelius Vandewater and Joseph T. Weyant. This was late in 1865, and by 1868 F. H. Weyant apparently planned to retire from the business and move to another town.

A public meeting was held at Hewlett's Hall, Hempstead, Thursday night, April 16, 1868, "for the purpose of taking such action as shall facilitate the completion of the projected connection of Hempstead with the South Side Rail Road at Rockville Centre."

No line was ever built between Rockville Centre and Hempstead, but the South Side Rail Road eventually reached Hempstead by a branch from Valley Stream, roughly following the route of the present West Hempstead Branch of the Long Island Rail Road. The South Side Rail Road had its own terminus not far from the present intersection of Peninsula Boulevard and Franklin Avenue, Hempstead, and for a few years Hempstead flourished as a railroad center served by three lines, the Long Island Rail Road, the South Side Rail Road and A. T. Stewart's rail road, which was usually simply called "the Stewart line." It was on the West Hempstead Branch of the old South Side Rail Road that one of the worst wrecks in the early history of Long Island railroads occurred a few years after the line was built. A heavy rain undermined a bridge across a stream at Lakeview with the result that the engine fell off the bridge, landing on its side and killing the engineer. The accident caused some injuries to passengers and other members of the crew, but the engineer was the only casualty.

Completion of the South Side Rail Road gave a great impetus to the growth of Rockville Centre. New families began moving to the village whose breadwinner, the man of the house, was employed in the City. This brought to Rockville Centre many men who were to become community leaders in later years and it produced a situation where the growth of the village was at a rate which doubled the population every few years. This growth continued decade after decade until about 1950, by which time most of the available land in Rockville Centre had been built up and its principal growth in the future would come from the erection of apartment houses.

One of the early developers who seems to have prospered was John P. Rhodes. A few years later during a Presidential election year a discussion of the various candidates' prospects took place at the Rockville Centre station and John P. Rhodes was quoted as having offered to bet anyone present $20,000 that Grant would be re-elected. The newspaper reported that there were no takers. Rhodes, however, was on solid ground for General Grant was re-elected.

John H. Reed published the Picket in Rockville Centre for five years, during one of the most exciting periods of its history. He also served part of this time as postmaster and as superintendent of the Sunday School at Christian Hook Methodist Church. In the Summer of 1870, however, he was in poor health and took advantage of an opportunity to sell the paper to a new owner who was to loom large in the affairs of this part of Long Island for approximately half a century.

The purchaser was George Wallace of Freeport, an erstwhile school teacher who had become a lawyer and who also cherished some political ambitions. The sale was made late in the Fall of 1870 for an undisclosed sum, except that there existed until a few years ago a receipt for $400 written the long way on a piece of legal paper about 18 inches long and eight inches deep signed by John H. Reed. James E. Stiles, who bought the newspaper in turn from George Wallace 48 years later, found the receipt in an old desk which he acquired with the paper and had it framed. For many years it hung in the office of the editor of the Nassau Daily Review-Star.

While we hope the $400 represented only a down payment on this pioneer journal and its printing plant there was a happy ending to John H. Reed's South Shore sojourn. He returned to Brooklyn to make his home and pursue his trade and apparently his health must have improved for he lived until 1906, at which time his death was reported in the newspaper he had founded.

South Side High School, the first high school on the South Shore, cost about $18,000 to build in 1893. Originally a red brick building, it has served as the Rockville Centre Municipal Building since 1924.

CHAPTER V

First Schools and Churches

WHEN GEORGE WALLACE BOUGHT THE PICKET from John H. Reed in the Fall of 1870 he moved the paper to Freeport and changed its name to "The South Side Observer." The Observer was published in Freeport for about 18 months before it moved back to Rockville Centre, but it remained essentially a Rockville Centre paper as this was the most important community in the area it covered.

The first issue under the new name, with a Freeport date line, appeared November 4, 1870. Beneath the name of the paper was the line, "The local newspaper for Rockville Centre, Pearsall's, East Rockaway, Valley Stream, Rockaway, Springfield, Oceanville, Baldwin, Freeport, Merrick, Bellmore, Ridgewood, Seaford, and for Queens County."

If this seems to be taking in a lot of territory it did not actually involve a very large population. There were less than 15,000 people in the entire Town of Hempstead in 1870 and the Observer did not include coverage of the Village of Hempstead, which was the most populous community in the Town.

The news content of the South Side Observer from the outset was broader than the Picket had attempted. George Wallace obtained correspondents in most of the communities listed above and regular columns under the name of the various villages appeared in almost every issue.

The Observer also embarked upon a more aggressive editorial policy. During the first year of his editorship repeatedly called for three things, better schools for Rockville Centre and the other villages, incorporation of Rockville Centre and creation of a new county out of the three Eastern towns of Queens County—Hempstead, North Hempstead and Oyster Bay.

The Observer also pointed out that the Town of Hempstead needed more than one Supervisor as the increasing population of the area required more attention than one Supervisor could give to the job.

In an editorial published April 10, 1874, The Observer proposed a division of the Town of Hempstead. He suggested the new town, which would include the area covered by Rockville Centre, Oceanside, Lynbrook, East Rockaway, Valley Stream and the Five Towns, be called "Atlantic," "Rockville" or "Rockaway." The editorial declared the Village of Hempstead, which was not incorporated at that time, dominated the town with the rest of the communities suffering from neglect.

The opening of service on the South Side Rail Road late in 1867 started an influx of population with the result that several churches actually were organized in the village before its first school was built. Most of the Rockville Centre natives had worshiped at the "Old Sand Hole" Church, which was officially the Near Rockaway Methodist Episcopal Church. This congregation dated from 1790 and was the third Methodist Church on Long Island. As both Rockville Centre and Pearsall's Corners increased in population a movement was started to divide the congregation by setting up new Methodist churches in both villages. Eventually the division took place. The Pearsall's Corners group established the St. James Methodist Episcopal Church and the Rockville Centre group established St. Mark's Methodist Episcopal Church. A third remnant of the Old Church remained there, establishing a Methodist Protestant congregation which still survives in the "Old Church" on Denton Avenue, Lynbrook.

St. Mark's Methodist Church was officially organized June 21, 1870, at a meeting in the parsonage of the Old Church, which stood until recently, with some alterations, on the point where Rocklyn Avenue, Lynbrook, runs into Merrick Road opposite the old cemetery. The old house was finally razed when Merrick Road was widened in the Middle 1960's.

The organizers of St. Mark's Church included names of prominent Rockville Centre residents which show up repeatedly in the history of the village. Present at the meeting were the Rev. John B. Merving, the Presiding Elder; the Rev. Charles Kelsey, pastor; and William Davison, Benjamin Pearsall, Nathaniel

Combs, Robert A. Davison, Oliver P. Miller and Wright Pearsall. The new congregation soon erected a crude structure, called "The Tabernacle," on the West side of Banks Avenue near Merrick Road where the first services were held.

Meanwhile, on November 4, 1870, Robert Pettit, the former merchant and postmaster of Rockville Centre, who had moved to New Brunswick, N. J., but who had been a member of the old Methodist Church, sold St. Mark's a plot of ground at the Southwestern corner of Village Avenue and Merrick Road for $700 as a site for the new church. This tract had 100 foot frontage on Merrick Road, 267 feet along Village Avenue to Lincoln Avenue and extended 178 feet along Lincoln Avenue.

A church was erected on this site the following year, at the corner of Merrick Road and Village Avenue, where it stood with subsequent additions until it was destroyed by fire in 1938. A parsonage was later built on the portion of this plot that was bounded by Village and Lincoln Avenues. The new church, which was of frame construction with an impressive steeple, was erected at a cost of $7,500, with a $4,000 mortgage. It was dedicated by Bishop Andrews on December 17, 1871.

Almost simultaneously with the creation of St. Mark's Methodist congregation a Baptist congregation was organized in the village. It held its early meetings in the Rockville Centre railroad station, or depot, where Sunday School classes also were held.

During 1870 the South Side Observer noted in one issue that two new churches were under construction in Rockville Centre, one by the Methodists and one by the Baptists. The Baptists built their church on the Merrick Road site which they still occupy, so that Rockville Centre's first two churches were within half a block of each other.

Rockville Centre did not get its own public school as fast as its own churches. Children of the village who went to school at the time attended an old school located at what would now be the northwest corner of Foxhurst and Oceanside Roads in Oceanside. In 1870 Foxhurst Road was called School Street and Oceanside Road was known as Christian Hook Road. This was a very primitive school, but it had a second floor that was improved somewhat for the "infant class" in 1860.

Spurred on by editorials in the South Side Observer the people

The Sixth Grade at Clinton Avenue School in 1910. The teacher, Miss Farmer, stands against wall in rear. Among the boys in this picture were Lucian Raynor and George Gumbs, both prominent in Rockville Centre in later years. (Picture was donated by Mrs. Edward Barnett, the former Ethel Schroeder, of Smithtown.)

of Rockville Centre began demanding their own public school and after much difficulty and delay got District 11 divided. District 21, the Rockville Centre district, was created finally in 1871, but not until after the people of the village had established their own private school, the Rockville Centre Institute.

The cornerstone of the Institute building was laid November 8, 1871, on the site at North Village and Hempstead Avenues now occupied by the Tudor Apartment House.

A public school was opened in rented quarters in 1872, after Robert White, Robert Rea and John R. Sprague had been elected school trustees at the first meeting of the new district held in January, 1872.

For more than three years the public school had a very unsatisfactory existence in a series of leased quarters, including the old Tabernacle that the St. Mark's congregation had built prior to the erection of its new church. When the school occupied a portion of the Tabernacle the remainder was being used as a barn.

There was a succession of teachers and in July, 1874, George Wallace, editor of the South Side Observer, a former school teacher himself, took charge of the school on an interim basis and served until February, 1875, meanwhile protesting through the Observer that Rockville Centre must have a modern school building of its own.

Eventually, late in December, 1875, a special committee that had been appointed to select a site, arranged to buy a plot on College Place, east of Village Avenue, now the site of St. Agnes School, for $700. The men who served on this committee were Alexander Davison, John R. Sprague and Clinton F. Combes. A contract for a school building to cost $2,383 was soon awarded to Mr. Sprague, of the committee, and the Rockville Centre School opened in its own building for the first time in September, 1876. The new school was a two-story building with a cupola, painted white with green shutters. Only the two rooms on the first floor were used at the outset and as the plot was only 150 feet square there was not much of a playground for the pupils. The new school was such an improvement over previous conditions, however, that the Institute, having served its purpose, soon closed. The calibre of teachers also showed a marked improvement after the new school was built, although it would be only a few years before this building was outgrown, so rapidly was Rockville Centre increasing in population.

In 1870 while Rockville Centre was acquiring its first churches and worrying about its dearth of educational facilities the Federal Census was taken. The results published early in 1871 in the South Side Observer showed Queens County was on the march. Its population had increased from 57,967 in 1865 (State Census) to 73,847 in 1870. Readers will bear in mind that Queens County in 1870 comprised all the area that now constitutes both Queens and Nassau Counties. Census figures showed the Town of Hempstead had grown more slowly, having increased from 11,764 in 1865 to 13,922 in 1870.

The Observer noted frequently the sale of houses to new residents, one of whom was R. B. Rosevelt (probably Roosevelt) editor of the Citizen and Round Table, who had been elected to Congress on the Democratic ticket. It seems likely he was elected from a Manhattan District, where he maintained his voting address, as there was no publication of this nature locally and no Congressman by this name appears in the history of Nassau County. This is believed to be the only instance, however, where Rockville Centre had a Congressman in residence.

A personal note in The Observer of May 17, 1872, stated that "Mrs. Sherwood has sold her home to C. W. Hayes of Brooklyn." The story continued to state that Mr. Hayes had been president of the C. W. Hayes Company of Brooklyn. Former Village President Edwin G. Wright, who knew Mr. Hayes well, recalls that he moved from the Williamsburg section of Brooklyn. His Rockville Centre home was on the South Side of Lincoln Avenue near the present Mansion House, or old Ketcham Lodge. A map of Rockville Centre published in 1895 with pictures of churches, business buildings and homes of prominent citizens around the border, shows that the Hayes home was an elegant Victorian mansion with a tower, many dormers and a porte cochere.

Early in January, 1875, the Observer reported that Mr. Hayes had retired from C. W. Hayes & Co., Williamsburg, and had left with his wife for a three months trip to the Everglades in Florida where he hoped to shoot some alligators.

More than 20 years after moving to Rockville Centre C. W. Hayes became the second president of the Village and serving for four years, from 1894 to 1898. He was an old man by that time, but his term of office was the fifth longest of any Village President or Mayor to date.

Mr. Wright says that after his term as Village President Mr. Hayes offered to sell the village all of the triangular block bounded by South Village Avenue, Merrick Road and Lincoln Avenue, except for the part occupied by St. Mark's Methodist Church, for a park. He wanted the village to pay him a small monthly sum each month as long as he lived. While the offer was declined, perhaps because the village law in those days may not have contained any provision for parks, it would have been a great asset to the community if the land had been acquired for that purpose.

Real estate news in the May 10, 1872, issue of the South Side Observer showed that John P. Rhodes had sold six lots on Banks Avenue to William Whitney, "who intends to build on them." Mr. Rhodes also had just sold two lots on Center Avenue, while a Mr. Brackett of New York had just purchased 13 acres in the area at a price of $300 per acre.

A well known resident of the village who is past four score years in age says that in his boyhood many of the largest and finest homes in Rockville Centre were on Center, Banks and Randall Avenues. This was the portion of the Village first subdivided and sold for village lots. It had been part of the Mordecai Smith farm. In the March 1, 1890, issue of the South Side Observer there appeared a letter from John P. Rhodes, describing his early real estate activities in the village nearly 40 years before. He stated that he and his partners paid $4,000 for the 60-acre Mordecai Smith farm, extending along the East Side of Smith's Pond and as far East perhaps as Village Avenue on the North Side of Merrick Road. This purchase was made about 1852, when Mordecai Smith died. Mr. Rhodes stated that after subdividing and disposing of the Smith property he and his partners bought the Israel Wright farm of 30 acres North of the Smith farm. This no doubt included part of the land now traversed by Lakeside Drive.

The South Side Rail Road got off to an auspicious start and its first few years were profitable ones. In 1871 the railroad had receipts of $408,615.10, expenses of $268,628.96 and a profit of $132,987.14. Any railroad in the country would be glad to show this ratio of earnings today. The South Side Rail Road also listed the following rolling stock in its 1871 report: 13 engines, 35 passenger coaches, 4 baggage cars, 20 house (box) cars, 60 flat cars, 12 grain cars, 3 cabooses and 13 hand cars.

The South Side's prosperity was shortlived, nevertheless. A few years later it was in receivership and ultimately sold in the final amalgamation of all the major Long Island railroads into the Long Island Rail Road Company, which had many years of successful operation before it became a subsidiary of the Pennsylvania Railroad.

CHAPTER VI

The Year of the Blizzard

Some years are so routine in their events from a community point of view they pass and are forgotten, except for individuals and families for whom they may have special significance.

The year of 1888 was not one of these. In the history of Rockville Centre it was marked by two events that made it a subject of conversation and recollection down to the present. One of these events was the Blizzard of '88 in which numerous Rockville Centre residents were particularly involved. The other was the "great fire," which destroyed a substantial part of the business section, and, as many fires do, resulted in an enforced modernization and improvement of the retail district.

There were other interesting events in the village during 1888, but the blizzard and the fire set it apart. While the blizzard affected a wide area Rockville Centre residents had gruelling experiences that by now have been passed down to the fourth generation.

The South Side Observer noted in its January 20, 1888, issue that Glentworth D. Combes was married on Wednesday, January 18, to Miss Hattie Aylesworth at the home of Mrs. L. M. Sanger. Glentworth D. Combes was the father of the late George D. A. Combes, founder of South Nassau Communities Hospital, and a president of the Bank of Rockville Centre. Glentworth D. Combes was a member of Rockville Centre's first village board. He conducted a lumber and hardware business on North Park Avenue and along Maple Avenue which George D. A. Combes later ran under the name of the G. D. Combes Estate.

The Observer also reported in its January 6 issue that Austin Corbin, president of the Long Island Rail Road, was having a large depot erected at the foot of 29th Street, Brooklyn, as part

53

of his plan of establishing a terminus for ocean vessels at Montauk Point. Corbin planned to dig a tunnel under the Kill von Kull between New Jersey and Staten Island so Philadelphia and Reading trains could bring freight to a point opposite his 29th Street station. The freight cars would be ferried across New York Harbor and sent on to Montauk. Corbin also wanted passenger vessels to dock in Fort Pond Bay at Montauk and send their passengers on to New York as fast Long Island trains. He claimed a whole day's traveling time between New York and Europe could be saved by this procedure. While the plan was tested on several occasions, even as late as the 1920's, it was never adopted.

The Blizzard of '88 started Monday morning, March 12, with a cold rain that later turned into snow. The snow continued intermittently for two days and nights, accompanied by high winds that piled up mountainous drifts in many places.

By 1888 Rockville Centre had many commuters and when they caught the Monday morning train to the City, after a cold walk to the station through the rain, they had little anticipation of the experience awaiting them.

By the time they got within a mile of Jamaica, however, the snow had piled up on the tracks enough to stop the first train that came along. Before many hours after that five trains were piled up at this point. There was not much fuel on the trains, which were heated by wood stoves, and there was less food.

Jamaica was only a small village in 1888. Even if the passengers had ventured to walk the mile into the village hotel accommodations would have been inadequate for all the passengers stranded on the trains outside the village. Some food and fuel were obtained, but the passengers, nevertheless spent a miserable 24 to 36 hours.

Among those trapped on one of the trains was Austin Corbin himself, without his pocketbook. When he left the train he borrowed $5 from Mrs. Acklund Boyle of Rockville Centre. A few days later he returned her money and in his letter of thanks he enclosed a complimentary railroad pass for Mrs. Boyle to use.

By Tuesday afternoon the storm had abated somewhat and 20 Rockville Centre passengers decided they would walk home. They had a miserable tramp along the old Jamaica Plank Road over which few vehicles had passed since the storm began. There was no beaten path for them. Some of the men who undertook this long hike were able to make it only because they were helped along by their companions.

Among those who walked from Jamaica to Rockville Centre was George Utter, who later served Rockville Centre as village clerk for many years. Mr. Utter, then a young man and un-married, was living with his mother, a widow, in their home on Randall Avenue, West of Center Avenue. Concerned because his mother was home alone, and because there was no way for him to get word to her about his own status, he became one of the hardy band that walked home from Jamaica that wintry night. The party reached Rockville Centre just as it was beginning to get dark, and there is no record that any of them suffered con-sequences as a result of this ordeal.

The snow was so deep that even residents who had not left the village had trouble getting to the stores for food and drugs. Train service between Rockville Centre and New York was not restored for several days.

As has happened many times since, the press and the public blamed the railroad officials for the plight of the trains. They charged that the snow plows were still in the car barns after the storm was over, and after the snow had piled up so deep and packed down so hard the plows couldn't be used anyway. The railroad officials, said the Observer, "acted like a group of school boys."

Rockville Centre's big fire started about midnight on May 17, 1888, in the store of Williams and Sault on Village Avenue, between what is now Sunrise Highway and the railroad. The cause of the fire is unknown and it was so far advanced before being discovered that a family living over the store barely escaped.

The fire soon spread from the Williams and Sault store to A. E. Kraemer's store, even though there was a 10-foot open space between the two buildings. The South Side Observer plant caught fire and burned down. Lotz' Hotel at Village Avenue and the railroad also burned, but volunteers, including the firemen, saved a lot of the furniture. The Eureka Hook and Ladder Company arrived soon after the fire broke out, but was unable to do much with the primitive equipment available. Rockville Centre had no water mains or hydrants in 1888, although the firemen could run their hose down into some wells in the business district. As the fire continued to spread Rescue Hook and Ladder Company arrived from Pearsall's Corners, but even with their help—they formed a bucket line—it was impossible to save the bottling plant. Geller's store also burned before the flames were finally brought under control.

The Observer reported subsequently that the fire lasted for about two hours and said it was the worst fire in the history of the South Side. It said that while it was insured for $5,500 this would not cover its loss.

Several of the frame buildings that burned that night were replaced with brick buildings. The Lotz Hotel was rebuilt with brick and stood at Village Avenue and the railroad until about 1930, having been used for business in its latter years.

The South Side Observer quickly moved its press into temporary quarters and ordered a fresh supply of type to replace that which had been ruined in the fire. The Observer then built a three-story brick building at the corner of Village Avenue and the conduit, which later became Sunrise Highway. When the Observer Building was completed it was one of the finest buildings in the village and when a street was opened along the route of the conduit subsequently it was called Observer Street, by which it was known for 30 odd years before it became Sunrise Highway in 1927.

The three-story Observer Building remained the home of the newspaper until James E. Stiles built The Review Building on Sunrise Highway (then Observer Street) in 1920. The building, under different owners and used for various purposes, is still standing at the Northeast corner of Village Avenue and Sunrise Highway, but following a disastrous fire about 20 years ago it was rebuilt as a two-story structure only. It now houses an insurance office.

In the January 4, 1889, issue The Observer, with pride, describes its new three-story structure. Besides the business office for the newspaper George Wallace had a law office there (he had offices in several places including New York City) and C. L. Wallace, part owner of the Observer, had a real estate office.

The recently-formed Rockville Centre Library and Improvement Association was using the second floor and the paper said it anticipated the Masons would use the third floor. On January 18, 1889, the Observer also stated that the Rockville Centre Brass Band had 18 members who rehearsed weekly on the third floor.

The Observer noted with pride that the new building had a hot-air furnace in the cellar, where the printing press also was located, and that this central heating was cleaner and less dangerous than having a stove in every room.

There were some pleasant and progressive events during 1888 despite the blizzard and the fire. In April J. M. Seabury of the American Electric Manufacturing Company spoke to Editor Wallace and other leading residents about a proposition to light the village with electricity.

Claude C. Van Deusen bought a plot of ground on Jamaica Avenue (Merrick Road) adjacent to Alexander Davison's property and built a handsome house. Claude C. Van Deusen many years later was Nassau County's Overseer of the Poor, which corresponds to the present Commissioner of Public Welfare. His house stood across the street from the present Rockville Centre post office and the land eventually became the Nassau Daily Review-Star's private parking field, years before it became the municipal parking field adjacent to the Rockville Centre Baptist Church.

On June 27, 1888, Hawkins Atheneum Hall held its grand opening. Atheneum Hall was a sort of local opera house, a tremendous, ugly building that stood at the Northwest corner of Village Avenue and Sunrise Highway. The old building, remembered in its final years as an eyesore, stood until the late 1920's. When it was opened, however, The Observer described it as the finest public hall on the South Shore, "a valuable addition to the village."

The opening night's entertainment included the Meigs Sisters, a quartet, and Alfred E. Pearsall, "elecutionist and humorist." Apparently Alfred was one of the local Pearsalls who had gone into the show business. The price of admission on the opening night was 75 cents.

The hall was crowded that night with residents of Rockville Centre, Baldwin, Pearsall's Corners, Freeport, East Rockaway and Oceanville (Oceanside). There were horses tied to all the hitching posts up and down Village Avenue, some of the more prosperous driving over in rubber-tired buggies.

Atheneum Hall continued to present regular programs for some years. In its December 28, 1889, issue the South Side Observer announced that Marshall P. Wilder was scheduled to appear at the hall under the auspices of the Rockville Centre Odd Fellows Lodge. It commented that Wilder was the most distinguished and highest-priced entertainer ever to appear in the village. Many members of the older generation no doubt recall the prestige Marshall P. Wilder enjoyed about the turn of the century when he was much in demand as a humorous speaker. He was also editor of an anthology of American humor in several volumes which enjoyed excellent distribution.

Rockville Centre in 1888 was still attracting executive-type new residents. The September 22, 1888, Observer noted that P. R. Jennings, a wealthy New York metal importer, had bought the villa of Miss Asman on Lincoln Avenue, which he intended to improve by adding a dining room with a bay window. The Observer added that Mr. Jennings was going to install a bathroom and would even have hot water in the kitchen.

While records are scarce concerning Rockville Centre's participation in the Civil War George Wallace, editor of The Observer, was one of the speakers at Memorial Day services held in the Rockville Centre Cemetery in 1888. Graves of Civil War veterans in the cemetery were decorated, with the D. B. P. Mott Post, G. A. R., of Freeport officiating. Prior to coming to Rockville Centre the post had decorated graves and held services in Freeport. The veterans took the train from Freeport to Pearsall's Corners and marched down Merrick Road to the cemetery. It seems certain that some Rockville Centre veterans were members of the Freeport G. A. R. post, as there was never a Grand Army post in Rockville Centre or Lynbrook.

During 1888 another church was added to the growing list of churches in Rockville Centre. The Church of the Ascension was originally authorized as an Episcopal Mission by Bishop Littlejohn of the Diocese of Long Island in 1885. The first service was held Sunday morning, April 12, 1885, in Institute Hall with about 25 families represented. Services continued to be held here for several years.

In February, 1888, however, the plot of ground where the Church of the Ascension now stands was purchased and plans made for the erection of a church. In August, 1888, the foundation was laid and Bishop Littlejohn appointed the Rev. Charles A. Jessup as Priest-in-Charge. The cornerstone of the church was laid on October 13, 1888, with Bishop Littlejohn in attendance and the building was in use by the end of the year.

The two Rockville Centre residents credited with persuading the diocese to launch a mission in the village are Sylvester Gildersleeve and Prof. Francis F. Wilson, who was also active in the early days of the Rockville Centre schools and the library.

A note in the South Side Observer of November 30, 1888, states that the Rev. Charles Martin Niles, rector of the Church of the Ascension, was editing a paper for the diocese called "The Church Messenger." The Church of the Ascension actually remained a mission for many years and was served by various pastors assigned by the Bishop before it gained parochial status in 1912. It had been incorporated in May, 1911, by the Rev. D. Herbert O'Dowd, priest-in-charge, William L. Merry and Charles V. Day. Charles V. Day was the father of former Village Trustee Charles V. Day, who served as chairman of Rockville Centre's 75th Anniversary Celebration Committee in 1968.

In the last issue of December, 1888, the Observer, in one of its frequent booster editorials, noted that there were now six churches in Rockville Centre. This was a substantial change from 20 years before when there was not a single church in the present village limits. These six churches represented the major churches, some at the same location, that are active in Rockville Centre in 1968, 80 years later.

SEA CAPTAINS
ON MAINE AND
VILLAGE AVENUES

Capt. Walter K. Whittemore No. 221

Maine

Avenue

Capt. Charles Coombes No. 207

Capt. Tristam Thurlow Corbett No. 208

Capt. Samuel E. Phillips No. 191

North Village Ave.

Prof. Francis F. Wilson

Capt. James Gallison No. 185

Old Rockville Centre Institute

The Wright Homestead

Hempstead

Randall Avenue

L.H. Butcher

CHAPTER VII

The Captains are Coming

A FEW YEARS AFTER THE CIVIL WAR when the completion of the South Side Rail Road made Rockville Centre definitely a commuters' village there was an influx of a particular class of new residents who gave the village a distinctive flavor and over the years contributed greatly to its development and status.

Rockville Centre has often been described as having been developed by retired sea captains. Actually Rockville Centre was a fast-growing, flourishing community by the time the first sea captains moved here. Moreover, some of the sea captains were not retired, but picked Rockville Centre because it was a high class community where some of their friends had already settled. They rated it as a pleasant community in which their families could live while they were away at sea.

The South Side Observer in its January 16, 1874, issue published a short article under the caption, "The Captains Are Coming."

Rockville Centre has long been noted for the many sea captains living in the village and the people heartily bid them welcome," said the Observer. Captain Gallison has this week sold four plots near the Institute."

In its July 3, 1874, issue The Observer stated that the new street linking North Village and Center Avenues had been named Maine Avenue in deference to the Maine sea captains residing there. It reported that Captain Gallison also was responsible for extending North Village Avenue through the woods North of his home, while the cross street, Maine Avenue, had been graded and improved. Of Village Avenue the Observer said, "It is to be hoped that public enterprise will be awakened to extend Village

Avenue to intersect the handsome road built by the Aqueduct company. This would give an excellent boulevard from Rockville Centre to Hempstead."

Before Hempstead Reservoir was built the Old Mill Road had been a rough lane through the woods linking Rockville Centre and Hempstead, but construction of the reservoir left portions of this road under water, so that in the early 'Seventies there was no direct road between Rockville Centre and Hempstead along the general route now followed by Village Avenue and Peninsula Boulevard.

The Captain Gallison mentioned above was Captain James Gallison who lived at 185 North Village Avenue, in a house just North of the Professional Building that is still standing. Captain Gallison acquired considerable property on North Village Avenue and sold some of it to sea captains. Eventually there were sea captains living on three corners of Maine and Village Avenues, others living on Village Avenue and others in various parts of the village.

Captain Gallison, perhaps not actually a sea captain at the time, had a tugboat business in New York and naturally became widely acquainted with sea captains. He was succeeded by his son, Forrest Gallison, who ran the business for many years. After Forrest Gallison's death, his widow contributed funds to build a memorial public library in Machias, Maine, the small town from which the family had come.

The late Willeby T. Corbett of 93 Grand Avenue, Rockville Centre, the son of Capt. Tristam T. Corbett, listed many of the sea captains who had lived in the village in an article by Mrs. Bernarda Timberman published by The News-Owl, April 21, 1944.

Captain Corbett's home was on the Southwest corner of Village and Maine, 208 North Village Avenue. Other sea captains, retired or still actively engaged in operating their own ships, who lived in the immediate area included Capt. Samuel E. Phillips, 191 North Village Avenue; Capt. Charles Coombes, 207 North Village Avenue; Capt. Walter K. Whittemore, 221 North Village Avenue; and Capt. C. D. Whittemore.

Capt. Austin Jayne lived at 96 North Village Avenue in a large

house just North of Washington Street. There was a steep hill
in those days from the present intersection of Hempstead and
Village Avenues going South to the village and the section where
Captain Jayne lived came to be known as "Barnacle Hill."

One of the most prominent of the sea captains who moved to
Rockville Centre was Capt. Edwin F. Wallace, grandfather of
former Village President Edwin W. Wallace. Captain Wallace
acquired a large tract of land on Maple Avenue and built a house
at 117 Maple Avenue where his grandson is now living.

According to Willeby T. Corbett, Captain Wallace came from
Millbridge, Maine, and was the first sea captain to settle in the
village. He became one of the original trustees of Rockville
Centre when it was incorporated in 1893.

Another captain who lived on Maple Avenue was Capt. James
W. Carty, whose home at 73 Maple Avenue was said to have
been shipped, piece by piece, from Harrington, Maine, where he
had worked as a ship's carpenter. Captain Carty was the last
survivor of the original sea captains to move to the village, having
lived until September 5, 1941. Captain Carty's ship was the
"Tillie Baker." After serving his apprenticeship as a ship's
carpenter he had gone to sea, won a master's certificate and finally
became owner of his own vessel.

Captain Austin Jayne's home on Barnacle Hill later was owned
by Capt. Alfred H. Laffin, who commanded the transport Burn-
side during the Spanish-American War, carrying troops from
Tampa, Fla., to Cuba. After the war the Burnside was converted
to a cable ship and laid the inter-island submarine cables in the
Philippines and later the cable from Seattle to Alaska. Captain
Laffin's daughter became Mrs. Arthur C. Martin, wife of Dr.
Arthur C. Martin, and they remodeled the old home on Barnacle
Hill and lived there for a time before moving to Garden City
and later to Westbury.

During the last quarter of the Nineteenth Century and the first
decade of the Twentieth Century the families of the old sea captains comprised one of the most prosperous sectors of the population of Rockville Centre. They lived in spacious houses, usually
with large grounds, and participated prominently in the cultural,
civic and business life of the village. Capt. Samuel F. Phillips, for

instance, was one of the organizers and later served as president of the Bank of Rockville Centre, the first bank on the South Shore of Nassau County.

Evidence that many of the captains were still going to sea after they moved to Rockville Centre is found in a news article in the South Side Observer of September 10, 1875, entitled "The Whereabouts of Our Sea Captains."

"Capt. Austin Jayne arrived a few days ago in Liverpool from Australia. Capt. W. K. Whittemore is on his way from Marseille, France, to South America. Capt. C. D. Whittemore is due in Bristol from New York. Capt. C. A. Coombes is now loading in Spain for the United States. Capt. James Gallison arrived recently in Stetine, Russia, from Philadelphia. Capt. Benjamin White arrived in Rotterdam from New York. Capt. Nathan S. Tracy sailed from New York to Lisbon. Capt. Edwin F. Wallace is rebuilding his bark in Maine. Captain Bedell is rebuilding his bark at Port Jefferson. He runs a steamer between New York and Washington, D. C. Captain Horn has retired from the sea and has gone into the chicken business. . ."

Capt. Benjamin White built a house on Morris Avenue, near Grand Avenue. He was the grand-father of Dr. Benjamin White Seaman, the Rockville Centre-born surgeon who was rated as the outstanding surgeon of Nassau County in the period between World War I and World War II.

Capt. Nathan S. Tracy once owned a 25-acre farm on the West side of Hempstead Avenue near DeMott Avenue. He had a son who was also a sea captain, Capt. Marcus H. Tracy.

Capt. Andrew Pierce, who owned a large house on Center Avenue North of the railroad, was master of a whaling vessel, one of the few of the old sea captains who had been in this business. Willeby T. Corbett recalled that once when his father took the rest of the family with him on a voyage he boarded at the home of Captain and Mrs. Pierce during their absence, no doubt so he could remain in school. After he had retired Captain Pierce served for a time as truant officer for the Rockville Centre schools.

Another seaman, Captain Moore, lived at the corner of Village Avenue and Merrick Road on the site where the Bank of Rockville Centre once stood. Captain Joseph Proctor, who lived on Lenox

Road, had several children who lived in Rockville Centre down to the present generation.

Capt. Tristam Thurlow Corbett, according to his son, Willeby T. Corbett, came to Rockville Centre from Machias, Maine, in 1885. He owned the 689-ton "Olive Thurlow" and frequently took his family with him on long sea voyages. Willeby T. Corbett's sister, Eugenie, who became Mrs. Morley K. Dunn, wife of a former village president of Rockville Centre, was born aboard the ship in the harbor of Noumea, New Caledonia. Captain Corbett sailed the "Olive Thurlow" for 20 years and then acquired the barkentine "Eleanor Williams." He died as a result of the shipwreck of his third vessel.

The Rockville Centre sea captains for the most part commanded "tramp" sailing vessels or steam cargo ships. When they went to sea with a cargo bound for a certain port they did not always return directly home. They might take on successive cargoes for different ports in all parts of the world. Often they were away as long as 15 months before returning to their home port. Many of the captains sailing their own vessels amassed comfortable fortunes in that era.

It is estimated that during the quarter of a century from 1870 to 1895 no less than several dozen sea captains lived in Rockville Centre at one time or another. Many spent their final years in the village while others lived here for a time and then moved elsewhere. A large number of prominent residents of the village today are members of the family of one of these various seamen.

Dr. Frank. T. DeLano, President of the Library Board for more than 30 years, served as President of the Bank of Rockville Centre longer than any other President.

CHAPTER VIII

The Rockville Centre Public Library

THE ROCKVILLE CENTRE PUBLIC LIBRARY, founded before the community had a high school or a bank, and more than a decade before the village was incorporated, is a pioneer institution that has been a source of pride and a major cultural and educational force for more than 80 years.

The Rockville Centre Library and Improvement Association, forerunner of the present library, was organized in 1882 and ever since that time books have been available to the residents of the village without charge. William H. Connell, a Village Avenue merchant, was the first president and Miss M. Antoinette Davison, the first secretary. William H. Connell was later police judge of Rockville Centre and is remembered as "Judge Connell," but Rockville Centre had no police judge at the time the library was formed. Miss Davison represented a family that has been prominent in Rockville Centre and this area since Colonial times.

Immediately after it was founded the Rockville Centre Library and Improvement Association established a circulating library and reading room that was later located on the second floor of The Observer Building at the Northeast corner of Village Avenue and Observer street. The Observer Building was erected following the big fire that destroyed a large part of Rockville Centre's business section in 1888.

The library must have had only a few dozen, certainly no more than a few hundred books at the time, which had been contributed by members and civic-spirited residents, but it proved so popular it soon outgrew its quarters in the Observer Building. When John W. DeMott, long afterwards a president of the Bank of Rockville Centre, erected a building on the West side of Village

Avenue near Merrick Road, and John T. Davison, grandfather of Surrogate John D. Bennett, erected an adjoining building, The Rockville Centre Library and Improvement Association moved into quarters provided by the second floors of the two buildings. The name, "Library," on the gable of the DeMott Building could be seen until the buildings on this block were razed to provide a site for the new home of the Bank of Rockville Centre Trust Company, now a branch of the Chemical Bank of New York. In the new quarters the ladies of the Association served as voluntary librarians. The reading room of the library also was used as a meeting place by various civic and cultural groups. During the Winter months formal receptions were held twice a month and occasional speakers were invited to address meetings there. There was a piano in the meeting room and other furnishings that had been given to the Association.

While members of the Association paid dues, rent and maintenance expenses absorbed most of this revenue, so the library

George Wallace (left), "Father of Nassau County," who published the South Side Observer from 1870 to 1918, and John Lyon, first village president of Rockville Centre and one-time County Comptroller. The latter's law office, on Front Street, was a training school for young lawyers, many of whom became prominent.

Professor Francis F. Wilson (left), *one of the founders of the Rockville Centre Public Library, also served as a director of the Bank of Rockville Centre, and Captain Samuel F. Phillips, active in all major civic projects in his lifetime. Captain Phillips served as President of the Bank of Rockville Centre from 1894 to 1900.*

was largely dependent upon gifts of books to supply reading material.

Dr. D. N. Bulson, who served on the library board from 1894 to 1902, once related that when he came to the village a group of men used to get together in the evenings for literary discussions. This group, comprising the intelligentsia of the village, included Alfred E. Ives, Sr., Prof. Francis F. Wilson, Robert A. Davison, William M. Hawkins, Dr. Bulson and others.

When Dr. Frank T. Delano, also a later president of the Bank of Rockville Centre, moved to the village and began meeting with the literary group he cited the need for the establishment of a tax-supported public library, such as existed in Westport where he had formerly lived.

Meanwhile a library had been established in the South Side High School for the use of the students and the two libraries were

combined in the establishment of the Rockville Centre Public
Library, as of May 22, 1894, under the auspices of the Rockville
Centre school district. The records show that the South Side
High School Library consisted of about 500 reference books and
other volumes, while the Association was able to contribute a
miscellaneous collection of 246 volumes.

The first board of the new Rockville Centre Public Library
consisted of Dr. Bulson, Dr. Delano, Prof. Francis F. Wilson,
Robert A. Davison and Capt. Samuel F. Phillips. A second floor
room was provided in South Side High School, now the Rockville
Centre Municipal Building, and the school district gave it an
appropriation of $50 a year. The library was open two afternoons
a week for one hour and on Saturday evenings it was open for
two hours. The librarian's salary was 75 cents a week, but it was
not long before she was provided with an assistant at 50 cents a
week.

The library was not entirely dependent upon its annual appropriation of $50. Many residents contributed books and periodicals
and cash gifts were received from the Rev. Thomas E. Carroll,
pastor of St. Agnes Catholic Church, and John Lyon, prominent
attorney of the village who had served as first village president.

Proceeds of some of the entertainments given by the school
children also helped to buy new books and subscriptions to six
of the leading periodicals of the day—North American Review,
The Forum, Century Magazine, Harper's Monthly, Review of
Reviews and St. Nicholas, the latter a popular children's magazine.
It is a commentary of the changing reading habits of the American
people and hazards of magazine publishing that only one of the
leading magazines of that day is still published.

The first librarian in the upstairs room at South Side was
Elmer S. Redman, the school principal, assisted by two high
school students, Sara S. Field, the late Mrs. Sanford A. Davison
of 75 Marion Place, Rockville Centre, and Grace W. Dana,
later a resident of Springfield, Mass.

Larger quarters were found for the library on the first floor of
the high school after Clinton Avenue School was built. The first
move by the library towards acquiring its own building was made
by Dr. Delano, then president of the Board of Education, in 1901

when he applied to the Andrew Carnegie Foundation for a grant of $10,000 for the erection of a library building. The request was approved with the usual provisions that the site be acquired locally and that 10 per cent of the Carnegie gift be raised every year for the maintenance and operation of the library.

Years passed before all these provisions could be met. Finally John Lyon gave a plot of land in the rear of his law office at the corner of Front Street and Clinton Avenue, on which the new building was erected, fronting on Clinton Avenue. John Lyon's law office was in a quaint one and a half story building that stood until about 1927 when it was torn down to provide a site for the Nassau County National Bank, now a branch of Franklin National Bank. Many prominent attorneys of Rockville Centre, Lynbrook, Freeport and other villages of later years had served their apprenticeship in John Lyon's office.

The school district appropriated $2,451.50 toward the new library to supplement the Carnegie Foundation gift of $10,000. The library building, exclusive of furnishings, cost $11,500 in 1912. It was formally dedicated December 21, 1912, and with additions and alterations served Rockville Centre and the school district for 50 years before it was replaced by the present modern library at North Village and Maine Avenues, which was dedicated December 2, 1962.

Civic-minded residents made some gifts to speed the opening of the library in 1912. A massive receiving desk, still in use about 40 years later, was the gift of Dr. Bulson. The library auxiliary provided four reading tables at a cost of $108 and the lighting fixtures costing a total of $155. Joseph Elias donated the heavy plate glass for the windows and the front door. The cornerstone of the new building was the gift of the Rockville Centre Civic Club. The family of Robert A. Davison contributed some of the furnishings as a memorial to the man who had been one of the prime movers in organizing the library.

The library when built in 1912 was estimated to have a capacity for 15,000 to 16,000 books and reading space for 35 to 40 persons. When the cornerstone of the new building was laid July 6, 1912, when the building was already well under construction, Judge William H. Connell, who had been the first president of the

Rockville Centre Library and Improvement Association 30 years before, was one of the speakers. Other speakers included the Rev. D. H. O'Dowd, Alfred T. Davison, attorney and son of Robert A. Davison, the Rev. George E. Bishop of St. Mark's Methodist Church, Dr. Bulson and Dr. Delano. George S. Skilton, president of the library board, presided at the dedication on December 21 of that year.

By the time the library occupied its new building on Clinton Avenue in December, 1912, it had acquired a full-time librarian, although it was still operating on a very small budget. The librarian was Miss Winona Caroline Martin, a gifted young woman who had been educated in Zurich, Switzerland, private schools in New York, and in Brussels, Belgium.

Miss Martin became Rockville Centre librarian in 1910. Under her leadership the Library Auxiliary was organized and the first children's story hour was introduced. She later published a book, "Twelve Tales of King Arthur," based on the material she used in her story hour. It was highly praised in book reviews as one of the best books of the kind that had been produced. Her story hour was so popular the room where it was held was often taxed to accommodate the children who crowded into hear her. Miss Martin also became one of the leaders of the Fortnightly Club of Rockville Centre, where her brilliant scholarship and rare sense of literary values were of great aid to the group.

Early in 1918, during World War I, Miss Martin took a leave of absence from the library to become a canteen worker under the auspices of the Y.M.C.A. in France. She sailed on February 3 from New York on the steamship "Chicago" for Bordeaux, France. While aboard she contracted scarlet fever and upon arrival was sent to the Claude Bernard Hospital in Paris to convalesce. She was killed on March 11, 1918, when the hospital was bombed by the Germans. The "Big Berthas" with which the Germans bombarded Paris in the last year of the war did little to aid their failing cause but caused wide-spread grief in Rockville Centre when such a popular public figure became a casualty.

A memorial service was held in Rockville Centre March 31, 1918, with Dr. Delano, president of the library board, presiding.

Addresses were made by Village President Edwin W. Wallace, Dr. James Sullivan, State Historian of New York; and Fletcher S. Brockman, Associate General Secretary of the National War Work Council of the Y.M.C.A. Tributes to Miss Martin were given by Mrs. Earl J. Martin, president of the Library Auxiliary; the Rev. Peter Quealy of St. Agnes Church and the Rev. Richard Hegarty of St. Mark's Methodist Church.

In July of that year a memorial plaque with a portrait of Miss Martin in bas relief was unveiled in the main room at the library. When the present library was opened the plaque was moved to the new building.

Before Miss Martin left for France, Mrs. Alice H. Decker, formerly of the Queensboro Public Library in Jamaica, had been appointed Acting Librarian. A short time after Miss Martin's death Mrs. Decker was appointed librarian, a post she was to fill for 32 years during a period of great expansion and growth in popular acceptance for the library.

By 1918 the library had grown to about 5,000 volumes, still only about one-third of its shelf capacity. It had 2,188 active borrowers and its circulation that year was 22,324. By the time Mrs. Decker retired in 1950 the library building had been greatly enlarged and it had 40,000 books on its shelves, 7,000 active borrowers and an annual circulation in excess of 170,000.

The library's first marked growth began in the late 'Twenties when its budget was increased to enable it to acquire more new books each year than it had in the past. The Junior Department was opened in the basement of the library building Thursday, September 10, 1931. Prior to that time this space in the basement, never having been developed into attractive quarters, had no regular use.

Cheerful decorations, new flooring and adjacent toilet and closet facilities, with its own entrance from the street, immediately made the Junior Department popular with the young readers of the village and added greatly to the soaring circulation of the library.

Dr. Robert K. Atkinson, a member of the Board of Education and one of Rockville Centre's most gifted speakers during that generation, spoke at the opening of the Junior Department. In

charge of the Department was Miss Margaret Davison, daughter
of Mrs. Sanford A. Davison, who had been one of the original
librarians in the old South Side High School quarters.

In the early 'Thirties much attention was attracted to the library
by a book review column in the Nassau Daily Review-Star,
through the courtesy of its publisher, James E. Stiles, and written
by three members of the staff, John Desmond, Frank A. Culver
and Seymour Marks. The book reviews always mentioned that
the books were available at the library and Mrs. Decker credited
the book column as being a factor in the growth of the library's
circulation by 200 per cent over a five-year period, even though
this was during the depression when the population of the village
was not increasing and many houses in the village were vacant.

John Desmond, a member of the New York Times editorial
staff, was still residing on Shellbank Place, Rockville Centre, in
1968 when this history was written.

The capacity of the library was more than doubled in 1934 by
an addition of similar architecture built in the rear of the original
building. Still before the inflated prices of the post World War II
period this addition cost about $15,000, with funds provided in
the school budget. It was opened in December, 22 years after the
library had been dedicated.

Over the years the staff of the library was gradually increased
and instead of the one-hour periods two days a week at the outset
it was now open five days every week, including some evening
hours, except on holidays. The library also was equipped to supply
books for branch libraries in all of the public schools of the village.

When current best-sellers of approved quality were in demand
the library sometimes had six or more copies of these books in
circulation and there was always a long reserved list of persons
waiting for them.

When John Steinbeck's famous book, "The Grapes of Wrath,"
came out in the 'Thirties the library had more than half a dozen
copies in circulation and Mrs. Decker said that on one occasion
a prominent resident of the village told her he had been waiting
for several months and his name had not been reached. He
threatened to go out and buy the book. She said that after such a
book had been reviewed and become a topic of conversation,

reservations would immediately be made by the dozen, from persons who had little chance of getting their turn at the book for months despite the numerous copies the library had in circulation.

While more than half of the library's books are in the non-fiction category, fiction always accounts for more than half of the circulation. This, in part, is explained that many reference books are used in the library and certain non-fiction books when taken from the library may be held for a longer period than is usually required to read a novel.

The big influx of population that all of Nassau County experienced after World War II also affected Rockville Centre. It was not long before all the remaining vacant land in the village was subdivided and even the few remaining vacant lots were bought up for new home sites. This was followed by apartment house building where one home on a large plot might be replaced by an apartment house capable of accommodating as many as 40 families. Rockville Centre, which had been a small village of about 3,000 population in 1900 passed 25,000 around 1950, half a century later.

It soon became apparent that Rockville Centre would need a larger library for its soaring population. Land was not available for any further additions on the Clinton Avenue site, even if it had been desirable from other points of view.

Shortly after World War II a drive was organized under the leadership of Allan B. Wright, a Rockville Centre attorney and a veteran of the war, to build a new memorial library in honor of those who served in World War II from the village, especially in honor of those who lost their lives during this conflict. Former Village President Edwin G. Wright, Allan Wright's father, accepted the chairmanship. It was hoped to obtain sufficient pledges to build the library largely with voluntary subscriptions. The old George A. Powers property at the Northeast corner of Morris and Grand Avenues was tentatively selected as a site for the new library. While numerous substantial pledges were made, eventually it became apparent that when a new library was built it would have to be financed by local taxes. The project had to be delayed, however, because the Rockville Centre school district was in the midst of a large building program, including the new South Side

High School and several new elementary schools.

In 1950 Mrs. Decker reached the age of retirement and resigned during the Summer after a tenure of 32 years, rarely equaled by a librarian in any community. She was succeeded by Miss Mary Kent, who had previously been a librarian with the Veterans Administration. She served for five years during which there was significant progress and expansion of the library services.

In the early 'Fifties, public libraries, including the Rockville Centre Public Library, began circulating records as well as books and periodicals. It was regarded as a cultural service to promote interest in good music as well as in literature.

Miss Kent was married and became Mrs. Grant while she was Rockville Centre librarian. In 1955 she resigned to move to another town with her husband. She was succeeded by the present librarian, William K. Harrison III, under whose administration plans for the new library on North Village Avenue were evolved.

The Nassau Library System also was set up during the 'Fifties. As a result patrons of the Rockville Centre Public Library now have access to thousands of books which may be borrowed from the system, if they are not in the local library. The Nassau Library System also has a stock of 16 millimeter films on various subjects which can be borrowed by local libraries, or by local groups through the library.

Mr. Harrison is a native of New York State. He attended Hampden-Sydney College in Virginia and then became a graduate of the Library School of Columbia University. He was associated with the American Library in Paris for a time and was later with the Ferguson Library at Stamford, Conn. He came to Rockville Centre from the latter post.

After several years of study, during which several possible sites were considered and various plans for a new library building reviewed, the Library Board, through the Board of Education of Union Free School District No. 21, ordered a referendum on a proposal to build a new library, costing approximately $500,000, on March 7, 1961. The site selected was the Patton property at the Northeast corner of Village and Maple Avenues, once the home of the old seaman, Capt. Walter K. Whittemore. Through the acquisition of some additional property the new library has landscaped grounds and space for parking approximately 40 automobiles. By re-designing the parking field space for an additional 20 cars was secured in 1968 without any additional land being used.

The new library was dedicated with an open house Sunday, December 2, 1962, and was open for all library services Monday, December 3. The new building is about two and half times as large as the old building on Clinton Avenue, which was sold to the Knights of Columbus of St. Agnes Church, for use as a club-house.

The new library was designed by the architectural firm of Gibbons and Heidtmann of White Plains, specialists in library design, in cooperation with Walter D. Spelman, Rockville Centre architect. The capacity of the new building is about 75,000 volumes, and as there were 74,672 volumes listed as of April, 1968, it is apparent that it has nearly reached capacity. The library acquires 8,000 to 10,000 new books each year, but thousands of volumes also are eliminated each year as they are worn out or become out of date. Some revenue is received each year from the sale of obsolete and discarded books.

In 1967 the library had a circulation of 325,038, and it has 14,748 regular borrowers listed in its files. Besides a Junior Department and a Reference Department under a special Reference Librarian, the new library has an enclosed reading room where current daily newspapers are available and smoking is permitted.

A study of the building and grounds already has been made by the architects of the library, so it can be enlarged when additional space becomes an acute requirement. The library has an attractive meeting room available to civic and cultural groups, equipped so that refreshments may be served, and with coat room and toilet facilities. This room is regularly used by the Rockville Centre Historical and Landmark Association, various Adult Education classes and New York University extension courses.

During the 74 years since the Rockville Centre Public Library was formed in 1894 by the merger of the high school library and the library of the Rockville Centre Library and Improvement Association only 37 persons have served on its five-member Board of Trustees, some of whom served continuously for more than 40 years.

Among those who have served on the Library Board were some

of the most prominent early residents whose leadership in business and civic affairs, including their service to the library, helped establish Rockville Centre as an outstanding community on Long Island, attractive as a place of residence for families of means and culture.

Prof. Francis F. Wilson, one of the original trustees, who served from 1894 to 1902 was a school man from New York City who resided in Rockville Centre for many years. Wilson Lane, Rockville Centre, perpetuates his name and two of his daughters resided on the South Side of this street until their deaths in the early 1960's. The Francis F. Wilson School also was named in his memory.

Capt. Samuel F. Phillips, who served from 1894 to 1908, was one of the founders of the Bank of Rockville Centre and served as its president from 1894 to 1900. Captain Phillips also served on the Board of Education.

Robert A. Davidson, also an original trustee, served only a few months on the Library Board. He lived on Merrick Road in a large house where the First National City Bank now stands. He was an organizer and the first president of the Bank of Rockville Centre.

Dr. D. N. Bulson, who served from 1894 to 1902, is remembered as the president of the Nassau County National Bank on Front Street, now a branch of the Franklin National Bank. Dr. Bulson also served Rockville Centre as village president and as a member of the Board of Education.

Dr. Frank T. Delano, who was a member of the Library Board for 42 years, from its inception until his death in 1936, was a prominent practicing physician in the village for many years before becoming president of the Bank of Rockville Centre about 1916.

Alfred E. Ives, a member of the original board who served until 1897, was a leader in many civic activities in Rockville Centre and many years later his son, Alfred E. Ives, Jr., served on the Library Board from 1921 to 1932.

William A. Martin, who served as Library Trustee from 1897 to 1900, is mentioned in many connections in the early history of the village.

Alfred T. Davison, who served as Library Trustee from 1900 to 1906, was the son of Robert A. Davison. He married a Freeport girl and lived in Freeport for many years, while serving as attorney for the Third Avenue Railroad in New York. Later he lived in Garden City, where he died in the early 1960's.

George S. Skilton, who served from 1902 to 1921, is mentioned in the record of many civic activities during that period.

Capt. Marcus H. Tracy, who served as trustee from 1905 to 1906, is mentioned in the history of the sea captains who lived in Rockville Centre.

William J. Bennett served from 1906 to 1909.

Mrs. Mary E. Earle, who served from 1907 to 1937, was the first woman member of the Board.

Willeby T. Corbett, who served 38 years from 1908 to 1946, was chairman of the Rockville Centre Draft Board during World War II, following his retirement as an executive of the United States Steel Export Corporation. He was identified with many civic activities during his long career.

Eugene P. Hawkins, who had the longest period of service on the Library Board, was appointed in 1909 and served for 46 years until his retirement in 1955. Mr. Hawkins conducted the hardware store on North Park Avenue which still bears his name.

Michael J. Madigan, who served as Library Trustee from 1932 to 1939, also served as a member of the Board of Education. He was editor of the Catholic News, the newspaper of the New York Diocese.

Mrs. Charles B. Mount, second woman to serve on the board, was elected in 1937 and served until 1945.

George D. A. Combes served from 1937 until his death in 1941. Mr. Combes, the son of Glentworth D. Combes, one of the first directors of the Bank of Rockville Centre and an original trustee of the Village of Rockville Centre, continued his father's hardware and lumber business on Park Avenue near the railroad. He led the drive to establish South Nassau Communities Hospital and was its first president. He was president of the Bank of Rockville Centre from 1936 until his death. A student of history and author of many papers and pamphlets on Long Island History, he was historian of the Town of Hempstead.

William J. Murray, who served as a Library Trustee from 1939 to 1955, served for many years as postmaster of Rockville Centre and as an officer and director of County Federal Savings and Loan Association.

Leonard H. Calvert, 1941–1951.

Mrs. Malcolm S. Spelman, 1945–1953.

Thomas M. Brennan, 1947–1953.

Jesse Henshel, 1951 to 1960, was president of the Unity Club of Nassau County and has been a director of County Federal Savings and Loan Association for many years.

Milton H. Cash, 1953–1955, resigned to become a trustee of the Village of Rockville Centre.

John P. Madigan, 1955–1962.

Members of the Library Board at the time the new library was opened in 1962 were Mrs. Sophi C. Silberberg, president, appointed in 1955; Charles V. Day, appointed in 1956, who later served as a member of the Village Board and in 1968 as chairman of the 75th Anniversary Committee; Mrs. Julia Cohill, appointed in 1955; Anthony Turano, appointed in 1960; and Judge Maurice J. Moore, appointed in 1962. Judge Moore served for many years as Police Justice of Rockville Centre and was also president of the Rockville Country Club for some years.

Albert D. Wood served from 1963 to 1967 and Mrs. John Seligman from 1963 to 1968.

The members of the Library Board in 1968 were Mrs. James S. Cox, Daniel M. Gilmartin, Duncan E. Longworth, Mrs. Milton G. Finfer and Mrs. Harold G. Kraus.

CHAPTER IX

Financial Center of Nassau County

In one of its January, 1888, issues, the South Side Observer commented that Rockville Centre should have a bank. The Observer pointed out what a convenience it would be to the farmers of the area as well as businesses located in the village, indicating that farming was still the principal occupation on the South Shore.

This comment no doubt was inspired by the fact the Hempstead Bank had been organized in 1887 and had proved successful from the start. The Hempstead Bank was the first commercial bank of Nassau County, although the Roslyn Savings Bank, formed in 1875, had already been in operation for 12 years.

The Observer's recommendation was not immediately acted upon, but a year later, in its March 1, 1889, issue The Observer reported that it had heard a building and loan association was to be formed in Rockville Centre, "the object of which is to enable its members by loan which may be repaid in weekly or monthly installments, to own their own homes, thus giving aid to those whose means and income are limited.

The Rockville Centre Savings and Loan Association actually did not get underway until the Fall of 1889, but on December 28, 1889, The Observer reported, "The Rockville Centre Savings and Loan Association has started off with a boom. Thirty-nine members have subscribed 285 shares."

The Rockville Centre Savings and Loan Association was the first of a series of financial institutions that made Rockville Centre the financial center of Nassau County for half a century, a status it enjoyed until the era of bank mergers deprived it of this rank in 1950.

The original subscribers to the Rockville Centre Savings and

Loan Association included the leading men of the community whose names have appeared in connection with many other activities. John Vincent took 10 shares, Alfred E. Ives, 10 shares; W. H. Connell, 10 shares; Francis F. Wilson, 5 shares; Dr. D. N. Bulson, 5 shares; John T. Davison, 5 shares; Capt. Edwin Wallace, 5 shares; C. W. Hayes, 5 shares; Glentworth D. Combes, 5 shares; David R. Longenecker, 10 shares; Capt. Samuel F. Phillips, 5 shares; P. R. Jennings, 10 shares; G. Byron Latimer, 5 shares; Jacob Van Vliet, 5 shares; John W. DeMott, 5 shares; William H. Pearsall, 5 shares. Other names not familiar to the present generation are included in the list of those who became members within the first few months of the Association.

The Rockville Centre Savings and Loan Association, later known as the Peoples Savings and Loan Association, and now a branch of the Nassau Savings and Loan Association, due to a

Hiram R. Smith (left), and John W. DeMott. Mr. Smith was President of the Bank of Rockville Centre from 1900 to 1915. He also served for many years as Supervisor of the Town of Hempstead. Mr. DeMott's building on Village Avenue at various times accommodated the Village Office, Public Library and Bank of Rockville Centre. He also served as President of the Bank of Rockville Centre, about 1916.

William H. Kniffin (left), *President of the Bank of Rockville Centre in the 'Forties, and George D. A. Combes, founder of South Nassau Communities Hospital and President of the Bank of Rockville Centre. Mr. Kniffin achieved prestige as a writer and teacher of financial subjects, while Mr. Combes attained distinction as a historian and genealogist as well as a public benefactor and banker.*

merger that became effective in 1968, acquired assets of approximately $150,000 in its early years and remained somewhat static for about a generation after that. For many years its headquarters were located in the real estate office of Frank P. Baylis, later Baylis and Johnson, on the West side of Village Avenue on part of the site now occupied by the Chemical Bank New York Trust Company. It was not until the late 1930's that the Rockville Centre Savings and Loan Association opened its office and renewed its drive for new members and savings, at a time when there was a rapid growth of savings and loan associations throughout the country. It effected a merger with the Mineola Savings and Loan Association, thus acquiring a second office, and for a time was known as the Rockville Centre-Mineola Savings and Loan Association before changing its name to the Peoples Savings and Loan Association. In 1967 the Peoples Savings and Loan Association acquired a third office in Smithtown Branch, Suffolk

Earl J. Bennett, vice-president of the Bank of Rockville Centre for a generation, also served as County Comptroller and Chairman of the Nassau County Charter Commission. Below, an early County Federal meeting. George W. Loft presents a savings account in County Federal Savings and Loan Association to James E. Stiles, Jr., then about eight years old. In the picture from left to right are Edward C. Daverennes, Adrian Hegeman, Gust Svenson, James E. Stiles, Frank Davis, Mr. Loft and "Jamie."

County. Its assets at the time of its merger with Nassau Savings and Loan Association were approximately $20,000,000.

Rockville Centre's next financial institution, and one that became a leader in County financial affairs over a period of many years, was the Bank of Rockville Centre, organized in 1890. The bank first opened for business on January 2, 1891, and in 1936, when the bank was 45 years old, the late George D. A. Combes, subsequently president of the bank, published a very complete history of the bank and the men who had served it as officers and directors.

The moving spirit in the organization of the bank, which became the second commercial bank of Nassau County and the first to open on the South Shore, was Robert A. Davison, whose home was on Merrick Road where the office of the First National City Bank now stands.

Mr. Combes says of Robert A. Davison in his history of the bank:

> Mr. Robert A. Davison, the first president of the newly-organized bank, was a lawyer of considerable repute at that time. He was a partner of the firm of Stillwell and Davison, with offices at 170 Broadway, New York, as early as 1871. He had a large practice and was probably considered the most outstanding man of this community. He was a descendant of Robert Davison, an early settler. . . . He was the father of George W. Davison, once President, now Chairman of the Board of the Central Hanover Bank & Trust Company.

Alfred T. Davison, whose name appears frequently in this history, also was a son of Robert A. Davison. It is interesting to note that both sons of Robert A. Davison became very wealthy men. Both were graduates of Wesleyan University at Middletown, Conn., and subsequently made substantial gifts to their alma mater. This was especially true in the case of George W. Davison, whose name is memorialized on the Wesleyan campus by an improvement he helped finance.

The original capital of the Bank of Rockville Centre was $25,000, which was raised by selling 250 shares at $100 a share. Mr. Combes states that the stock was in such demand that there were two purchasers for every share. A limit of 10 shares was set by the organizers and some subscribers purchased only two shares. There were 54 original stockholders, most of whom were from Rockville Centre, but there were also subscribers from Baldwin, Freeport, Oceanside, Lynbrook, East Rockaway and Hewlett. The stock of the Bank of Rockville Centre was always closely held, often by descendants of the original subscribers. In 1941, when the bank observed its 50th anniversary, the late Mrs. Sarah Baylis Johnson, who became a pioneer woman bank director when she was elected to its Board, told this writer that there were only 68 stockholders, whereas many other banks in the County as of that date numbered their stockholders in hundreds and even thousands. The $1,000 that some of the original subscribers paid for 10 shares eventually enriched the purchasers or their descendants.

Among the original subscribers are the following familiar names:

Robert A. Davison, 10 shares; Thomas G. Knight, 10 shares; John Vincent, 10 shares; Prof. Francis F. Wilson, 5 shares; Capt. Samuel F. Phillips, 10 shares; John W. DeMott, 5 shares; C. W. Hayes, 5 shares; Charles L. Wallace, 10 shares; Capt. Edwin Wallace, 2 shares; John T. Davison, 10 shares; Glentworth D. Combes, 5 shares; Hamilton W. Pearsall, 5 shares.

Charles L. Wallace, who lived in Freeport, was publisher of the South Side Observer at that time. He was a brother of George Wallace and had become a partner in the ownership of the paper. Charlie Wallace also was an outstanding real estate salesman and is said to have been responsible for attracting many prominent residents to Rockville Centre.

Hamilton W. Pearsall, who lived at Lynbrook, still known as Pearsall's at that time, later organized the Lynbrook National Bank and became its first president.

The organization meeting of the bank was held November 15, 1890, in the rooms of the Rockville Centre Library and Improvement Association on the second floor of John W. DeMott's insurance building on the West side of Village Avenue. The original Board of Directors consisted of Robert A. Davison, Thomas G. Knight, John Vincent, VanWycke Hewlett (of Hewlett), Glentworth D. Combes, Wesley B. Smith, Charles Davison, Charles L. Wallace, Charles W. Hayes, Austin W. Cornwell, Samuel F. Phillips, Francis F. Wilson, John W.

DeMott, John T. Davison, Oliver Davison, Edward T. Thurston, and Hamilton Pearsall.

Robert A. Davison was elected president, John Vincent, vice-president, Hiram R. Smith of Freeport, cashier, and Captain Phillips, assistant cashier. The original offices of the bank were in the rear of John W. DeMott's building and one of the first expenses of the bank was to erect gratings on the back windows at a cost of $35.

Hiram R. Smith, who later served as president of the bank and then as Supervisor of the Town of Hempstead, was paid $1,200 a year as cashier. An ambitious young man who had done well in business in New York City, Hiram Smith was one of the "Rock" Smiths of the same original stock as Mordecai Smith, founder of the village. Hiram Smith's father was Nelson Smith, a Freeport merchant. In the original sale of stock, Hiram Smith bought five shares and his father bought three shares. Captain Phillips' salary as assistant cashier was only $200 a year, but he probably did not work full time.

One of the first employees of the bank was Bergen T. Raynor of Freeport, a young man who was employed as bookkeeper at a salary of $9 per week. Mr. Raynor, who later resided on Morris Avenue, Rockville Centre, and became an officer of another Rockville Centre bank, died in the Summer of 1967 at the age of 95 years, the last surviving man of those associated with the Bank of Rockville Centre during its first year.

When the bank opened for business on January 2, 1890, its first day's deposits totaled $4,036.62. At the meeting of the Board of Directors on January 15, 1891, however, deposits had increased to $23,520.39 and the bank had already made loans aggregating $7,675.23. The bank prospered from the start, but had a narrow escape during the Depression of 1893 when the value of its securities declined and there was a serious decline in deposits. The prospect of going into receivership was discussed, but Captain Phillips, among others, insisted that the bank remain open and try to recuperate its fortunes. Robert A. Davison served as president from 1891 to 1894. He then resigned and was succeeded by Captain Phillips, who served as president until 1900. Hiram Smith was elected president in 1900 and served until 1914, resigning

The three-story Bank of Rockville Centre, at the Northeast corner of Village Avenue and Merrick Road, was the finest business building on the South Shore when it was built in 1908. Building was razed in early 'Sixties when bank moved into its new quarters in the center of block across the street.

after he had been serving on the Board of Supervisors for about one year. John W. DeMott then became president, serving in 1914 and 1915. Subsequent presidents of the bank until its merger with Chemical Bank New York Trust Company were Dr. Frank T. Delano, George D. A. Combes, William H. Kniffin and Oscar Gast. Dr. Delano had the longest tenure of any president, serving from 1916 until his death in 1936, or for more than 20 years.

In 1907–08, the Bank of Rockville Centre built the three-story building at the Northeast corner of Village Avenue and Merrick Road, which it has occupied for more than half a century. This building, which is remembered by most of the present residents of the village, was the finest building on the South Shore at the time it was opened.

In 1925 the bank was granted fiduciary powers and its name

was changed to "Bank of Rockville Centre Trust Company." A brochure issued in 1951 when the bank was 60 years old showed its deposits as of October 1, 1950, as $14,367,187. Total resources as of December 31, 1950, were $16,299,396.09.

In the late 1950's, the bank acquired all the property along the west side of Village Avenue between Merrick Road and Sunrise Highway as a site for a new building, with parking space for its customers. This building was completed in the early 'Sixties. Shortly afterwards the bank was merged with the Chemical Bank New York Trust Company. By this time the total resources of the bank had grown to approximately $42,000,000 and it had acquired branch offices in Oceanside and West Hempstead.

One of the best known men associated with the Bank of Rockville Centre during its long history was William H. Kniffin,

West side of Village Avenue about 1900. Some of the stores in this picture were razed when the City of Brooklyn extended its conduit through the village, along the route now followed by Sunrise Highway. Edwin G. Wright, who donated this picture, says the pipe line beneath what became Observer Street and later Sunrise Highway was 72 inches in diameter.

executive vice-president for more than 20 years, and president from 1942 until his death in 1951.

The men who founded and operated the Bank of Rockville Centre during its formative years were local business and professional men. Even Hiram R. Smith, the first cashier and later president for many years, had had no previous banking experience when he assumed his office when the bank opened.

Mr. Kniffin was invited to join the bank in an executive capacity about 1918 when the need for professional management became apparent. He had been associated with a Jamaica bank, but had been a banker all his life. Mr. Kniffin, whose son, Vance Kniffin, is manager of the Rockville Centre office of the Chemical Bank New York Trust Company, was rated throughout his period of residence in the County as one of Nassau's outstanding bankers. An author, he had published several books on banking. He taught banking at both Rutgers and New York Universities. He was active in the Nassau County Boy Scout and Red Cross organizations and had other associations which made him one of the best known men of the County. Mr. Kniffin also was about 80 years old at the time of his death, and up to his final illness apparently had given no thought to retirement.

The founding of the Bank of Rockville Centre, second commercial bank in Nassau County, ushered in a period of bank expansion that was slow at first, but reached boom proportions in the 1920's. The Freeport Bank was organized in 1892, about a year after the Bank of Rockville Centre opened. Charlie Wallace, one of the owners of the South Side Observer, but a resident of Freeport, became a director of the Freeport Bank, although he also served on the board of the Bank of Rockville Centre. During the Nineties, a number of other banks were organized throughout Nassau County, but it was 16 years before a second bank was established in Rockville Centre.

Late in 1907, however, the First National Bank of Rockville Centre was organized, opening for business late in the Fall. Advertisements for the new bank began to appear in the South Side Observer in November, 1907. The Bank of Rockville Centre, which had been running a small "institutional" advertisement each week took notice of the competition by publishing some

GEO. V.
LOFT
with
Compliments
FROM

Vin
FULLER

SARATOGA

larger ads. In one of these the Bank of Rockville Centre pointed out that its resources exceeded $1,300,000 and that it was the largest village bank in New York State. This might well have been true, as many Upstate cities are actually smaller than Rockville Centre, and were even at that time, even though it was in 1907, as it is today, only an incorporated village.

The First National Bank of Rockville Centre was organized with $25,000 capital, which seems to have been the regular amount for organizing new banks in that era. The first Board of Directors consisted of Girdell V. Brower, Judge William H. Connell, C. D. Davison, John H. Carl, Alfred T. Davison, Robert C. Gillies, Robert H. Homan, Henry Hebenstreit, Dr. J. Ensor Hutcheson, William H. Holloway, G. Byron Latimer, George W. Loft, Edwin Patten, Isaac Terrell and George J. Quinn.

The first officers of the bank included G. Byron Latimer, president; John H. Carl, Vice-President; and Gabriel Toombs, Cashier.

The founders of the First National Bank of Rockville Centre were prominent men. G. Byron Latimer, the first president, also served as village president at a later date. John H. Carl, who lived on Grand Avenue, Baldwin, was a wealthy contractor. Dr. J. Ensor Hutcheson, son of Dr. Robert Hutcheson of Merrick Road, Rockville Centre, where the Rockville Centre post office now stands, became in time the outstanding surgeon of Nassau County and it is said he trained Dr. Benjamin W. Seaman, also a Rockville Centre boy, so well that Dr. Seaman succeeded him as the leading surgeon of Nassau County between World Wars I and II. George W. Loft, owner of the Loft Candy Company at the time, owned a handsome estate on Merrick Road in Baldwin, near the Rockville Centre line. He served for many years as treasurer of Tammany Hall in New York and was Congressman from a New York district for two terms. In later years, Mr. Loft was to assume a more dominant role in Rockville Centre affairs.

The First National Bank of Rockville Centre began its career as an aggressive competitor of the Bank of Rockville Centre. It advertised that it was more convenient for commuters, as its building was on Village Avenue between Observer street and the railroad. It also advertised that its deposits were insured, even though there was no Federal Deposit Insurance Corporation until many years later. The First National Bank also started advertising that it would pay 4 per cent on time deposits, whereas the prevailing rate was 3 per cent or less. It soon dropped back to 3 per cent, however, as its advertisements in the Observer showed. A statement of condition published December 13, 1907, a few weeks after the bank opened showed total resources of $70,000 compared to the $1,300,000 claimed by the older Bank of Rockville Centre.

During 1907 three other banks were organized in Nassau County. Hamilton Pearsall of Lynbrook, a director of the Bank of Rockville Centre and related by marriage to some of its other directors, led in the organization of the Lynbrook National Bank and became its first president. The records show, however, that Mr. Pearsall remained, for a time at least, also a director of the Bank of Rockville Centre. Banking laws today would not permit an individual to serve on the boards of two banks in such proximity of each other.

Two banks also were organized in Farmingdale in 1907, the Bank of Farmingdale and the First National Bank of Farmingdale. It has often happened that two groups simultaneously would try to organize banks, with the result that one group would seek a state charter and the other a Federal charter. This ultimately resulted in Nassau County having 13 First National Banks.

Two or three years after the First National Bank of Rockville Centre was organized, it received what might be classed as unfavorable publicity. Some of its stockholders became unhappy with the knowledge that members of the Board of Directors, which included 16 men, were paying themselves Directors' Fees for every meeting of the Board. It appears that the Directors' Fee in question was $5 a meeting and that the Board usually met once a month, but the unhappy stockholders thought the $80 a month should be distributed more widely in the form of higher dividends or used to build up the undivided profits.

Eventually John H. Carl became president of the First National Bank of Rockville Centre and served until his death in the late 1920's at the age of more than 80 years. In the late 1920's Mr. Carl also was influential in erecting a new skyscraper home for the bank at the Northwest corner of Park Avenue and Sunrise Highway. Unfortunately, Mr. Carl became ill and died before the bank was able to move into its new home. This building is now owned and occupied by the Catholic Diocese of Rockville Centre. After Mr. Carl's death Frank B. Gardner, a local automobile distributor and a member of the bank board, became president for a short time. He was succeeded by Cadman H. Frederick, a former Freeport real estate man who had moved his headquarters to Babylon, where he later was organizer and head of the Suffolk County Federal Savings and Loan Association.

The First National Bank of Rockville Centre built its expensive new home just at the outset of the depression, which started after plans for the building were already under way. It proved an unfortunate move as the upper floors were not immediately rented and the building became a drain upon the bank. In the early 1930's it became one of the first banks to succumb to the depression. News of its difficulties resulted in special meetings of the Nassau County Bankers Association and establishment of the Nassau Clearing House Association, by which the local banks hoped to come to each other's aid in emergencies to maintain confidence in the local banks.

Ultimately the First National Bank of Rockville Centre had to close its doors. Its assets were taken over—for liquidation, not as a merger—by the Bank of Rockville Centre and depositors were ultimately paid in full although the stockholders did not fare so well.

Ten years after the First National Bank of Rockville Centre was established, Rockville Centre got its third bank. A great deal of history had been made during the 10 years from 1907 to 1917, however. Rockville Centre, no doubt, had doubled in size. The country was in the midst of World War I and there was a booming war economy.

The Nassau County National Bank, organized in 1917, was able to make the same claim the First National Bank had originally made. It was most convenient for the commuters as it was located on Front Street opposite the railroad station.

The bank opened for business late in 1917. The South Side Observer, then nearing the end of its long career, reported in

January, 1918, that at the annual meeting the following men had been elected, or re-elected, members of its Board of Directors: John Lyon, County Judge Lewis J. Smith (who lived in Hempstead), Dr. D. N. Bulson, Herman Veit, Edwin W. Wallace, Francis J. Mulgannon, Francis G. Hooley, Townsend Southard, Dr. Aaron L. Higgins, Edgar H. Steenken, Joseph Elias, Henry Hessner and George D. Smith.

Officers of the new bank, elected at this meeting, were Dr. Bulson, president; Judge Smith and Francis J. Mulgannon, vice-presidents; Edwin W. Wallace, cashier; and Earl H. Proctor, assistant cashier.

This was also a distinguished group of men. John Lyon, Dr. Bulson and Edwin W. Wallace all served as village president. Judge Smith and Francis G. Hooley both ultimately became Supreme Court Justices, while Mr. Wallace served with distinction for many years as a member of the Assembly when there were only two Assemblymen in Nassau County, one for the North Shore and one for the South Shore.

Mr. Wallace apparently served only briefly as cashier of the bank. It was not long before Bergen T. Raynor, who had become cashier of the Bank of Rockville Centre and a member of its Board of Directors, began a long association with the Nassau County National Bank as cashier. Earl H. Proctor, a son of Captain Proctor, mentioned as one of the old sea captains who lived in the village, also retained his association with the bank until it was merged with the Franklin National Bank in the early 1950's.

Dr. Bulson served as president of the Nassau County National Bank from the time it was organized until his death about 30 years later. He was known as a president who made a habit of standing in the lobby or near the door of the bank where he could greet all the customers as they came in. Dr. Bulson did not give up the practice of medicine for many years after he became president of the bank. With a beard and old-fashioned clothes he was a familiar figure on the streets of Rockville Centre, especially in the 'Twenties, when he drove a Ford runabout so slowly many wondered if he knew the speed limit had been increased above the original eight miles an hour established in the early 1900's.

Dr. Bulson was still president of the bank when he died in 1945 at the age of 90. In the lobby of the former home of the Nassau County National Bank, now the Front Street office of the Franklin National Bank, there is a bronze memorial plaque erected by the Board of Directors in 1949. The plaque bears a bas relief portrait of Dr. Bulson and an inscription written by the author of this history at the request of James E. Stiles, publisher of the Nassau Daily Review-Star, who had become a director of the bank in the late 1940's.

The text of the inscription on the plaque, inspired by the wording of a plaque in Christ Church Cathedral at Lexington, Ky., mentioned by the once-popular novelist, James Lane Allen, in one of his Kentucky stories, is as follows:

Dr. Devillo N. Bulson

1855-1945

Founder, Nassau County National Bank

President 1917-1945

Physician, Banker and Civic Leader

Esteemed and beloved by the Community,

He was a kind and gracious man who

exemplified the basic virtues of integrity

and honesty in a long and useful life;

He was honorable in his business dealings,

able in his professions and tolerant in

his attitude toward his fellow men

Bergen T. Raynor retired from his position as cashier of the Bank in 1950 when he was nearly 80 years of age. Mr. Raynor continued to live at his home on Morris Avenue, near Grand Avenue, until his death in the Summer of 1967 at the age of 95. Starting as a clerk in the Bank of Rockville Centre when it opened in 1891, his career had covered 76 years of banking history in the village.

In the late 1940's the Nassau County National Bank took over the Roosevelt National Bank, which became its first branch. In

Dr. D. N. Bulson, Village President 1912–16, and President of Nassau County National Bank, 1918–45.

the early 1950's it obtained permission to open a third office in Uniondale.

Early in 1955 the Nassau County National Bank was merged with the Franklin National Bank, which thus acquired a second office in Rockville Centre. Two of the directors of the Nassau County National Bank—Supreme Court Justice Francis G. Hooley and William J. Sullivan, later Supreme Court Justice—became members of the Board of Franklin National Bank at the time of this merger and continued to serve for a number of years.

The last two financial institutions established in Rockville Centre were the work of the same man—George W. Loft, who founded the South Shore Trust Company in 1929—the year the depression began—and County Federal Savings and Loan Association in 1937.

In the late 1920's, Mr. Loft had the misfortune to lose control of the Loft Candy Company. The story at the time was that he had been speculating in his own stock, was caught short and squeezed out. It appears that he made money in the deal, but lost the company that bore his name. Mr. Loft had one son, Leon Loft, who had been running the candy company for his father at a salary reported to be $25,000 a year. When the new management dismissed Leon, Mr. Loft opened a chain of food stores— early supermarkets—in Westchester and put Leon in charge at a salary reported to be $25,000 a year. Unfortunately, within a year or two the son became ill and died.

Loss of the candy company is believed to have inspired Mr. Loft to open a bank in Rockville Centre. He was spending less time in New York City politics and living almost entirely on his estate on Merrick Road, Baldwin.

Mr. Loft had been a director of the First National Bank of Rockville Centre for many years, but he had quarreled with his former friend, John H. Carl, and resigned from the Board. Mr. Loft's brother-in-law, John McMahon, had been an employee of the First National Bank, but was dismissed after Mr. Loft left the Board.

When the South Shore Trust Company opened on Village Avenue in 1929 the First National Bank of Rockville Centre had already moved into its new skyscraper home at the corner of

Arthur T. Roth, the Rockville Centre resident who built the Franklin National Bank into a two billion dollar institution.

Sunrise Highway and North Park Avenue. Mr. Loft invited Mayor Charles E. Richmond to become president of the bank, but he appointed his brother-in-law, John McMahon, to a position corresponding to Executive Vice-President. Mr. Loft became chairman of the board.

The South Shore Trust Company grew rapidly. Mr. Loft proved to be an aggressive banker. The bank also profited from his political connections. Mr. Loft was a close personal friend of the Democratic State Comptroller, Morris Tremaine, and he was able to have the South Shore Trust Company named a depository for State funds, which inflated his statement of condition during most of the life of the bank.

When the First National Bank of Rockville Centre had to close its doors after a period during which it steadily lost deposits through massive withdrawals it was reported that the South Shore Trust Company was well fortified if a run developed against banks in general. Mr. Loft was said to have moved a large sum of cash in the bank to be ready if a run developed.

During the early 1940's when all of the banks of Nassau County were growing in assets, compared to the $3,000,000 to $5,000,000 class in which they had operated for about 20 years the two largest banks in the County were the South Shore Trust Company and the Franklin Square National Bank, now the Franklin National Bank, and then operated by Arthur T. Roth of Rockville Centre who is now chairman of the board of the Franklin National Bank.

At one time when both banks had assets of approximately $18,000,000, they ran a series of advertisements in the Nassau Daily Review-Star in which each claimed to be the largest bank in Nassau County.

Mr. Loft died about 1945, when he was past 80 years of age although still in vigorous health until his final illness. Five years later his widow, Mrs. Julia Loft, sold her controlling interest in the South Shore Trust Company to the Franklin Square National Bank, which became the Franklin National Bank about this time as it expanded beyond its original locale. Mr. Loft's estate was estimated to exceed $10,000,000 with some placing it as high as $14,000,000, of which his equity in the South Shore Trust Company must have been a substantial part.

Eight years after he founded the South Shore Trust Company, Mr. Loft sponsored the establishment of the last financial institution to be founded in the village. A law had just been passed providing for the chartering of Federal Savings and Loan Associations to help promote the Roosevelt New Deal administration's policy of increasing home ownership.

During the Spring of 1937, Mr. Loft organized a group to seek a charter for the County Federal Savings and Loan Association which Mr. Loft no doubt expected to advance the status of the South Shore Trust Company in various ways, one of which was by serving as a depository for its funds.

Mr. Loft engaged Mayor Theodore Ornstein of Long Beach, who was then practicing law in New York City, to handle the legal work connected with obtaining the charter. He invited various men to become members of its Board of Directors and offered the presidency to James E. Stiles, publisher of the Nassau Daily Review-Star. Mr. Stiles became one of the most enthusiastic of the founding group, asking his executives and other associates to make pledges toward the fund of $100,000 needed to get a charter for the association.

In due time the charter was granted and the final organization of the association completed. Fifteen original directors were elected at a meeting held June 30, 1937. The first County Federal Savings and Loan Association Board of Directors consisted of George W. Loft, Adrian Hegeman, Gust Svenson, Joseph Goldman, Harry B. Carter, James E. Stiles, Edward C. Devarennes, William N. Clurman, Dr. Manfred J. Gerstley, Ralph P. Schley, Joseph C. Lembo, J. Myles Flynn, Arthur E. Gross, Felix P. Nicklas and Richard A. Brennan.

A large number of these men were associated with Mr. Loft through the South Shore Trust Company or other enterprises, but the list also included several prominent business and professional men.

James E. Stiles, then publisher of the only daily newspaper on Long Island outside of Greater New York, was one of the prominent men of Nassau County and widely known in newspaper and political circles throughout the State.

Harry B. Carter, owner of the Bee Bus Company, was a pioneer among the bus line operators on Long Island and one of the most successful.

Adrian Hegeman was an attorney and builder. He built some of the first apartment houses erected in Rockville Centre, including the one that stands at the Southeast corner of Sunrise Highway and Forest Avenue.

Joseph Goldman, owner of Consumer Coal and Oil Company, had been a popular and successful local business man for many years. Mr. Goldman was to be the last of the original directors to serve on the County Federal Board. He retired and became a Director Emeritus in 1967 after 31 years of service on the board.

Edward C. Devarennes was president of the South Shore Trust Company at the time, and consequently one of Mr. Loft's employees. He was highly regarded as an able professional banker.

William N. Clurman was a capitalist engaged in various enterprises. He once owned the old skyscraper home of the First National Bank of Rockville Centre, for which no profitable use was found during the depression. It was reported that Mr. Clurman bought the building for $37,000, or about one tenth of what it cost to build it.

Dr. Manfred J. Gerstley was an outstanding ear and nose specialist with a handsome home and office on Hempstead Avenue, Lynbrook. Mr. Loft was one of his patients. Dr. Gerstley also had an office in New York. During World War II he became an officer in the U.S. Navy and afterward moved upstate near Syracuse. Some of his former Long Island patients thought so highly of him they traveled Upstate for treatments.

Ralph P. Schley and Felix P. Nicklas were Rockville Centre real estate brokers at the time County Federal was established.

Joseph C. Lembo operated a business that leased heavy road building and construction equipment. His headquarters was on Sunrise Highway near the intersection with Merrick Road.

J. Myles Flynn, who lived in Baldwin, was best known as a naturalist. He contributed many articles and letters to the Nassau Daily Review-Star. He was well known to Mr. Loft through St. Christopher's Roman Catholic Church, which both attended.

Arthur E. Gross was an accountant who practiced his profession in Rockville Centre and vicinity for many years.

Richard A. Brennan, who had just purchased an old house on Lenox Road, Rockville Centre, and moved to the village, was president of the Breevort Savings Bank of Brooklyn.

Gust Svenson, who subsequently was to serve as president and later as chairman of the board of County Federal, was a builder. When Mr. Loft decided to develop the 30 or more acres in his estate on the Merrick Road at Baldwin Mr. Svenson was the man who built most of the homes in the Loft Estates. The association must have been a pleasant and profitably one as Mr. Loft and Mr. Svenson remained good friends throughout Mr. Loft's lifetime.

County Federal Savings and Loan Association opened for business July 6, 1937, in a single store at 49 Front Street. Its principal employee was Frank Davis, who probably had only one assistant during the first year of operations.

Mr. Loft became chairman of the board while James E. Stiles became president of the association. A few weeks after County Federal was opened Mr. Brennan resigned, evidently finding that it was either not legal or not appropriate for a savings bank executive to serve as officer of a savings and loan association.

Mr. Stiles, as president, invited John H. Glass of Rockville Center to become a member of the board. Mr. Glass was an advertising executive of the New York Daily News. He had lived in Lynbrook for many years, but the previous year, in 1935, he had purchased a home in Rockville Centre and was well known both to Mr. Stiles and to Mr. Loft.

One of the major contributions made by Mr. Glass in the early years of the association was to encourage some of the directors to patronize his tailor. Known as one of the best dressed men of the village, Mr. Glass had his suits made by D'Andrea Brothers, who operated out of Rockefeller Center in New York, but were both residents of Rockville Centre.

Mr. Stiles and Mr. Svenson were both large men, considerable in excess of 200 pounds, and their appearance was noticeably improved when they began ordering their suits from the D'Andrea Brothers.

County Federal prospered in a mild form from the outset. Having been established in the depths of the depression when unemployment was high and many houses in the area were vacant and for sale at a fraction of their original cost, it managed to show impressive gains, percentage wise, each year.

The association of George Loft and "Jim" Stiles as chairman and president respectively of the same organization was not entirely harmonious. While both remained enthusiastic about the progress and future of County Federal they did not see eye to eye on many matters. There was some evidence they did not trust each other, but the main factor was that both men were accustomed to running anything with which they were associated and it was hard for County Federal to have two bosses.

In his enthusiasm to promote the savings and loan association Mr. Stiles published many advertisements in the Nassau Daily Review-Star which he contributed to County Federal. Mr. Loft, however, wanted to be sure they were contributed and it was reported that he asked Mr. Stiles to sign a paper to that effect to be put into the record so that a bill for the advertising could not be produced at some later date.

The association between Loft and Stiles continued for several years, nevertheless, before Mr. Stiles resigned as president and as a member of the board, on the plea that the pressure of his publishing business and other interests made it impractical for him to continue.

There was no prolonged coolness between Mr. Loft and Mr. Stiles as a result of the resignation. With less to quarrel about they became better friends and Mr. Loft actually began inserting County Federal advertising in the Review-Star and paying for it.

Mr. Loft did not live to witness the spectacular growth enjoyed by County Federal after World War II when gains of a few hundred thousand dollars a year in savings accounts were replaced by gains running into millions. County Federal was just under $10,000,000 in assets when Mr. Loft died in 1945. Eight years later it passed $100,000,000 in assets. In one year, 1952, County Federal increased its assets from $52,000,000 to $94,000,000 as a high dividend rate—3 per cent—attracted savings from all parts of the Metropolitan Area. As a pioneer Federal savings and loan association County Federal achieved its growth before the drive for savings became as competitive as it is today.

As County Federal's resources assumed large proportions the

original headquarters at 49 Front Street had to expanded. The store next door was acquired and the space on the second floor over the two stores, as well as the basements beneath them were all developed to accommodate increasing business and personnel.

In the early 1950's County Federal acquired the site at 53 North Park Avenue and built its present skyscraper headquarters. This building was completed in the Fall of 1952. Meanwhile County Federal began an expansion program by which it acquired four branch offices. An office was opened in Valley Stream March 17, 1951; a Wantagh office was opened June 2, 1956; a Levittown office July 19, 1958; and an office in Kew Gardens Hills (Flushing) was opened July 1, 1964.

During the years since it opened on July 6, 1937, with resources of $106,000 at the end of the first day's business to the end of 1968 when its resources were approaching $400,000,000, County Federal has had five presidents. James E. Stiles served from 1937 to 1942; Adrian Hegeman served from 1942 to 1943; Eugene Bird Coler served from 1943 to 1949; Gust Svenson served from 1949 to 1953; Mr. Coler again served as president from January to November, 1953; while H. B. Diffenderfer has served as president since November, 1953.

In 1953, following an uprising by a group of directors who deposed Gust Svenson as president, the Federal Home Loan Bank Board intervened and proposed that an institution as large as County Federal had become should have a trained, professional banker to direct its operations. None of the men who had served as president up to this time had had any previous banking experience. After interviewing a number of prospects, including some local commercial bankers, the Board of Directors of County Federal picked Mr. Diffenderfer and invited him to become president. Mr. Diffenderfer at the time was a vice-president of the Federal Home Loan Bank of New York and had many years of professional banking experience. When Mr. Diffenderfer assumed his duties Mr. Svenson was elected chairman of the Board of Directors and continued to serve in this capacity until his death in 1962 when he was about 80 years of age. Besides serving as president and chairman of the board, Mr. Svenson, as a builder, had supervised the construction of County Federal's main office in Rockville Centre and its branch office buildings in Valley Stream and Wantagh.

John H. Glass, who has risen in the Daily News organization over the years to become Advertising Manager and subsequently Advertising Director, succeeded Mr. Svenson as chairman of the board and served until he died in December, 1965, at the age of 75. Although he had retired as Advertising Director a year or two prior to his death, Mr. Glass was still driving into New York to the Daily News, where he was retained as an advertising consultant, until two weeks prior to his death. He had been serving as president of the Rockville Country Club for a number of years in addition to his association with County Federal and the New York Daily News.

After Mr. Glass died Julius Kassover of DeMott Avenue, Rockville Centre, became chairman of the board. Mr. Kassover was one of the founders of the Vim Electric Company, with his brothers, and has other business interests in real estate and related fields, Mr. Kassover had been a director of County Federal for more than a decade when he became chairman. Other members of the Board of Directors who live in Rockville Centre or work there are Dr. Alfred J. Cereste, Assistant Superintendent of the Rockville Centre Public Schools; William R. Gibson, Jr., who has been in the building and real estate appraisal field throughout his career; Jesse Henshel, a retired executive of the Bulova Watch Company; William J. Schmidt, a retired executive of the Long Island Lighting Company; and William W. Schwenke, Senior Vice-President of County Federal, who has been an officer of the association for more than 20 years.

Due to its early, aggressive role in the savings and loan field, County Federal at one time was one of the 25 largest savings and loan associations in the United States. When the savings and loan associations of California and Florida gained impetus it lost some ground in the national field, but as of today ranks as the largest savings and loan association in the four Long Island counties, second largest in New York State and about 31st in size in the United States.

For almost half a century Rockville Centre could claim to be the financial center of Nassau County as the total resources of its

John H. Glass, an Advertising Executive of the New York Daily News, was chairman of the Board of County Federal Savings and Loan Association and president of the Rockville Country Club.

financial institutions exceeded those of any other village in the County. During the 1940's when Rockville Centre had three independent commercial banks and two savings and loan associations, with total resources aggregating $100,000,000 or more, it was outstanding in this respect.

The 1950's saw a great change come over the banking picture in Nassau County. This was the era of bank mergers. From about 60 independent banks in 1950 Nassau dropped to less than 20 independent banks in 1960. This first merger of large proportions occurred in 1950 when the Franklin National Bank acquired the South Shore Trust Company. Within a short time after this merger the Franklin National Bank became the first Nassau County financial institution to pass $100,000,000 in assets and thereafter the financial center of Nassau County would be the village which Franklin designated as its home office.

In 1960 the New York State Legislature passed a bill allowing New York City commercial and savings banks to open branches in Nassau and Westchester Counties. The law provided, however, that a branch could not be opened in a village where a local independent bank had its home office. This protected Rockville Centre from city branches for several years as the Bank of Rockville Centre Trust Company had its home office in the village. When the Bank of Rockville Centre Trust Company was merged with the Chemical Bank New York Trust Company a year or two later, however, the way was opened for City branches to open in Rockville Centre. For a while branches of Bankers Trust Company and the First National City Bank of New York were within a few doors of each other on Sunrise Highway. In 1967 the First National City Bank moved its office to Merrick Road where it had erected a new building on the site of the old home of Robert A. Davison, founder and first president of the Bank of Rockville Centre. During the same year, farther east on Merrick Road, the Dry Dock Savings Bank of New York opened a branch. It began to look as if Rockville Centre were going to recover its old status as the financial center of Nassau County.

CHAPTER X

Rockville Centre is Incorporated

Aᴌᴛʜᴏᴜɢʜ Gᴇᴏʀɢᴇ Wᴀʟʟᴀᴄᴇ, new owner and editor of the South Side Observer, proposed as early as 1870 that Rockville Centre become an incorporated village and repeated this recommendation at least once a year thereafter, it was not until 1893—23 years later—that incorporation took place.

The South Side Observer on Friday, July 14, 1893, published a legal notice of the election to be held the following day, but this was simply a legal requirement that had to be met. Incorporation had been the subject of a heated controversy for some months at the time and every resident of the village must have been aligned on one side or the other. The names of those who signed the petition for the election to decide the issue of incorporation showed the strength of the movement, nevertheless.

The text of the notice in the South Side Observer was as follows:

NOTICE OF ELECTION
to vote on
Incorporation of Rockville Centre

Notice is hereby given that between the hours of ten o'clock in the forenoon and three o'clock in the afternoon on the 15th day of July, 1893, at Atheneum Hall, Rockville Centre, an election will be held to determine whether the proposed hereinafter described shall be incorporated as a village.

That part of the Town of Hempstead, Queens County, New York, not in an incorporated village proposed to be incorporated and to be known as the incorporated Village of Rockville Centre is bounded and describes as follows:

Beginning at a certain oak tree standing on the easterly side of Mill River between lands owned by Charlotte Mount and land owned by Henry R. Cade; thence running South 60″ 20′ east one thousand three hundred and seventy-six (1376) feet to a stake at the intersection of the Westerly line of the road leading from Oceanside to Hempstead with the northerly line of the road leading from Ocean Side to Rockville Centre; thence running North 35″ 00′ east seven hundred and twenty-five (725) feet to a stake at the intersection of the westerly line of the road leading from Oceanside to Hempstead to a stake there driven in the ground; thence running North 302 03′ East one thousand eight hundred and fifty (1850) feet along the westerly side of the highway; thence South 60″ 35′ East eight hundred and seventy-one feet to a stake there driven in the ground; thence North 68″ 19′ East three thousand and seventy-four (3074) feet to a stake driven in the ground on the edge of Parsonage Creek; thence running Northeasterly along the westerly side of said creek one thousand nine hundred feet (1900) until it comes to a stake driven in the ground at a point two hundred feet North of Seaman Avenue; thence running North 64″ 42′ west three thousand three hundred and eighty (3380) feet to a certain marked tree; thence North 61″ 18′ west two thousand three hundred and forty-one (2341) feet to a stake there driven in the ground; thence running North 45″ 00′ West one thousand six hundred and ninety-seven (1697) to a stake under the fence on the Westerly line of land beloning to the City of Brooklyn; thence running South 2″ 18′ East seven hundred and eighty-three feet to post standing in the fence; thence running South 52″ 00′ West nine hundred and forty-four (944) feet to a post there standing in the fence; thence running South 30″ 31′ West eight hundred and forty-two feet to a post there standing in the fence; thence running South 5″ 10′ West two hundred and eleven (211) feet to a stake there driven in the ground; then running South 80″ 49′ East one hundred and sixty-seven (167) feet to a stake there driven in the ground; thence South 30″ 41′ West one thousand and eighty-two (1082) feet to a stake there driven in the ground; thence South 33″ 12′ West three hundred and seventy-nine (379) feet to a stake there driven in the ground; thence running South 49″ 20′ West two hundred and sixty-six (266) feet; then South 58″ 44′ West three hundred and fourteen (314) feet; thence South 87″ 44′ West five hundred and ninety-nine (599) feet until it comes to the Easterly line of the highway leading from East Rockaway to Washington Square; thence running South 19″ 40′ West seven hundred and twelve (712) feet to a stake there driven in the ground; thence running South 9″ 52′ East four hundred ninety-seven (497) feet to a stake there driven in the ground; thence South 1″ 10′ East three thousand nine hundred ninety-one (3991) feet to the point or place of beginning, containing within said bounds according to a survey made by Alvin G. Smith C.E., May 1893, one and 99301/100000 square miles of land.

The amount to be expended the first year of incorporation for ordinary expenditures shall not exceed $500.

The annual election of officers of the corporation, after the first election, shall be held on the first Monday of August in each year.

Dated Rockville Centre, June 7, 1893.

This legal notice was signed by 26 prominent citizens who had called for a vote on incorporation. The signers were John V. D. W. Turner, T. J. Sammond, W. D. Whittemore, G. Byron Latimer, W. H. Connell, John Lyon, Oliver B. Tuthill, Edwin Wallace, Alfred E. Ives, Robert A. Davison, E. T. Thurston, Frank Hunter, John T. Davison, John Vincent, William M. Hawkins, John T. Runcie, Jacob Van Vliet, Samuel F. Phillips, George B. Mount, John S. Church, Nelson L. Seaman, John J. Purdy, D. N. Bulson, M.D., Francis F. Wilson, Charles F. Grim and Dr. J. Ensor Hutcheson. With such backing the proposal could hardly fail to pass.

The man who made the survey, Alvin G. Smith, a resident of Freeport, was serving as Town Engineer of the Town of Hempstead more than 30 years later. Alvin G. Smith founded the surveying firm of Smith and Malcolmson which under a different name is still in existence. The present firm, Baldwin and Cornelius, formerly identified itself as "Successors to Smith and Malcolmson" on its stationery and in other ways.

The area described in the survey represents less than half of the present incorporated limits of the village. Roughly the Northern boundary was originally DeMott Avenue, the Eastern boundary went some distance East of Oceanside Road and the Western boundary went as far as Ocean Avenue South of Merrick Road. A substantial part of the village from the outset has been South of Merrick road. The areas North of DeMott Avenue were not taken into the village for many years later, as they were not extensively developed for more than 40 years after the village was incorporated.

Proponents of incorporation carried the election by a substantial majority, but it proved to be an exciting day. The South Side Observer reported in its issue of Friday, July 21, 1893:

> Saturday last was a day of much interest to the people of Rockville Centre, and quite an earnest contest was had on the question of incorporation. At ten o'clock the polls were opened by Supervisor Townsend and Town Clerk Brill, and Frank Hunter was sworn in as poll clerk. The opponents of incorporation made a bitter fight, but the friends of the measure were in the lead all day and clinched their victory at half past two when a large reinforcement came in from the City on the train. There were 219 votes polled, of which 139 were in favor of incorporation, 79 against, and 1 blank, making

a majority of 60 in favor of incorporation. Those who fought the measure felt their defeat keenly, but in a day or two all were good natured again; and the general impression is that Rockville Centre takes a new start in life.

Incorporation having been approved, the first village election was held August 19 at Atheneum Hall, also from 10 a.m. to 3 p.m. The more or less official ticket consisted of John Lyon for village president; Capt. Edwin Wallace and Edwin D. Seabury, trustees for two years; Glentworth D. Combes, trustee for one year; Nelson L. Seaman, village treasurer; and John T. Runcie, tax collector.

A second ticket was nominated, but was held to be illegal. All of the official candidates were elected except John T. Runcie, who was defeated for tax collector by write-in vote for Charles A. Spedick. There was also a write-in vote for Walter H. Jones for village president, but he received only 34 votes while John Lyon received 153. Glentworth D. Combes, unopposed, received 186 and Nelson L. Seaman received 187 for village treasurer. The village treasurer is now appointed by the Village Board, not elected, and the Village Clerk, who is also appointed is officially tax collector for the village.

Two of the men involved in the first village election of Rockville Centre had sons who became distinguished physicians. Nelson L. Seaman, who ran a bakery in Rockville Centre about where Al Dowd's Steak House now stands on Lincoln Avenue, was the father of Dr. Benjamin W. Seaman and John T. Runcie was the father of Dr. William H. Runcie, who practiced in Freeport and later served as Deputy Commissioner of Health of Nassau County.

The first meeting of the new village board was held at the home of Captain Wallace on Maple Avenue on August 26, 1893, at 8 p.m. The trustees decided they should meet every Monday night at the Wallace residence.

The following committees were named at the first meeting:

Lyon and Wallace—Village Ordinances
Seabury and Combes—Public Highways
Lyon and Wallace—Assessment Roll
Combes and Seabury—To Pick Village Clerk and Street Commissioner.

Several days later, apparently at a special meeting of the board, Trustees Combes and Seabury presented three names to be balloted upon for village clerk, Edgar Southard, H. R. Williams and W. H. Connell. Connell received two votes on the first ballot while Southard and Williams received one each. On the second ballot Connell was picked by three votes to one for Williams, and was declared the first village clerk of Rockville Centre.

William H. Connell was a hardware merchant, with a store on Village Avenue in about the middle of Sunrise Highway, as this street had not been opened at that date. Later Connell was to serve as police justice and be known as "Judge Connell." The village clerkship was not to be a full-time job for many years.

Trustees Combes and Seabury also appointed George R. Mount to be Street Commissioner. There was no other candidate for this job, which was to be about the most important in the new village government. The South Side Observer, in advocating incorporation, had pointed to the sad condition of village streets and declared the Town could not be expected to work on any of them except major thoroughfares leading through the village.

Both Connell and Mount agreed to serve in their respective capacities without pay.

The Rockville Centre Village Board also appointed a Board of Health consisting of Alexander Davison, C. E. Gritman and H. R. Williams. It will be noted that none of these men was a doctor.

Rockville Centre was merely following a developing trend when it became an incorporated village. The year before Freeport had been incorporated, while on the North Shore Glen Cove had become a village and Floral Park was in process of becoming a village. Glen Cove, a city for the last 40 years or longer, was an incorporated village for upwards of 30 years before it obtained a city charter after World War I.

Interesting things were occurring elsewhere on the South Shore, then called the "South Side," as Rockville Centre set up its village government. The new residents of Pearsall's, formerly known as Pearsall's Corners, desired a less countrified name. An election was held Saturday, August 12, after the residents had petitioned the Long Island Rail Road to change the name of the station. The issue was whether Pearsall's should henceforth be known as Lynbrook or Windermere. H. R. Jaques served as secretary of the election and the residents who voted cast a majority of votes in favor of changing the name to Lynbrook. Most of Lynbrook's new residents had moved there from Brooklyn and they chose the name for their new home by reversing the spelling of the one they had left.

H. R. Jaques was the grandfather of Dr. Alan Jaques, Rockville Centre surgeon. His father, Dr. Arthur D. Jaques, who lived on the boundary of Lynbrook and East Rockaway—on Atlantic Avenue—served the Village of Rockville Centre as health officer for many years, and was a founder both of the Lynbrook National Bank and South Nassau Communities Hospital.

During 1893, the South Side Observer announced that Dr. Robert W. Hutcheson was going to build a big house on Jamaica

Home of Alexander Davison at Northwest corner of Merrick Road and South Park Avenue. The Fantasy Theatre was built in what used to be Mr. Davison's backyard. Rockville Centre Baptist Church in foreground, at left.

The spacious home of Dr. D. N. Bulson at South Park and Lincoln Avenues, still occupied by his niece, Miss Elizabeth Snyder, cost nearly $5,000 about 65 years ago.

Avenue, which actually was Merrick Road. Dr. Robert W. Hutcheson was the father of Dr. J. Ensor Hutcheson. His Merrick road home was sold many years later as a site for the present Rockville Centre post office. Dr. Robert Hutcheson owned a large tract that extended back to Lincoln Avenue. When Dr. J. Ensor Hutcheson was ready to practice medicine and get married, his father gave him a lot fronting on Lincoln Avenue where Dr. Ensor Hutcheson built a handsome home, which he occupied until his death in the 1930's.

In 1893, the South Side of the village having been developed rapidly in recent years, it was first proposed that South Park Avenue be extended all the way to Ocean Avenue by building a bridge across Mill River.

One of the first ordinances adopted by the Rockville Centre Village Board fixed the speed limit within the village limits at eight miles an hour. There were no automobiles in the village in

1893. The speed limit was set to keep young bucks and others from racing their buggies and light wagons through the streets. One of the purposes for desiring slower speeds was to keep fast moving vehicles and horses from kicking up too much dust. While the principal streets of the village may have been macadamized they were nevertheless dusty in the Summer and early Fall. The fine for exceeding the speed limit was fixed at $5.

Other ordinances adopted during the first months after the village was incorporated included one requiring that peddlers should obtain licenses and another requiring that all dogs running at large must be muzzled. It is questionable if the latter was enforced any better by the first village board than it has been in subsequent years.

There was a bad fire in Rockville Centre in the Fall of 1893. The barn in the rear of Simon Stiner's store on Village Avenue caught fire on the night of October 4. The South Side Observer in reporting the fire had high praise for the Live Oak Engine Company. "Give those boys plenty of hose and plenty of water and the company will be very useful at a fire," it declared. At the Simon Stiner fire the boys had very little of either. Rockville Centre had no water mains in those days. The water used in fighting the fire came from a well that had been dug near the curb in that block. It was called a "fire well." Men formed a bucket brigade that night to supplement the stream the Live Oak hose played on the fire with a hand pumped engine and between them they saved the village, although the barn was damaged beyond repair.

In December, 1893, the Village Board hired its first policeman. Joseph Shelly took the job at an annual salary of $500 a year.

In the meantime copies of the village ordinances had been printed on a large sheet by the Observer printing plant and the Board ordered that copies be posted in the post office, at Trustee Glentworth D. Combes hardware store on North Park Avenue and on the large tree in front of Simon Stiner's store on Village Avenue.

In October, 1893, the Village Board received a communication from the Supervisor of the Town of Hempstead (there was only one then) inquiring the amount of the village debt. Village President John Lyon ordered the village clerk to notify the Town Board that Rockville Centre had no debt.

Bills began to trickle in, nevertheless. The Village Treasurer presented items showing that it had cost $119.10 in various fees to have the village incorporated. Street Commissioner George R. Mount presented a bill November 2 for $51.85 for work he had done on the streets. The bill was approved and ordered paid.

Mr. Mount was a builder and contractor by profession. He received no salary as street commissioner, but was paid for work he did on the streets with his employees and equipment. The month before, at the meeting of September 11, Trustee Combes called the Board's attention to an obstruction the Street Commissioner had made in the middle of Village Avenue, apparently while working on a private job.

While the first few meetings of the Board had been held at the home of Trustee Edwin Wallace, in September the Board began meeting at the law office of President John Lyon and by the next year the Library on Village Avenue became the regular meeting place.

In November, Trustee Wallace offered a resolution authorizing the Public Light Committee to take action, or at least make a study, of better lighting for the village streets.

This was followed in December by the two fire companies of the village asking for a conference with the Village Board on the question of a better water supply, while G. Byron Latimer and Walcott C. Foster applied for permission to organize a water company to serve the village.

Thus within six months of incorporation the Village of Rockville Centre tackled the twin problems—water supply and lighting—out of which grew the municipal utilities that have made it an outstanding community.

The Village Board spent the latter part of 1893 working out the first village budget—for 1894—and when all the chips were down, it was found that it was going to cost $1,300 a year to run the village, of which it was anticipated $800 would be spent on the streets. The board mentioned a general tax levy of 13 cents on each $100 of assessed valuation and a special levy of 22 cents per $100 for highway improvements.

CHAPTER XI

Municipal Water and Light

Rockville Centre municipal utilities—its water department and its electric light department—dating respectively from 1895 and 1898—were planned at the outset to serve the business district.

There had been many disastrous fires in the village prior to its incorporation and although by 1895, two years after the village was incorporated, there were about five volunteer fire companies they were greatly handicapped in their work by lack of an adequate water supply.

Street lighting also was an early concern of the Rockville Centre Village Board and when the municipal electric light department was set up in 1898 its primary purpose was to provide street lights.

When the water department was established in 1895 the village bought a plot of ground at the Southeast corner of Maple and Morris Avenues from Capt. Edwin Wallace, a member of the first Village Board. The lot extended along Morris Avenue from Maple to the railroad right-of-way and there was 50 feet frontage on Maple Avenue.

On this site the village erected a small pump house and installed a double-action steam pump, which is now on display as a museum piece adjacent to the municipal storage tank up near Mercy Hospital. Water was obtained from a shallow well right on the property. Water mains were first laid in the business district, but gradually extended so all residents could have running water in their homes.

Public Works Commissioner Charles P. Ketler reported in

1968 that when the village was razing some old homes in the urban renewal area it found that one of them had water tap No. 3, indicating that area was one of the first to obtain water service. The streets involved in the urban renewal area had some of the finest homes in the village at the time.

Eventually Rockville Centre had three shallow wells, ranging in depth from 30 to 50 feet. The old steam pump pumped water from these wells into a wrought iron standpipe beside the pump house. The old standpipe, probably 60 per cent of the height of the village storage tank that now towers over it, is still in use. It is used as part of the cooling system for the diesel engines in the municipal power plant.

The shallow wells were discontinued about 1927 in anticipation of the village installing sanitary sewers, most of which actually were laid in 1929. The village then began digging deep wells. Three deep wells were dug in the vicinity of the old village incinerator on Sunrise Highway near Ocean Avenue. Water was first pumped from them into the municipal storage tank that was erected on the Maple and Morris Avenue property beside the old standpipe. Later a second municipal storage tank was built on the incinerator property, while the big storage tank near Mercy Hospital was added years later. There are now 10 deep wells supplying the village with water.

In 1898, three years after the water department had been organized, the village built its first municipal power plant somewhat as an addition to the water department, and on the same site which is still occupied by the main village generating plant.

A small building to house the generator, with its own boiler and pump, was erected on the same plot adjacent to the Water Department building. When the electric wires had been strung on poles throughout the business section and other parts of the village residents were permitted to tap these wires for electricity in their homes. They paid a flat fee for this service, based on how many lights they proposed to use, but the generator operated only at night. It started about sundown and was operated until dawn. There was no daytime service.

There is a tradition, reasonable to believe, that St. Agnes Church was responsible for the ultimate introduction of electric service during the day. It is reported that a prominent couple were to be married at St. Agnes and the priest in charge requested that the generator be operated that day so the church could be lighted by electricity during the service. Having demonstrated that electricity could be generated in the daytime as well as at night it was decided to provide 24-hour service. No doubt the rates went up when this was done.

Not all residents elected to have their homes wired for electricity during the early years. It was a matter of local gossip and comment when any resident had his or her house wired for electricity, as it later became when the more affluent and progressive citizens began buying automobiles.

Records in Commissioner Ketler's office showed that in 1905, seven years after the municipal electric department was set up, the power plant produced 206,183 kilowatt hours of electricity for 285 subscribers during the entire year. This is about what the present power plant produces every day in 1968.

The evolution of both the municipal water department and the municipal electric department can be traced in the minutes of the Rockville Centre Village Board, which during the early years were usually quite short and are still preserved in their original ledgers in the clear handwriting of the successive village clerks.

John Lyon served only one year as Village President. In August, 1894, he was succeeded by Charles W. Hayes, who remained in office four years and had the pleasure seeing the Water Department established and plans for the Electric Light Department well advanced before he retired in March, 1898. Village elections have been held in March since that time. Mr. Hayes was succeeded in March, 1898, by Edwin D. Seabury, who was in office when the Municipal Electric Light Department went into operation. Actually limited service started about the middle of February, 1898, shortly before President Hayes retired.

Mr. Seabury was the last of this group of men to die. In later years he moved to Roosevelt, where he was still living at the time of his death in the late 'Twenties. He was Village President for only one year.

The minutes of the Village Board for October 4, 1894, noted that the Board had voted to organize a Board of Water Commissioners. A meeting on the subject of setting up a Water Department, to which the residents would be invited, was set for November 26, 1894. The minutes noted that a legal notice of the meeting would appear in the South Side Observer for the three issues preceding that date.

Apparently not much was accomplished at the November meeting, for another meeting was called for April 1, 1895, at Atheneum Hall to vote on the proposition to levy a tax to provide a water system for the village. The voters at this meeting approved the proposition by a vote of 59 to 35.

An indication that progress on the Water Department had been made during the Summer is noted in the minutes of September 19, 1895, when the Village Board approved a motion to order 700 feet of hose.

In August, 1895, looking forward to the establishment of the Rockville Centre Fire Department, Live Oak Engine Company offered the village all of its property as a beginning of the department. It noted in its communication that it was changing its name to Live Oak Engine and Hose Company. It will be noted that the village acted almost immediately to provide the hose.

In October, Live Oak Engine and Hose Company had "No. 1" added to its name and was admitted to the Rockville Centre Fire Department. Eureka Hook and Ladder Company became No. 2 and in November, 1895, Alert Hose Company became No. 3. A formal resolution creating the Rockville Centre Fire Department was adopted by the Village Board October 8, 1896. The application of Defender Hose Company had been received by the Board on December 5, 1895.

The fire companies had anticipated the Village Board by electing officers several months earlier, the trustees having indicated they would accept the Fire Department when it had completed its organization.

The first officers of the Rockville Centre Fire Department, elected in the Summer of 1896, consisted of John R. Sprague, Chief Engineer; Thomas J. Sammond, Assistant Engineer; Chauncey Langdon, Secretary; and Freeman E. Gager, Treasurer. Each company was asked to submit to the village board a complete list of its members.

On July 11, 1896, Trustee Edwin Wallace moved that the Village accept the Fire Department, its organization having been completed. The budget of the Fire Department for the forthcoming year was fixed at $2,000. This meeting was held at the home of Trustee Glentworth D. Combes, and appears to have been a special meeting called for this purpose. The records show that at the time Eureka was admitted to the Department its full name was Eureka Hook, Ladder and Bucket Company. "Bucket" was dropped, apparently, as soon as the water mains were laid through the streets.

In a re-shuffle of titles later in the year the official designations of the four companies were as follows:

> Live Oak Engine Company
> Eureka Hook and Ladder Company
> Defender Hose Co. No. 1.
> Alert Hose Co. No. 2

About this time the Village Board voted to sell 10 $200 bonds, one to be retired each year over a 10-year period, "to provide and equip fire houses." In December, 1896, the Village Board adopted a resolution thanking the original officers for helping to set up the fire department and providing for their replacement, the first officers apparently having been temporary during the formative period.

The new officers of the Fire Department, announced shortly after this meeting, were Thomas J. Sammond, Chief Engineer; Oliver H. Tuthill, Assistant Engineer; E. A. Gager, Secretary; and W. C. Crain, Treasurer.

It was the custom of the various companies to submit to the Village Board a list of their members, and nearly every meeting received a supplementary list of new members that had joined the respective companies.

In March, Mr. Crain resigned as Treasurer of the Fire Department, it having been discovered he was not even a member of the Department. Mr. Crain accepted his fate with reservations, however, for in April he submitted proof that he had just become a member of Live Oak Engine Company.

The creation of the Rockville Centre Fire Department, with

four companies, almost simultaneously with the establishment of a Water Department and installation of water mains shows that the move by the Village had generated a lot of interest in the fire companies, some of which had been organized years before but had been forced to carry on their work with extremely limited facilities.

Meanwhile Rockville Centre was moving by various steps towards the establishment of its electric light department, which over the years and down to the present probably has been the village's greatest asset.

In November, 1893, shortly after the village was incorporated Trustee Edwin Wallace offered a resolution that the Public Light Committee take action toward better street lighting.

George Wallace, owner of the South Side Observer, but also a practicing attorney, appeared before the Village Board on October 17, 1895, and presented a request from the Town of Hempstead Electric Light and Power Company for permission to erect poles and string wires on the streets of the village to provide street lights and electric power. This request was referred to the Light Committee, and it appears that the request may have been premature, as the Hempstead company up to that time had no facilities for generating electricity.

At the December 10, 1895, meeting of the Board, however, on recommendation of the Light Committee, the Trustees agreed the Town of Hempstead Electric Light and Power Company could erect poles and wires once the company was incorporated and had built a power plant. The promoter of this company was a man named A. Garcia. We wonder which representative of the Village Board took this message to Garcia.

Apparently nothing came of the Hempstead proposal, but the idea of electric lights for the Rockville Centre streets became a major issue with strong support. On August 18, 1897, 25 residents qualified to vote asked the Village Board to hold an election on the proposition of setting up a Municipal Electric Light Plant. They proposed a referendum on a proposition to issue $12,000 in bonds to erect a plant and put up poles and wires. The Village Board called such an election for September 7, 1897, and the proposition was carried by 47 to 38 with three votes having been

thrown out as having been cast by unqualified voters. The Board
at an adjourned meeting held at John T. Davison's house at the
Northeast corner of Merrick Road and Park Avenue September
15 voted to go to Amityville to inspect an electric light plant
there.

It should be pointed out that 70 years ago Amityville was a
more important village than Rockville Centre. It was an older
community, long established in a prosperous farming area with
many residents also making their livelihood from the bay. It was
also a popular Summer resort with several large hotels on the
waterfront. A few years later it would be linked with Farmingdale, Huntington, Babylon and other Suffolk villages by a short-
lived trolley line.

Another modern improvement made its appearance in Rockville
Centre about this time. In October, 1897, two telephone companies asked permission to erect lines in the village—the South
Shore Telephone Company and the New York and New Jersey
Telephone Company. Both companies were granted permission to
extend service to the village, one of the conditions being that the
Rockville Centre Village office get a free telephone and that the
companies must make provision to link their service with other
companies lines.

On October 6, 1897, the Board voted to sell $12,000 in bonds
to be retired at the rate of $1,000 annually, starting with the fifth
year and ending on the sixteenth year. Interest was to be paid on
the bonds semi-annually at a rate not to exceed 4 per cent. Subsequently, on December 6, 1897, the entire bond issue was sold
to Isaac W. Sherrill of Poughkeepsie, N. Y. The same day the
Village Clerk, John R. Mangles, told the Board that the new
free telephone in the Village office was not giving satisfactory
service. The Board a few weeks before had rented space in
John W. DeMott's building on Village Avenue at an annual
rental of $80. When it moved in the Village bought its first safe
for $85.

On October 14, 1897, weeks before the new bond issue was
sold the Village Board engaged Daniel D. Smith of Oyster Bay
to draw plans and specifications and supervise construction of an

electric light plant. It was agreed that Mr. Smith would be paid $500 upon acceptance of the plant by the village.

Bids for the new power house were opened November 3, 1897. They were as follows:

William E. Whitney	$1,750.00
Charles H. Robinson	$1,475.00
John B. Lenmily	$1,270.00

On motion of Trustee John T. Davison the low bid was accepted and Mr. Lenmily got the job. Trustee Marcus H. Tracy moved to advertise for 500 poles to carry the electric wires, and he suggested that this work ought to be completed by December 1, 1897. However, the power plant would not be in operation for months as a generator had to be ordered as well as the new plant constructed.

Daniel D. Smith who got the contract to draw plans and super-vise construction of the power plant was a pioneer electrical engineer who had a part in setting up Freeport's municipal power plant as well as several on the North Shore. By marriage he was an uncle of Former Trustee, Village Clerk and Village Treasurer Arthur D. DeMott.

Before the new power plant was finished John B. Lemily, the contractor, was authorized to build a coal shed and outside toilet, "water closet," adjoining the plant for the sum of $170.

The village proceeded to start erecting light poles, but on January 17, 1898, it authorized the New York and New Jersey Telephone Company to erect poles and string telephone wires on Village Avenue, Center Avenue and Lincoln Avenue with the provision that it could put its electric wires on, the same poles, while the telephone company would be authorized to put telephone wires on poles the village had erected provided it would pay something for the use of them.

The present generation of Rockville Centre residents does not remember when the village had telephone and electric poles on its business streets, as they are all underground, but the poles existed for a long time, being both unsightly and dangerous, before the wires finally went underground.

On January 17, 1898, shortly before Rockville Centre got its first electric lights George W. Rorer, Walter D. Whittemore and Freeman E. Gager, the enumerators, finished their census of the village. They reported that there were 1,750 persons, more or less, living within the village limits and another 1,750 living in the community just outside the village limits. The enumerators were paid for their work at the rate of one cent per name. It appears that they split $35 for their work.

Village Clerk John R. Mangles, who had been a popular official, although only in office for a short time, died suddenly February 9, 1898. The Village Board held a special meeting and adopted resolutions of tribute. The Board ordered the village office to be draped in mourning for 30 days. It was nearing village election time, so John W. DeMott agreed to serve as village clerk on an interim basis.

The minutes of the Village Board during this period show the successive moves taken in anticipation of completion of the electric light plant. The Village Clerk on November 1, 1897, was authorized to purchase a record book for the Electric Light Department.

At an adjourned meeting held at the home of President Hayes on Lincoln Avenue November 8, 1897, the Village Board considered the bid of George R. Mount to furnish electric light poles. Mr. Mount's bid was as follows:

For poles 30 feet long	$2.95 each
For poles 35 feet long	$3.20 each
For poles 40 feet long	$3.45
For poles 45 feet long	$4.00

G. Christian submitted a bid to supply 30-foot poles at $3.35 each. Trustee Seabury moved that George R. Mount was the lowest bidder and be awarded the contract. The village had specified that these poles must be set five feet in the ground and advised that no crooked poles would be accepted.

It was noted at this meeting that Isaac W. Sherrill of Poughkeepsie, who bought the Municipal Electric Light Bonds, had sold seven of the $1,000 bonds to the Mechanics Savings Bank of Fishkill-on-Hudson.

Daniel D. Smith notified the Village Board on November 15, 1897, that he had ordered a transformer and wire, and would appear Wednesday night with bids for the engine, dynamo and other items needed in setting up the new Power House. Mr. Smith subsequently stated that he had both the engine and boiler built to special specifications, based on his experience in setting up previous power plants.

Frederick R. Sammis of Oyster Bay offered to put cross arms on the Electric Light poles at a cost of 28 cents each and was awarded the contract.

Rockville Centre was having other headaches about this time. Numerous complaints were received about the muddy streets, paving not having been introduced. On December 17, 1897, President Hayes reported Contractor Charles Hart was damaging the streets hauling heavy pipe to be used in connection with the reservoir of the City of Brooklyn, the reservoir being what is now known as Hempstead Lake. It appears the pipe had been shipped to Rockville Centre by rail and was being hauled North over Village and Centre Avenues. The Board voted to ask contractor for a certified check of $200 as surety he would repair the damage, otherwise he would be required to obtain a license for each horse-drawn dray or wagon used on the job.

Wright Pearsall submitted a bill for $3.20 to the Village Board on January 3, 1898, for furnishing six chairs for the village office in the John W. DeMott building.

The South Side Observer for January 14, 1898, reported that wiring for the street lights was about completed and many of the lamps had been put up. "The dynamo has arrived and the engine is expected in a few days, but the boiler has been delayed," said The Observer. It said that three arc lights would be erected on the business part of Village Avenue. The other lights throughout the village were to be incandescent and would number about 300.

The Observer reported that the Village Board of Light Commissioners had established the rates it would charge.

By contract—for stores only—the rate would be 60 cents per month for each 16-candle power lamp, if paid on or before the tenth of the month. If paid after the tenth the rate would be 65 cents per lamp.

All hotels, churches, halls and residences furnished with lights through a meter would pay 12 cents per 1,000 watts. The meters would be furnished by the village at a rental of 20 cents per month. The Observer continued:

"The basis upon which the Board has fixed the meter charges for dwellings, etc. is upon an estimate that a 16-candle power lamp will burn 50 watts an hour. Thus a lamp burning four hours each night for a month of 30 days would consume 6,000 watts, costing 72 cents, averaging three-fifths of a cent per hour for a lamp.

The Observer noted that many residents were having their houses wired. It said the Electrical Equipment Company of which M. W. Tracy was manager had wired the dwellings of Dr. Robert W. Hutcheson, Village Trustee Seabury, Village Trustee Marcus H. Tracy, John W. DeMott, William E. Whitney and George Mount. Jacob Van Vliet also had had his store wired.

Despite its enterprise in setting up an electric light plant, Lynbrook had street lights before Rockville Centre. Lynbrook and East Rockaway were not incorporated villages then, but that area established a lighting district and it appears that gasoline lamps were used. The Observer complimented favorably upon the new lamps, but later pointed out that they had proved very expensive.

It became evident early in 1898 that the original appropriation of $12,000 for electric lights would not complete the job. The money was running out before the new plant went into operation. The South Side Observer of February 11, 1898, reported:

> The Village Trustees have heard a great deal of criticism lately about the new lighting plant. It is said the appropriation is exhausted, the plant incomplete and no prospect of getting the work completed. A trustee said the village had already wired two miles more than the original plans called for, had the dynamos placed, boiler and engine in position and over 300 street lamps erected. He said when all bills were paid there would be a surplus in the treasury. He said lamps in stores and residences when the plant is put into operation will give the village an income of $75 a month. This trustee pointed out that the same engineer and fireman will run both the light and water plant, so that the village will have an economical set-up with the prospect of additional income as more people have their houses wired.

This trustee undoubtedly was Capt. Marcus H. Tracy, the

spokesman for the Electric Light Commissioners. In order to quiet the adverse criticism and have a heart-to-heart talk with the people the Village held a meeting on Monday, February 28, 1898, to review the status of the plant. The plant by then was in operation, as the Observer reported on March 4, 1898, that the street lights had been burning each night for the past two weeks. It said the incandescent lights were satisfactory, but that the 2,000-watt arc lights on Village Avenue were not coming up to expectations. It noted, however, that the arc lights were put up on trial and if not satisfactory the village would not have to pay for them.

Forty taxpayers attended the meeting called by the Village Board. Trustee Tracy was the chief spokesman. He said the village originally planned to put up seven miles of street lights, but actually had erected 10 miles. He said more wire was needed, there must be a condenser for the boiler and the Village had to have some money to buy meters. Captain Tracy estimated $1,600 or $1,700 would do the job.

The old sea-captain, now turned utility expert, did a good selling job. Within a week the Village Board got a petition from "31 qualified electors" calling upon the Village to issue $2,000 additional bonds to complete the electric light plant "to furnish electric light to the village and inhabitants." The first name on the petition was that of Capt. Samuel F. Phillips, then president of the Bank of Rockville Centre. Among the signers were Dr. Bulson, Dr. DeLano, Capt. Wallace and most of the members of the Village Board, including Captain Tracy and even John B. Lemily, the contractor who built the power plant.

It was decided to hold a referendum on this proposition March 15, 1898, at Live Oak Engine House between the hours of 2 and 6 o'clock p.m. The proposition was carried 101 to 32 after 13 votes had been thrown out. That same day George W. Rorer was elected the new Village Clerk and his salary was fixed at $40 per month.

The Board decided to raise the $2,000 by selling four $500 bonds to be retired on the fifth, sixth, seventh and eighth years after issued. Isaac Sherrill again appeared and bought the bonds. He had anticipated receiving 5 per cent interest on them, but when the Bank of Rockville Centre offered to take them for 4.95 per cent annually Mr. Sherrill agreed to accept a rate of 4.9 per cent and consummated the deal.

In March, 1898, the Huntington Long Islander quoted Daniel D. Smith, who built the Rockville Centre Power Plant, as saying it was one of the most efficient on Long Island. He said the village already had 400 incandescent street lamps in use. Mr. Smith was interviewed as he prepared to leave to supervise the erection of another electric light plant, at Milburn, N. J.

The Rockville Centre Village Board, having successfully completed the installation of a power plant, now turned its attention to other pressing problems. On June 7, 1898, the Board authorized a committee to study the propriety of purchasing a street sprinkler. The sprinkler was either purchased or a contract given, for on July 5, 1898, the committee reported regular sprinkling on Village Avenue from Lincoln to Washington Avenue, Front street by the railroad station and on Observer street from Village Avenue to the Alert Fire House. The committee said the merchants and residents were paying about two-thirds of the cost.

Sprinkling was so popular that on July 26, 1898, the Village Board received a request from the Long Island Rail Road for permission to tap the water main at the railroad tracks and Village Avenue so it could sprinkle its roadbed and allay the dust kicked up by its fast trains as they whizzed through the village. The Village Board agreed the railroad could tap the water main and use what water it needed for this purpose at a cost of $11 per year payable in advance on May 1 of each year.

After a wet spell in September, 1898, the Electric Light Committee suggested that ashes from the power plant be placed on the sidewalk in front of the village property along Morris Avenue. The fireman agreed to do it for a small additional compensation. He probably used a wheelbarrow.

Mrs. Louisa Loomis complained to the Board on July 1, 1898, that the Long Island Rail Road was hauling manure from the City and dumping it on a lot next to her property on Oceanside Road. Mrs. Loomis said this was creating a nuisance and health menace, and she also wanted a street light erected in front of her house.

In the 'Nineties and for many years before, when horses were the chief means of transportation in New York City, manure was one of the City's chief exports. It was hauled to Long Island by both trains and boats for use on the farms, especially the potato fields in the center of the Island. The railroad A. T. Stewart built to Garden City and on out on Hempstead Plain was eventually known as "the manure line."

The minutes do not say what the Village was able to do about the manure pile next to Mrs. Loomis' house, but they do say steps were taken to extend electricity to her place.

CHAPTER XII

South Side High School Established

Dⁿᵁᴿᴵɴɢ ᴛʜᴇ 'ɴɪɴᴇᴛɪᴇꜱ when the first bank was established in the village, Rockville Centre was incorporated and its municipal water and electric light systems were established, educational progress was being made and a chapter of the Masonic Lodge was granted a charter after many years of effort.

The school that had been opened on College Place in 1876 became overcrowded and inadequate in about a decade, due to the steady growth of the population. Principal Frank W. Lindsley called a special meeting of the Board of Education on November 16, 1889, and suggested that the school be named "The South Side Union School," because now that it was proposed to offer academic as well as elementary education students from other villages on the South Side of the Island would be attracted, and would pay tuition if they lived outside of the school district. Rockville Centre was then in course of establishing the first high school on this side of the Island, even though its facilities were inadequate.

A few months later, on July 17, 1890, the Board of Education received a petition signed by 50 citizens pointing out that a new, modern school building was badly needed. The Board of Education had aready rented space in another building for some of the classes.

From this petition South Side High School evolved over the period of the next two years. The building that was erected, also on College Place, now houses the administrative offices of the Village of Rockville Centre, with comparatively few additions to the original structure.

A bond issue for $18,000 was approved at a special meeting and a committee of five, consisting of Samuel O. Wright, C. W. Hayes, H. E. Smith, Austin Jayne and I. F. Phillips, was named to advise and assist the Board of Education, then called "trustees," with the new school.

The site, also on College Place, was purchased for $1,200 and plans for a two-story brick building were approved from several sets of plans submitted, some of which called for another wooden school house. No provision for toilets or electricity was made. Capt. Samuel F. Phillips, then president of the Bank of Rockville Centre, advanced the money to buy the site with the understanding he would be repaid when the old school was sold.

The $18,000 bond issue was sold to the Far Rockaway Bank, to bear interest at the rate of 4 per cent per annum. The contract for the building went to Henry H. Vought, the lowest bidder for $17,350.

The old school down the block was sold at public auction Saturday, October 17, 1891, by Clarence Matthews, auctioneer. An advertisement of the sale in the South Side Observer showed that Alfred E. Ives, Jr., was then the clerk of the Board, his father Alfred E. Ives, Sr., being a member of the Board.

The old school was bid in for $2,250 by the Rev. Patrick McKenna and became the first St. Agnes Roman Catholic Church of Rockville Centre. St. Agnes now owns all the land from Clinton Avenue to North Village Avenue, along College Place. In the original purchase of the old school, however, the land acquired was 160 x 150 feet in about the middle of the block.

The total cost of the new South Side High School, now the Village Hall, was $20,365.45 with land, building, furniture and legal fees. When it opened February 20, 1892, there were 281 resident pupils and 35 non-resident academic pupils. In time the non-resident high school students would run into a much higher number. The new building still used kerosene lamps and had toilets in the back yard.

Tuition charges for non-resident pupils were as follows: Primary grades, $14 a year; intermediate grades, $16 per year; pre-academic, $18 per year; and academic, $20 per year.

Principal Lindsley resigned at the end of that year, to accept a higher salary elsewhere and was replaced by Elmer S. Redmond at a salary of $1,200 a year.

In 1898, about five years later, the South Side Observer noted that seven teachers from Rockville Centre had resigned at the end of the school year to accept better-paying jobs in other districts and even in other states. It commented that they could make $50 to $100 a year more in other places, indicating that Rockville Centre was paying about $500 for a classroom teacher while there were places which were paying as much as $600 a year.

The new South Side High School was crowded in less than five years after it was built, partially due to the non-resident pupils it attracted. There are prominent residents in Valley Stream, Lynbrook, Baldwin, Freeport and points out East today who got their secondary education at South Side High School.

The congestion of the '90's was relieved by building the Clinton Avenue School in 1895 and 1896, in time for the opening of school in September, 1896. The Clinton Avenue School, authorized to be a two-story brick structure containing eight class rooms, was built by J. B. Lemily for $10,700. It will be recalled that Mr. Lemily also built the first municipal power plant several years later. Fred P. Smith was awarded a separate contract to install two large hot air furnaces in Clinton School for a sum not to exceed $800. Again the Board of Education spent $185 for privies, enclosed by high board fences.

The first attempt to organize a Masonic Lodge in Rockville Centre in 1876 met with failure. The Grand Lodge would not give the Rockville Centre group a chapter. Morton Lodge in Hempstead is a pre-revolutionary chapter and presumably it was deemed adequate still to serve this area. Josiah Martin, who built "Rock Hall" in Lawrence, for instance, was a member of Morton Lodge, although the record seems to indicate he might have lived in Hempstead a while before Rock Hall was finished.

In 1880 another attempt was made to get a Masonic Lodge formed in Rockville Centre, but without success. In 1888 Robert A. Davison, founder of the Bank of Rockville Centre and an outstanding attorney, led an unsuccessful attempt to form a lodge.

Finally a group received permission to organize Massapequa Lodge, Free and Accepted Masons, in 1896. The first meeting was held January 23, 1897.

The first officers of Massapequa Lodge were as follows: Master, Thomas R. LeCount; Senior Warden, William H. Connell; Junior Warden, George Wallace; Treasurer, C. W. Hayes; Secretary, Edwin D. Seabury; Senior Deacon, Marcus H. Tracy; Junior Deacon, Platt Conklin; Senior Master of Ceremony, Dr. Frank T. DeLano; Junior Master of Ceremony, Herman J. Martens; Chaplain, Austin Jayne; Tyler, William T. Odell; Trustees, William H. Kennedy, John H. Carl and George P. Bergen.

It can be seen from this list that almost everybody who was anybody in Rockville Centre at that time joined the lodge. Not all the members came from Rockville Centre. Platt Conklin, the Junior Deacon, was a prominent resident of Freeport, as was George Wallace, one of the owners of the South Side Observer, while John H. Carl lived in Baldwin.

Freeport later organized a Masonic Lodge and the two lodges had a parallel history in an interesting way. Before so many country clubs were organized many villages had local clubs for civic and social affairs. The Rockville Centre Club obtained a house on Lincoln Avenue, originally built by John P. Rhodes, as its clubhouse. Years later the Massapequa Lodge acquired this property, where its lodge rooms are now located. The auditorium it built back of the old home, and still used as a lodge room, was once the scene of some exciting athletic events when Rockville Centre had a crack basketball team.

The Freeport Masonic Lodge eventually acquired the old home of the Freeport Club at the Southwest corner of Grave Street and Sunrise Highway, which it still holds.

In 1898 while Rockville Centre was completing the task of getting its municipal electric light plant into operation events of a much broader character forced their attention on the residents. The Spanish-American war broke out and a bill was introduced to create a new county—Nassau County—out of the three Eastern townships of Queens County, North Hempstead, Oyster Bay and Hempstead.

Big headlines in the South Side Observer featured the course of the war with Spain. These stories did not appear in the front page of The Observer, which was largely devoted to "boiler plate," but ran on an inside page each week. The Spanish-American War was a short war. The Observer carried a headline in its April

22, 1898, issue which read "War With Spain." It had previously reported the sinking of The Maine and other events leading to the war. By August it was able to report that the war was over.

Camp Black, named after the Governor of New York State at the time, was established on Hempstead Plains, about where Mitchel Field is now located. The Observer reported that between 8,000 and 9,000 men were in the camp. It appears that the State Guard was first assembled there and gradually these units were mustered into the U.S. Army...

Archer B. Wallace, son of George Wallace, wrote letters to The Observer from Camp Black. In a letter addressed later to "Uncle Charlie," C. L. Wallace who was then editing The Observer, Archer wrote from Tampa, Fla., that his unit—Co. K, 71st Regiment—were soon to embark for Santiago, Cuba. He mentioned that Greaves, Carman, Gombert and Asmus—local boys— were in the camp with him and all were doing well.

The Wallace family suffered one casualty from the war, however. George Wallace had a brother, Alexander H. Wallace, who was living in Prescott, Arizona, when the war broke out. He joined Col. Theodore Roosevelt's "Rough Riders" and while in Cuba contracted either typhoid fever, or yellow fever, from which he never recovered. He came to George Wallace's home at Freeport while ill on his return from the war and died there. He was buried in Greenfield Cemetery at Hempstead with military honors. The Rough Riders had returned from Cuba and were at Montauk Point when he died. An honor guard was sent to take part in the funeral.

Willeby T. Corbett, son of Capt. Tristam Corbett, also served in the Spanish-American War. He enlisted in the U.S. Navy and served aboard the Kanawah in Cuban waters, but his ship was not involved in any fighting. When he returned after peace was declared The Observer reported that Mr. Corbett would return to his job with the Illinois Steel Company. A year or two later this company was one of many companies that were merged to form United States Steel. Mr. Corbett eventually became an executive of the United States Steel Export Company and served until his retirement about the time of World War II, during which he was a member of the local draft board.

By the 'Nineties George Wallace had given up editing The Observer and was practicing law with marked success. In 1898 he was an Assemblyman from Queens County was introduced the bill to erect Nassau County. In a letter to The Observer Mr. Wallace stated that he did not write the bill, but introduced it as a result of a mass meeting held in Mineola which appointed a committee to draw up such a bill. He introduced the bill February 24, 1898, and it passed the Assembly on March 25, 1898, with a margin of three votes. After initial opposition by the Democrats in the Senate the bill finally passed the Senate unanimously and was quickly signed by Governor Black.

In describing the bill to readers of The Observer Mr. Wallace wrote, "It was prepared with great care and the argument (in its behalf) of Mr. Halstead Scudder before the committee was unanswerable as to the merits of the bill and the necessity of its passage."

Actually Queens was already a divided county. Its Western townships had already been created into a borough of the City of New York. As a county, however, it still included the three townships that became Nassau County. They were too rural to be annexed by Greater New York and it was confusing for Queens to try to administer them when the greater part of its population was a part of New York City.

The Board of Supervisors of Queens County opposed the bill, nevertheless, and when a hearing was held Townsend Scudder, Halsted Scudder's younger brother, appeared as counsel to the Board and spoke in opposition. The Scudder brothers were thus a family divided on the issue of creating Nassau County. In his argument Townsend Scudder cited the fact the Spanish-American War then in progress and said it was not an auspicious time to set up a new county.

Despite the opposition that developed, however, Governor Black signed the bill and there was widespread excitement and interest as the work of nominating officers for the new county began. The first Nassau County officers were elected in November, 1898, and took office on January 1, 1899. In addition to electing officers plans had to be made for erecting a court house, but first the new County had to choose a County seat. Three villages vied for the honor—Mineola, Hicksville and Hempstead—with Mineola winning by a slight plurality.

While George Wallace successfully introduced the bill that created Nassau County and was frequently called "the Father of Nassau County" afterwards, he took greater pride in his own bill that helped wipe out the tramp racket in Nassau County.

As a rural area close to New York City, Nassau County used to be overrun with tramps and migrant workers during the Summer. Most of these men were harmless, but it was the policy of local authorities to arrest them for vagrancy unless they could prove they were working for some farmer. Constables received a fee for each tramp convicted and sent to the Long Island City jail—the Queens County jail—for vagrancy. They were also paid to transport them to the jail. Soon constables and magistrates had a wholesale business going every Summer. Tramps by the hundred were convicted and hauled to Long Island City with great profit to some of the authorities.

John Lyon, first village president of Rockville Centre, also spoke out against this racket and contributed to the work of ending the abuse. George Wallace's bill helped wipe out the racket—to some extent—but it made him many enemies along the way.

After the Governor had signed the bill creating Nassau County George Wallace hoped to be rewarded by being elected the first County Judge. He was nominated by the Republican Party and carried the Town of Hempstead by a big margin, but disgruntled officials in North Hempstead and Oyster Bay worked against him and he was defeated by a handful of votes, losing the election to Robert Seabury of Hempstead, who became Nassau County's first County Judge. Mr. Wallace had a thriving law practice, nevertheless, and was probably better off financially as a result of losing the election.

In May, 1898, the Village of Freeport celebrated the opening of its municipal electric light plant. Rockville Centre's plant had been in operation a few months already and members of the Village Board were guests of Freeport at the celebration. Village President Edwin D. Seabury of Rockville Centre spoke briefly, congratulating Freeport on joining the ranks of progressive communities that provided their own electric power for street lighting and commercial and residential lighting.

About the time it was announced that St. Mark's Methodist Church of Rockville Centre was having electric lights installed.

Early in 1898 a group of women led by Mrs. Mary B. Haight organized the Fortnightly Club of Rockville Centre, which, now in its 71st year, has long been recognized as one of the outstanding women's clubs on Long Island. There were eight charter members. Besides Mrs. Haight they were Mrs. H. Chapin, Mrs. John B. Dewsnap, Mrs. E. Heath, Jr., Mrs. John E. Hutcheson, Mrs. George S. Skilton, Mrs. M. Strickler and Mrs. W. B. Woolley. It is possible that Mrs. John E. Hutcheson was the same as Mrs. J. Ensor Hutcheson, wife of the prominent Rockville Centre surgeon, who lived on Lincoln Avenue. Mrs. Hutcheson was host to the club in 1899 when it marked its first birthday.

Mrs. George S. Skilton was the first president of the club and in later years most of the charter members served as presidents. In 1899 the Fortnightly Club joined the Long Island Federation of Women's Clubs and at least one president, Mrs. Glenn C. Pettit, served also as president of the Long Island Federation. The club was incorporated in 1926.

The Fortnightly Club, which holds most of its meetings at the Masonic Temple on Lincoln Avenue, has brought many famous men and women to Rockville Centre as guest speakers. In the early 'Thirties the Long Island author and essayist, Christopher Morley, addressed one of its meetings which this writer, as a newspaper editor, was invited to attend.

The Fortnightly Club observed its 50th anniversary April 6, 1948, with an elaborate program at the Masonic Temple. At this meeting Mrs. William F. Bigoney had on display the original records of the club, including minutes taken by its early secretaries. Mrs. Bigoney, then residing in Baldwin, was close to her girlhood home when she came to the Masonic Temple, as she had lived in a house adjacent to the temple before her marriage.

CHAPTER XIII

The Trolley Comes to Town

THE EXCITEMENT GENERATED by the introduction of electric lights for streets, places of business and residences had hardly died down before a new use for electricity began to attract the attention of progressive citizens.

The larger cities of the country had had street cars for many years. They were horse drawn—in many cities mules were used as they seemed to have greater stamina than horses—and naturally traveled at a rather slow pace. When electricity was developed as a new source of power cities began electrifying their trolley systems. This speeded up the service and made it possible to extend service to outlying areas that had not been served before.

It was only a step from this point to envision electric cars providing inter-city rapid transit. The era of the Interurbans was dawning. Long Island was to prove a pioneer in developing such service. Eventually many Suffolk County villages were connected by trolley lines as well as those which were built to serve Nassau County. There was one trolley line, for instance that ran all the way from Amityville through Farmingdale to Huntington, while another connects South Shore Suffolk villages all the way from Amityville to Patchogue.

Talk of establishing a trolley system to serve Nassau villages started in the late 'Nineties. A group of local business men announced before 1900 that they were going to establish the Nassau Belt Lines Company with a capital of $300,000. The company proposed to build a line from Mineola through Garden City and Hempstead to Freeport, then along the South Shore to Valley

Trolley car at Centre Avenue Station, near Lincoln Avenue, about 1910. The small building at the extreme left was the real estate office of Charles Brindley. The popular Merdes stationery store next door was used as a waiting room for trolley customers. It cost 15 cents to ride from Rockville Centre to the connection with the New York subway (elevated) at Ozone Park. (Picture donated by Harold Brindley.)

Stream, where the line would turn North along the right of way of the West Hempstead Branch of the Long Island Rail Road and go back to Mineola by this route. Promoters of the company pointed out that this "belt line" would serve 80 per cent of the population of Nassau County.

Local men involved in the company, as investors and directors, were John W. DeMott, Austin Cornwell, Charles L. Wallace and Capt. Samuel F. Phillips, then president of the Bank of Rockville Centre.

George Wallace and his brother, Charles L. Wallace, both had substantial incomes in addition to whatever they may have made out of the South Side Observer. George Wallace had built up a lucrative law practice, while Charlie Wallace was a very successfull real estate broker, even while serving as editor of the South Side Observer. Charlie Wallace, for instance, at one time served as a director both of the Bank of Rockville Centre and the Freeport Bank.

The local capitalists had hardly announced their intentions, however, before another company, backed by New York City capitalists, announced plans to build a trolley system over approximately the same route. The New York company was called the Mineola, Hempstead and Freeport Trolley Company, and it proposed to raise at least $1,000,000 to build its line.

The South Side Observer noted that on May 16, 1899, a delegation of Rockville Centre citizens attended a hearing on the proposed routes before the State Board of Railroad Commissioners in Manhattan. This was before the day of the New York Public Service Commission.

The commissioners did not play favorites. They gave both companies permission to go ahead with their plans. The tedious task of obtaining necessary franchises from the town, villages and from private property owners then began. An editorial in the South Side Observer on April 13, 1900, made this comment:

> The proposition for a trolley on the side of a business street is a bad one, although it may do very well for a country road. Merchants and others don't want an arrangement that will prevent customers from driving their vehicles up in front of their place of business and letting their vehicles stand close to the curb.

This sentiment apparently helped move the trolley lines to the center of the street where they ran through business sections.

Somewhere along the line the Nassau Belt Line Company gave up the effort. It never got a system into operation. The Mineola, Hempstead and Freeport Company proceeded to obtain the necessary franchises and build its line. On September 22, 1902, it changed its name to the New York and Long Island Traction Company, a name which survived for approximately a quarter of a century. The company built its first line from Mineola through Hempstead to Freeport. Service on this portion opened May 18, 1902. The company also built a line all the way down South Main Street, Freeport, to the waterfront. This was to connect with the Point Lookout ferry. There was no paved road from Long Beach to Point Lookout in 1900, but many Nassau residents had Summer cottages at Point Lookout which they reached by ferry from Freeport. The Point Lookout connection was not profitable to the trolley company, however, and the service was abandoned as early as 1905.*

The New York and Long Island Traction Company began building toward the West as soon as its Mineola-Freeport line was in operation. Service to Park Place, Rockville Centre, was started September 21, 1903. This gave Rockville Centre residents their first cross island public transportation to the County Seat. There had been a stage line between Rockville Centre and Hempstead at one time, but it is claimed that before the trolley line was opened there were grown men and women in Freeport, Baldwin and Rockville Centre who had never made the trip to Hempstead or Mineola. Most of them had been to New York and Brooklyn by train, but they had never driven across the Island in the horse drawn conveyances available up to that time.

Gradually the New York and Long Island Traction Company built Westward through Lynbrook and Valley Stream, past Rosedale and one to Jamaica. The proposed line along the West Hempstead Branch to Mineola seems never to have materialized as that had been a plan of the Belt Line Company which failed.

The New York and Long Island Traction Company served as a feeder for the Long Island Rail Road rather than a competitor. In some instances the traction company arranged to run its cars over the Long Island Rail Road tracks for a fee.

Rockville Centre did not benefit from the trolley line to the extent that might have been expected. Actually the trolley passed some distance from the retail district of the village. It ran along the railroad line between Rockville Centre and Lynbrook to about Windsor Avenue, Rockville Centre. Then it turned at an angle to reach Woods Avenue and veer South to Oceanside. Finally it ran along Atlantic Avenue through Baldwin Harbor and Freeport to Bedell Street, Freeport, where it turned North to Main Street and on up North Main Street and Nassau Road through Roosevelt and on to Hempstead. The closest point the

---

*A complete, detailed history of the New York and Long Island Traction Company was published in 1952 by Vincent F. Seyfried and is available at the Nassau County Museum, East Meadow, and various Nassau public libraries.

trolley came to Rockville Centre's retail district was about a block South of the Junction of Lincoln Avenue and Merrick Road. Old residents of the village say there was a paper store and one or two retail establishments near this point, but the main business section of Rockville Centre was Village Avenue, Observer Street, Front Street and later Park Avenue. Residents of Baldwin Harbor and Oceanside found it much easier to go on to Lynbrook for their shopping, because the trolley ran along Stauderman Boulevard and crossed Atlantic Avenue, Lynbrook's main retail street, right next to its principal stores.

Valley Stream had no retail district to speak of in those days, so Valley Stream residents also did their principal shopping in Lynbrook in cases where they were dependent upon the trolley. As a result there was a time when Lynbrook had a larger business district than Rockville Centre. Its streets were crowded on Saturday night, the principal shopping night of the week in those days, compared to a much smaller throng on the streets of Rockville Centre.

Rockville Centre benefited from the trolley in many ways, nevertheless. A $100,000 power plant was built on Ocean Avenue at what would now be the Northeast corner of Ocean Avenue and Sunrise Highway, although Sunrise Highway was not built until the trolley was out of business.

Oceanside and Baldwin Harbor commuters used to use the trolley line to get to Rockville Centre to catch a train to the City, which brought some business into the village. The Rockville Centre village office for many years was on Merrick Road, near the intersection of Lincoln Avenue, and fairly convenient to the trolley line.

Former Village Trustee Charles V. Day states that as a boy he used to see local attorneys taking the trolley, Eastbound, to go to Mineola to attend court. Sometimes rival attorneys in the same case would take the trolley together, along with their respective witness and perhaps the complainants and defendants. All had to ride together in the same car all the way through Freeport and Hempstead to get to the County Court at Mineola.

A report published in the South Side Observer three months after the line between Mineola and Freeport opened showed it was making money. Presumably it prospered for many years as the service continued until 1926. In its latter years, however, the trolley was a perpetual source of gripes and criticism.

When James E. Stiles established the Nassau Daily Review in 1921 one of his first crusades was against the poor service of the traction company. By 1925 the traction company was suffering acutely from bus line competition. The Bee Bus Company, established by the late Harry B. Carter, first ran between Rosedale and Jamaica. Eventually it ran along the Merrick Road through all the South Shore villages and on into Jamaica. It was much more convenient for most riders than the trolley.

During its final years Gen. Lincoln C. Andrews was in charge of the New York and Long Island Traction Company for a time. He was later given a job with the U.S. Treasury at Washington, which then had charge of enforcing prohibition. General Andrews pointed out, to the press, that the company was not getting enough revenue to service its debt and make the improvements the line needed so badly.

After General Andrews left his successors found the task hopeless. The bonds of the company were held in Cleveland and no additional money was forthcoming from that source or the local banks. Service deteriorated during the Winter of 1925–26 and in the late Spring the Public Service Commission gave the company permission to stop operations and liquidate its assets. It was years, however, before all the old rails were torn up and sold for scrap iron. Much of the rolling stock was in such bad condition it had to be burned. The Nassau Daily Review in the Summer of 1926, when this writer was its City Editor, carried a story of a big bonfire near the Ocean Avenue power house, which disposed of various assets of the defunct line.

The era of the interurbans in America was short-lived, as the history of the New York and Long Island Traction Company proves. It was typical. Yet the New York and Long Island Traction Company for at least 20 years of its 24-year history, played an important part in the development of Nassau County and to a lesser extent in the growth of Rockville Centre. It was a link between the horse and buggy days and the coming era of paved highways and two cars in every garage.

Major Andrew J. MacElroy, who founded The Owl about 1908 and published it until his death more than 50 years later. The Major is shown here in his uniform as an officer in the U. S. Air Force during World War I.

CHAPTER XIV

Competition for the Observer

Although george wallace and his brother, Charles L. Wallace, published The South Side Observer for 48 years, from 1870 to 1918, it was not destined to run this half-century without local competition. While The Observer was undoubtedly the most influential newspaper on the South Shore throughout this period, it appears from old records available that two other Rockville Centre weeklies were launched about 1908.

Bound files of the Long Island News and The Owl were destroyed in a fire at the plant more than 30 years ago, but an old copy of The Owl given to this writer by Former Village President Edwin G. Wright is dated Saturday, May 25, 1912, and is listed as Volume 4, No. 21.

This would indicate The Owl was started sometime in 1908. Old-timers in Rockville Centre believe that the late Major Andrew J. MacElroy first published The Owl as a bulletin for the Rockville Centre Club, which had its clubhouse in the building now occupied by Massapequa Lodge, F. & A.M.

In his history of Rockville Centre schools Former Superintendent Floyd B. Watson states that the first school paper was issued in February, 1910, when a copy of The Owl was published by Major MacElroy on Washington's Birthday that year. It is entirely likely that Major MacElroy used the same name both for issues of the paper for the club and for the schools.

Andrew J. MacElroy first came to Rockville Centre as principal of the high school in 1903 at a salary of $1,600 a year. He continued until April 1, 1905, when he resigned to go into business. His title as "Major" dated from the rank he held in the U.S. Army during World War I.

After experimenting with issues of The Owl while engaged in some other business Major MacElroy at length organized a company subsequently known as the Acorn Publishing Company, and launched a regular weekly newspaper called The Owl. The issue of The Owl for May 25, 1912, showed it was a full-sized newspaper of seven 14-pica columns. This was the standard size of New York City dailies at that time. Later they all used eight 12-pica columns until tabloid-sized newspapers became popular.

A copy of The Owl for Friday, March 12, 1915, shows the company was then named The South Side News Company, Acorn Building, Rockville Centre. A. J. MacElroy, President and Editor; A. M. Leavens, Vice-President and Treasurer; E. M. Fratz, Secretary.

Austin M. Leavens retained his interest in The Owl until the 1940's, although he had moved out of the village before that time. Edward M. Fratz was an old-time Long Island printer who was later employed at the Lynbrook New Era after it had been acquired by Col. Lloyd C. Griscom, who was building up a chain of Nassau weeklies. Mr. Fratz later founded The Lynbrook Leader, which he published until his death, probably in the early 1950's. A copy of the Owl for 1916 shows that Fratz had left The Owl and a man named E. Herbert Herlihy was listed as Managing Editor.

There are also copies available of a weekly newspaper named The Herald, which in 1909, was publishing Volume 1, No. 45, dated Thursday, October 28, lists E. T. Berg as president and A. R. Wood as treasurer and manager of The Rockville Centre Publishing Company, Inc. There are also copies of The Herald as late as 1914, but the 1909 issues suggest it may have been sponored by Senator William H. Reynolds to help promote the sale of Long Beach to the company he had formed to develop that beach into the present City of Long Beach. There are also available issues of The Herald with a Lynbrook dateline, as though it might have been brought out with Reynolds propaganda in several communities.

An old-time South Shore newspaper man named Frank Bang

Edwin W. Wallace, Village President on three separate occasions, Assemblyman and Nassau County Commissioner of Welfare. Mr. Wallace was the youngest President the Village had ever had when he first took office in March, 1916.

once told us he edited the first weekly newspaper in Rockville Centre that used headlines. The Observer, for instance, up to that time had published its late news on inside pages, using its first page largely for short items of national interest, short storeis, etc.

Frank Bang, who was a correspondent for Metropolitan newspapers in this area in the 1920's, was the father of Henry Bang, who became well known on Long Island during the 1960's as commercial manager for the New York Telephone Company.

The only one of these weekly newspapers that was destined to have a long life was The Owl. In 1915 the masthead of The Owl featured a drawing of an owl, around which was the legend "As Wise as an Owl and Harmless as a Dove." The Owl also proclaimed that it was "a newspaper for the progressives of Nassau County" and it had wrested the official designation for the village from The Observer.

Major MacElroy was an admirer of President Theodore Roosevelt and followed him when he organized the Progressive Party in his try for the Presidency in 1912. By 1916 The Owl apparently had seen that the Progressive cause was hopeless, for by then it proclaimed itself "a newspaper for all the people of Nassau County." It had also become the official newspaper for the Village of East Rockaway as well as continuing to be the official newspaper of Rockville Centre. The Owl was one of the first Nassau newspapers to suggest that Hiram R. Smith, president of the Bank of Rockville Centre, should be elected Supervisor of the Town of Hempstead to give the people a business administration. Major MacElroy used to write some spirited editorials on Town and County affairs and they were widely quoted in other Nassau weeklies. George Wallace acknowledged the stature of The Owl by arguing with it, or with the Major, in his own editorial contributions to the Observer.

It appears that Major MacElroy never devoted full time to The Owl. While he had a small office in its building on Front Street up to the time he died in the early 1960's, he was for many years representative of a textbook publishing company, traveling widely in this capacity.

While he was in the Army during World War I Major MacElroy met a sergeant named Guy Bacon, who was also a printer.

Major MacElroy invited him to come to Rockville Centre and take over the mechanical and job printing responsibilities for the company. Somewhere along the line The Owl acquired a newspaper, which no one seems to remember, called The Long Island News, and changed its name to The Long Island News and The Owl, which it bears today. Guy Bacon became a part owner of the company and ran it with marked success. Major MacElroy was about eighty-six years of age when he died in the early 1960's. Mr. Bacon survived him only a vew years, but in the meantime he had razed the old Acorn Publishing Company building and erected the modern building now occupied by the newspaper and printing company on the same site.

It was Major MacElroy's distinction to publish a Rockville Centre weekly for more than half a century, even longer than the Wallaces published The South Side Observer. Major MacElroy, like George Wallace and John Lyon, the first village president, also come to the area as a school teacher.

During the first decade of the 1900's the Rockville Centre Village Board was concerned primarily with the improvement of the streets. Rockville Centre, like other American small towns, had been a muddy, dusty town since it was founded. In the 'Nineties the village commenced sprinkling the streets in Summer to help keep down the dust. During the decade from 1900 to 1910 the village began oiling the streets. After several oilings a waterproof coating developed so the water ran off instead of causing mud after every rain. The Spring thaw usually went through this coating, however, so the roads had to be scraped and oiled again in the early Summer.

During this decade Rockville Centre spent a lot of money macadamizing its principal streets with Peekskill gravel, a process that was to continue for about 20 years. The Village Board also gave considerable attention to the construction of crosswalks at the main intersections, so pedestrians could walk across without wading through the mud even though the rest of the block was not paved. For many year's Rockville Centre appropriated about $1,000 a year for crosswalks, which probably cost less that $50 apiece, as they were also built with Peekskill gravel.

A typical resolution for street improvements during that decade is one which proposed to spend $1,000 for graveling South Park Avenue, beginning at Merrick Road and going as far South as the $1,000 would permit. There was a similar separate provision for each street to be graveled and it must have been frustrating to residents living down the road away to find that the money gave out just before it reached their property.

On February 19, 1909, George S. Vandewater, a prominent architect of the village and leading member of St. Mark's Methodist Church, and 16 others submitted an inquiry to the Village Board as to why Lenox Avenue was not macadamized. The Board's official reply was that it was authorized by a previous referendum to grade the street, not macadamize it and that funds for such purpose were not available. The Board said, however, it hoped to have funds for this purpose in its next budget.

Mr. Vandewater once told this writer that he was raised in one of the better homes on Washington Avenue, which today does not have any homes, with one possible exception. One of Mr. Vandewater's last jobs was to build a fine home for Dr. DeLano on Cornwell Street, just off Harvard Avenue.

On March 3, 1909, the trustees proposed a $4,500 special levy to improve and expand the electric light system and plant, using also an unexpended balance of $6,300 in the light fund, as shown by Village Treasurer Bergen T. Raynor in his annual report, published as a legal notice in the South Side Observer.

One reason the trustees wanted to expand the electric light plant was that electricity was becoming a source of power as well as light. The village, of course, was growing, but on March 25, 1907, Village Clerk George W. Rorer was directed to get samples of an electric flat iron, coffee percolator, heating pad and electric shaving mug to put on display in the village office to show the consumers of the municipal power plant the new uses for electricity.

In 1909 the village started numbering houses as the community was now so large it was impossible for everybody to know where everybody else lived. The Village Board ordered that Southern Boulevard (presumably Merrick Road) be the dividing line between the North and South for streets that crossed it.

On December 3, 1907, the Village Board received a letter from

William Richensteen, Village President from 1909 to 1911, in front of old village offices on Merrick Road.

Mrs. E. F. Bigoney of the Civic Club requesting that large trash cans be placed about the village in order that people might throw waste paper in the cans instead of on the streets, as had heretofore been the custom. The Village Clerk was directed to file the letter and write Mrs. Bigoney that the Board was studying the matter. Subsequently it asked Mrs. Bigoney to submit a list of places where the civic club thought the trash cans should be set down, but warned her that servicing of the cans might cost the village hundreds of dollars a year.

On January 14, 1908, the village Board received a new application from the South Shore Traction Company for a franchise along Lakeview Avenue through the village. The South Shore Traction Company had earlier failed to get its line built. By that time the New York and Long Island Traction Company had been operating through the lower part of Rockville Centre for several years, but the revived company felt it could do a good business with a line along Seaman Avenue, Lakeview Avenue and Hendrickson Avenue between Freeport and Valley Stream, running Northward from Freeport through Hempstead to Mineola, and from Valley Stream through Norwood (Malverne), Lakeview and West Hempstead to Mineola.

John T. Davison and a group of prominent citizens appeared before the Board at a hearing and spoke in favor of the project. The franchise undoubtedly was granted by the village but the line again failed to materialize.

The telephone in 1908 had come into such wide use that the poles with many wires were an unsightly hazard on the business streets of Rockville Centre. On March 23, 1908, Counsel Edwin G. Wright was ordered to ascertain if the Village had the authority to make the telephone company put its wires in underground conduits through the village, a move that was subsequently accomplished. On May 19, 1908, the Village Board asked the Long Island Rail Road to erect crossing gates at the Merrick Road crossing between Rockville Centre and Lynbrook. The railroad ultimately had gates at Center, Village and Park Avenues, but no crossing protection was provided at Morris and Forest Avenues until the late 1920's after Former Village President and Former Bank President G. Byron Latimer had been killed in an accident at the Morris Avenue crossing.

The Village Board in 1908 also took up the question of extending a new street through the village along the right-of-way of the North Pipe Line. While today's Peninsula Boulevard runs through the Village of Lynbrook along the right-of-way of the North Pipe Line, Rockville Centre never succeeded in getting a road built over it. Observer Street, now Sunrise Highway, through Rockville Centre was built over the main pipe line of the old Brooklyn Water Supply all the way from Rosedale east as far as it went. Mr. Edwin G. Wright recalls, however, that they previously had difficulty getting a bicycle path established along the right-of-way because certain city authorities wondered if the extra weight of all these wheels might not crush the pipe line.

In the decade starting with 1888 two now familiar churches were added to the list of Rockville Centre religious organizations —the Holy Trinity Lutheran Church and the Rockville Centre Presbyterian Church.

Prior to 1898 there had been a Congregational Church in Rockville Centre—not the present Congregational Church, however. It had a church building at the Northwest corner of Lincoln and South Park Avenues, the site now being occupied by a gasoline filling station.

A group of Lutherans had also been worshiping in this building when in 1898 the small membership of the Congregationalists caused them to disband. The Lutherans, faced with the prospect of having no place to worship, decided to form a regular congregation and take over the church, if practical. Thus the English Evangelical Lutheran Church of the Holy Trinity was officially organized January 4, 1899. The leader in the organization of the congregation was the Rev. Dr. C. Armand Miller, pastor of Holy Trinity Lutheran Church in New York City. As a compliment to him the church took the name of his city church. Local founders of the congregation included William Horton, Herman Luning, John Kellerman, Fred Meinke, Sr., John Bookman and Charles Weber.

The Mrs. Bigoney previously referred to as desiring the village to put waste cans on the streets was the daughter of Fred Meinke, Sr., who lived on Lincoln Avenue in an old home near the present Pettit-Clayton Funeral Home.

The Congregational Church building was sold at auction by the dispersing congregation, and bought by Herman Hasler, who offered the Lutherans the building if they would move it off the site. Through the efforts of Henry Wilkens, Sr., who was not then a member of the Lutheran congregation, a site directly across the street was purchased for $2,250. The church was moved to this site and served the congregation for more than 50 years.

The first regular pastor of Holy Trinity Lutheran Church was the Rev. William H. Steinbicker, who had supplied the pulpit occasionally since June, 1898. He became a full-time pastor in June, 1899, after he had graduated from the Seminary. He remained until November 1, 1901, when he married the church organist,

Miss Elsie Luning, and accepted a pastorate in Brooklyn. The people of Holy Trinity always had an affection for the Reverend Steinbicker. He preached the sermon at the 25th anniversary in 1924 and was also among the guest speakers at the 50th anniversary in 1949. In January, 1924, he was pastor of St. Luke's Lutheran Church at Farmingdale, L.I., and in January, 1949, he appeared as one of the distinguished guests who spoke at the anniversary. Other speakers at this event included Mayor W. Harry Lister and Jacob Wagner, who had been a member of the Rockville Centre Board of Education for many years.

The pastor best remembered by this generation is the Rev. Carl W. Nutzhorn, who came from the Valley Stream Lutheran Church to become pastor of Holy Trinity in 1924 and remained until his death in 1958 after thirty-four years of service. Pastor Nutzhorn's final years were crowned with success. He lived to see the completion and dedication of the handsome new Holy Trinity Lutheran Church at Lincoln and Woodland Avenues. This church was dedicated Sunday, March 4, 1956.

In a letter to George D. A. Combes, who was a prominent member of the church, written in December, 1938, Mrs. Carrie E. Wilkens, wrote that when Miss Luning married Pastor Steinbicker and moved to Brooklyn she became voluntary organist, expecting to serve a few weeks, but actually served 10 and a half years. During the last two or three years, she said, she received $50 a year for her services.

On Sunday, April 12, the carillon in Holy Trinity Church on Lincoln Avenue was dedicated "in living memory of the Rev. Carl W. Nutzhorn," who had died the year before, having had the privilege of occupying the pulpit in his new church for about two years.

The Rockville Centre Presbyterian Church was officially organized in 1909. The first recorded meeting of the congregation was held in December, 1908. In January, 1909, a Presbyterian Sunday School was started in Reliance Hose Fire House on Forest Avenue. Preaching services were instituted in February and the first Communion Service held in July. There were then 35 members. In 1911 the original church building, a small frame structure, was completed and dedicated. It stood on the site of the present church at the Southeast corner of Morris and Lakeview Avenues.

Plans for the present church were made in 1926 and the cornerstone laid in November of that year. The first service in the new building was held in October, 1927. The old church, having been moved back on the lot to provide space for the new brick structure, was completely destroyed by fire in May, 1928. In January, 1955, ground was broken for the new building for the church school and on September 28, 1955, it was opened and dedicated. On the committee were three men—Harold Brindley, Sr., Lester G. Chapin and William J. Wallis—who had held similar posts when the new church was built nearly 30 years before. Major Andrew J. MacElroy, the publisher of the News and Owl, and James Spiers, Sr., were honored at the fortieth anniversary dinner held in 1949.

The Rockville Centre Presbyterian Church has had only five pastors during its sixty years. The Rev. Harry Vaughn Mathias, the present pastor, was installed on November 23, 1945, and has thus completed nearly a quarter of a century as pastor of the church. The Reverend Mathias, who is active in civic affairs, has served for many years as one of the chaplains at South Nassau Communities Hospital.

The four previous pastors were the Rev. Arthur H. Rennie, January, 1910, to January, 1921; the Rev. Nelson B. Chester, November, 1921, to July, 1923; the Rev. Clifford J. Young, July, 1923, to January, 1929; and the Rev. Edward Ono Williams, June 1929, to April, 1945.

Congregation B'nai Sholom of Rockville Centre, one of the oldest Jewish congregations in Nassau County, was organized in 1907. For many years it worshipped at a synagogue on Windsor Avenue, just South of Merrick Road. This general area is now largely covered by the bridges erected about 1950 in the separation of grades at the intersection of Merrick Road and Sunrise Highway. As there were no Jewish synagogues in neighboring villages during B'nai Sholom's early years many residents of Lynbrook, Oceanside, Baldwin and other villages also worshipped there. As the old trolley line ran past the synagogue it provided a convenient method of transportation for the members from other

South Shore villages. During the 'Twenties and early 'Thirities Rabbi Mortiz Speier of Congregation B'nai Sholom achieved County-wide prestige for his scholarship and eloquence. He was often invited to participate in dinners and public meetings at the County level. The present handsome temple of B'nai Sholom at Hempstead and Lakeview Avenues was built in 1950, but has been substantially increased in size by subsequent additions for its school and other purposes. In 1967 Congregation B'nai Sholom marked its 60th anniversary.

CHAPTER XV

World War I

By THE ERA OF WORLD WAR I the automobile was dominating the American economy to an extent that would not have been thought possible even 10 years before. In the decade between 1900 and 1910 the purchase of an automobile by a Rockville Centre or South Shore resident was a newsworthy event, regularly reported in the South Side Observer.

By 1913 and 1914 the pages of the Observer were almost monopolized by automobile advertising. This must have been a bonanza for The Observer, as its volume of advertising increased substantially in this period. During 1913, for instance, there were large display advertisements from numerous firms, some of them advertising automobiles that are no longer built and hardly remembered.

The Baldwin Garage advertised the Maxwell, which was also sold by Frank J. Goodwin at his garage on Merrick Road, Rockville Centre. The Gardner Garage and Motor Company, also on Merrick Road near Windson Avenue, advertised that it was "distributor for the Cole, Maxwell, Marion and Mercer." Gardner and Goodwin were across the street from each other, but in the early days there might be more than one distributor for an automobile in the same community.

In later years Frank and Arthur Goodwin built up a big business as distributors for the Dodge automobile. Frank B. Gardner, who lived until about 1950, enjoyed many prosperous years as agent for the Packard. A low-score golfer at the Rockville Country Club, Frank B. Gardner also served for a brief period as president of the First National Bank of Rockville Centre.

Other automobile dealers using The Observer in 1913 were the Rockville Centre garage, agent for Buicks; Charles E. Edwards of 154 Merrick Road, who sold Overlands; G. Bennett Smith of Merrick Road, Freeport, agent for the Studebaker; Hutcheson Brothers of Hempstead, "Jackson"; and C. W. Vandeveer of 40 Hendrickson Avenue, Rockville Centre, agent for the Paige-Detroit. Herbert E. Pearsall of Merrick Road advertised the Oldsmobile.

Vandeveer's agency was somewhat removed from the heart of Rockville Centre, but had the advantage of being near the Rockville Centre stop of the old trolley line that served the South Shore at that time.

As might be expected Rockville Centre's Village Board was chiefly concerned with street improvements, and was still using Peekskill gravel. The Town and County also were beginning to build roads and since a lot of money was being spent it was inevitable that some road scandals developed, but fortunately no Rockville Centre residents appeared to have been deeply involved.

When it was proposed to improve, or pave, Long Beach Road the South Side Observer pointed out that this would chiefly benefit the real estate development of Senator William H. Reynolds at Long Beach, and that it should be a toll road.

The Rockville Centre Village Board several years later took notice of the increasing use of the automobile by adopting a village speed limit of 15 miles per hour. The ordinance also provided that no automobile should be operated after dark unless it was equipped with headlights.

Another serious problem also developed almost simultaneously with the outbreak of the first World War. On February 25, 1918, members of the Rockville Centre Fire Council appeared before the Village Board and reported that it had become almost impossible to obtain horses to draw fire engines to the fires that broke out in the village. The members pointed out that once the equipment was light enough for a group of men to pull it to the fires themselves, but that the new equipment was too heavy for the men to draw.

This resulted in the Village Board deciding to submit a proposition to the people for $7,500 for new fire equipment, to be repaid in three annual instalments of $2,500 each. The money would be spent for three purposes:

1. To buy a tractor to pull the equipment of Eureka Hook and Ladder Company.

2. A chassis for the Defender and Alert Hose Companies.

3. New motorized apparatus for Reliance Hose Company.

This proposition, subsequently approved and activated, marked the beginning of the era of gasoline-powered fire apparatus in the village.

Charles L. Wallace, who had been part owner of the South Side Observer and its editor for many years, died in Nassau Hospital May 31, 1913, of diabetes, in his 63rd year. While Charlie Wallace lived in Freeport, he was a popular figure in Rockville Centre and one of its leading real estate brokers. It was stated after his death that Mr. Wallace never opened his office or sold real estate on Sunday, as most of the brokers did, but that he usually made more sales than any of his competitors in spite of his refusal to do business on Sunday.

About 1912 Hiram R. Smith, who had been an officer of the Bank of Rockville Centre since it opened in 1890 and its president since 1900, was elected to the Board of Supervisors. He remained president of the bank for about a year after he was elected to office. In 1913 when he ran for re-election he was opposed by Augustus D. Kelsey of Lynbrook, who ran on the Progressive ticket, supported by Major MacElroy of the Rockville Centre Owl, and Paul W. F. Lindner of Malverne, the Democratic nominee. Mr. Smith was re-elected and continued to serve as Supervisor until his death in 1925.

Augustus D. Kelsey later served as Republican sheriff in Nassau County. He had also been the first village president of Lynbrook and one of the founders of the Lynbrook National Bank and Trust Company. In the late 'Twenties Mr. Kelsey, already about 70 years of age, became president of the Lynbrook bank and served for nearly 20 years. When he died in the early 1950's he was past 90 years of age and had attended meetings of the Board of the Lynbrook bank, of which he was chairman, until shortly before his death.

One of Hiram Smith's achievements as Town Supervisor was

the erection of the original Hempstead Town Hall on Front Street, Hempstead. When discussion of the Town Hall first began, The South Side Observer suggested it ought to be erected in Rockville Centre, as this was a more central location of the Town. Hempstead had long been established as the Town seat, however, and The Observer's suggestion brought no results. The $75,000 Town Hall was built beside the historic Horse Brook in Hempstead. Subsequently large wings were added on each side and in May, 1968, the new Hempstead Town Hall, costing several million dollars, was dedicated.

John Lyon, first village president of Rockville Centre, had been serving as comptroller of Nassau County for a number of years when he announced his retirement in August, 1913. The Observer paid a tribute to Mr. Lyon, stating that he had saved Nassau County thousands of dollars by his honesty and "business acumen." Mr. Lyon by that time had become known as "Honest John" Lyon.

Almost immediately, Mr. Lyon accepted the Republican nomination for Assemblyman from this district, but like his outstanding contemporary, George Wallace, who had lost a bid to become the first County Judge of Nassau County, Mr. Lyon was defeated by LeRoy J. Weed of Garden City. Mr. Weed was no mean opponent. An able man, successful in the publishing business in New York, he lived with high prestige until an advanced age, serving for years as one of the early trustees of Hofstra College, now Hofstra University.

In April, 1913, there was an epidemic of scarlet fever in Rockville Centre. Ten cases were reported at one time, but fortunately they were light cases that produced no fatalities. Dr. A. D. Jaques, the village health officer, although he was a resident of Lynbrook, was requested by the School Board to examine all children returning to school after an illness of two days or more to see if they could spread the disease. The schools apparently were not closed.

In the Spring of 1913 the Rockville Centre Public Library announced that it had received a copy of "The Inside of the Cup," a best seller by the American Winston Churchill, who became one of the most popular novelists of his time.

The village was beginning to need playground space for the

children as vacant lots and open fields were disappearing. Village Trustee Edwin W. Wallace, grandson of Capt. Edwin Wallace who has once been on the Village Board, donated the use of a lot at Maple and Morris Avenue, which he had inherited from his grandfather, to be developed as tennis courts and the School Board opened the Clinton Avenue School playground in the Summer for the first time.

Edwin G. Wright was president of the village when the United States entered the World War in 1917. As railroads began to be taxed carrying troops and military supplies, Rockville Centre developed a serious coal shortage, especially for the operation of the municipal electric light plant. As a move to conserve coal street lighting was curtailed.

George D. A. Combes, who was operating the hardware, coal and lumber business established by his father Glentworth D. Combes, offered to sell the village two carloads of coal to help tide it over. Harry C. Major, in charge of the power plant, reported he had ordered 10 carloads of coal and hadn't received a single car weeks later.

President Wright was authorized to buy five to 10 carloads of George's Creek coal from a New York man who offered it at $8.65 per ton, above the going price at that time.

Edwin W. Wallace succeeded Mr. Wright as Village President in 1918, when the war was on in earnest. Shortly after becoming Village President, Mr. Wallace reported a chance to get 3,500 to 4,000 tons of coal at $6.25 a ton. The Village Board authorized the purchase of that amount at the lower price, and since some of the $8.65 coal had not been delivered the Board voted to cancel that order.

Harrison B. Wright had been serving as Police Justice of Rockville Centre until he left to enter the service. The Police Justice received no salary, but was paid on a fee basis. During 1918, or late in 1917, Harrison Wright submitted the village a bill for about $200, representing his fees for cases he had tried.

When Harrison Wright left office, John S. Thorp, a local insurance man, was appointed Police Justice. The law did not require that the Police Justice be an attorney. Shortly after taking office, Judge Thorp appeared before the Village Board and requested that his salary be fixed at $50 a month, pointing out that the fee system was generally being abandoned as a means of paying public officials. Judge Thorp was given $50 a month, but by the end of the year the work had increased to the point he came back and requested $100 a month. The Board was somewhat reluctant to double the Judge's salary, but after a lengthy discussion, a resolution was offered that the salary of the police Justice be fixed at $900 a year, or $75 a month. Trustee Lee Greiner offered an amendment that the salary be fixed at $1,000 a year, which was adopted. The salary of the Village Police Justice has been increased from time to time since that date and is now $6,000 per year.

George A. Powers was appointed chairman of the Liberty Loan Drives in Rockville Centre. Mr. Powers, an officer and director of the Bank of Rockville Centre, lived at the Northeast corner of Morris and Grand Avenues for many years. Mr. Powers came from a family that had a fortune in Brooklyn real estate and later had David R. Longenecker, also a one-time Village President, build him a handsome home at the Northeast corner of Hilton Avenues and Fourth Street in Garden City. This was some years after World War I, however.

After one of the Liberty Loan Drives there had been adverse comment on the Village Board's participation. When the matter was brought to the attention of the Village Board at one of its meetings, Trustee Richardson stated that he had not been invited to sit on the platform at the bond rally, but that he had driven his own automobile in the motorcade that preceded the rally. Village President Ed Wright had been seated on the platform, it was pointed out.

When the next Liberty Loan Drive came along Ed Wallace had become Village President. He instructed Village Clerk George Utter to send Mr. Powers a communication offering the services of the Village Board as a group to help sell Liberty Bonds.

President Wallace also appointed a Home Garden Committee, after receiving such a request from the New York State Food Commission. The request also urged that the people raise poultry and swine. Mr. Wallace named Judge William H. Connell chairman of the Home Garden Committee. As members he named Edwin G. Wright, Treadwell D. Carpenter, Mrs. L. H. Rockwell, J. R. Spellman, Mrs. George F. Metcalf, Frank P. Baylis, Robert

H. Taylor, George F. Spinney and A. T. Powell.

Judge Connell died shortly after he was appointed chairman of the committee. He had been the first village clerk and had served as Village Police Justice in the early days of the village. The Village Board adopted a resolution of sympathy, a copy of which it directed Village Clerk Utter to send to his family.

In May, 1918, Capt. James W. Carty appeared before the Board with a design for a service flag in honor of men from the village who were in the armed forces. He said there would be 140 stars on the flag, as the village had that many men in uniform up to that date. Trustee Joseph Russ also recommended that the Village begin considering what type of memorial it should erect in honor of men in the service, including those who might lose their lives in the service.

Rockville Centre was hard hit by the Spanish influenza in the Fall of 1918, about the time the Armistice was signed. Dr. Jaques ordered schools, churches, and motion picture theatres closed, and all public meetings banned during the epidemic.

At its meeting on November 20, 1918, the Village Board received a request from the U. S. Government to supply electric power for the Naval Ordnance plant it was opening on Milburn Avenue, Baldwin. The Armistice had been signed two days before the meeting, but the Navy proceeded with the plant, later known as the "Star Shell Plant" and it was operated for many years, standing adjacent to the Coral House restaurant, just North of Merrick Road on Milburn Avenue.

While Edwin W. Wallace was Village President, Robert W. Nix of Hempstead Avenue appeared before the Board at one meeting and suggested the Village get the Long Island Rail Road to build a tunnel under the tracks at the Rockville Centre Rail Road station, so homecoming commuters would not have to walk across the tracks to get to Front Street. Such a tunnel was built eventually, but it was about 20 years later, probably after Mr. Nix had died. The tunnel was used until the tracks were elevated about 1950.

Robert W. Nix lived in a handsome Southern Colonial type home on the large plot now occupied by St. Mark's Methodist Church.

During World War I, but before the United States entered the war, leading residents of Rockville Centre had an important role in the formation of the Nassau County Historical Society. The South Side Observer on June 11, 1915, announced that a meeting would be held the following night, Saturday, June 12, in the Rockville Centre village office for the purpose of discussing the organization of a Nassau County Historical Society. The call for the meeting was signed by Dr. D. N. Bulson, Capt. James W. Carty, Glenn C. Pettit, William S. Covert, the Rev. Edwin B. Richmond, Rand W. Sutherland and Thomas L. Murphy.

Outside of Rockville Centre the leading spirit in the organization of the society was Dr. James S. Cooley, a medical doctor who was then Superintendent of Schools of Nassau County. Dr. Cooley presided at the meeting held at the Rockville Centre village office, which was attended by about 25 persons, at least half of whom were from Rockville Centre.

When the organization was completed, Dr. Cooley became the first president and two Rockville Centre men were elected officers. George D. A. Combes was elected treasurer and Robert M. Darbee was named secretary. Robert M. Darbee was a cultured resident of the village whose name frequently appears in the files of the South Side Observer of that period. He subsequently left Rockville Centre for Brooklyn, where he became president of the Bay Ridge Savings Bank, serving in that post until his death in the 1940's. Mr. Combes, who later became a bank president himself, served as treasurer of the Nassau County Historical Society until his death in 1942 and was one of the ablest contributors to its publication, the Nassau County Historical Society Journal. The first issue of the Journal contained an article by Mr. Combes on "The Battle of the Hempstead Swamps."

It is interesting to note in passing that two subsequent presidents of the Nassau County Historical Society, Preston R. Bassett and Arthur L. Hodges, who are collaborating in the preparation of this history, were residents of Rockville Centre. While Mr. Bassett is now living in Ridgefield, Conn., his home was on Broadway, Rockville Centre, during the years he was head of the Historical Society.

CHAPTER XVI

The Nassau Daily Review-Star

LATE IN 1917, George Wallace sold the South Side Observer to James E. Stiles, who was publishing a weekly he had founded in Freeport in 1914 under the name of The Nassau Post. The change of ownership became effective at the beginning of the year in 1918, thus ending nearly a half century of The Observer's ownership by George Wallace and members of his family.

Originally The Observer had been the only newspaper on the South Shore of Nassau County. By 1918 there were weekly newspapers in all of the South Shore villages and The Owl of Rockville Centre was providing The Observer with strong competition in its home community.

The masthead of The South Side Observer early in 1918 included the following names: James E. Stiles, President; Wilbur Raynor, Vice-President and Superintendent of Printing; Charles D. Lewis, Secretary; Archer B. Wallace, News Editor.

All of these men lived in Freeport. Wilbur Raynor had worked for the South Side Observer before Mr. Stiles bought it. He continued to work for the paper as long as he lived, becoming superintendent of the Job Printing Department after the paper had become a daily. Charles D. Lewis was a brother-in-law of Mr. Stiles, while Archer B. Wallace was the son of George Wallace. He had been running the paper for his father and he stayed on in the same position for a few months after the new owner took over.

Purchase of the South Side Observer by James E. Stiles brought to the Rockville Centre business community a man who was to become one of the most prominent men of the village in a career lasting for more than 40 years. It was to make Rockville Centre the seat of the first daily newspaper on Long Island outside of Greater New York and become a factor in the development of the community in many ways.

George Wallace did not long survive the sale of his paper. He continued to contribute his weekly column to the Observer after he had sold the paper, but in February, after a trip to Albany, he suffered a serious attack from which he never fully recovered. His death occurred at his home in Freeport May 7, 1918. Several columns covering his brilliant career appeared in the Observer, along with an editorial which this writer recognizes as having been written by James E. Stiles himself.

George Wallace was a brilliant man. He had become one of the leading citizens of Nassau County and was well known in legal circles in New York where he maintained a law office for many years. On one occasion he ran for Mayor of New York City on a single tax ticket. He collected some of his writings into a book which he called "The Disinherited." This author has a copy of the book presented to him by Archer B. Wallace many years after his father had died. Mr. Wallace had been successful in business as well as in the law. Despite an expensive family and a fondness for travelling abroad the Observer stated that his estate was estimated at between $150,000 and $200,000. Edwin G. Wright of Rockville Centre, who was one of the executors of the estate, said years later that the estate exceeded $100,000 but was somewhat smaller than had been anticipated at his death.

After Mr. Wallace's death, John Lyon wrote a tribute on his character which he sent to the Observer. This tribute concluded with the sentence, "In the words of the Latin poet, 'Nothing of interest to humanity was foreign to him'."

James E. Stiles had one of the most meteoric careers of his generation on Long Island and at the height of his career he was a leader among the daily newspaper publishers of New York State and highly respected and watched with interest at the national level. He was a pioneer daily newspaper publisher in the suburban field.

A native of Saratoga Springs, the Stiles family later resided in

John M. Greene, left, Managing Editor, and Arthur L. Hodges, Editor, served the Nassau Daily Review-Star, Long Island's first daily newspaper outside of Greater New York, for approximately 25 years prior to its sale to the Newhouse chain. This picture was taken in the early 'Thirties.

Brooklyn and then moved to Freeport in time for James E. Stiles to become a graduate of Freeport High School and a member of its football team. He attended Wesleyan University at Middletown, Conn., where he graduated with the Class of 1913.

When James E. Stiles founded the Nassau Post a few months after graduating from college he had no capital for the venture. The Nassau Post never had its own printing plant. It was always printed in the plants of other weeklies until Mr. Stiles bought the South Side Observer and its printing plant. The Post prospered in a small way, nevertheless, partially by receiving the designation to publish public printing which was to remain a large source of income for Mr. Stiles throughout his publishing career.

The South Side Observer and its mechanical equipment was sold to Mr. Stiles for about $18,000. The three-story building at the Northeast corner of Village Avenue and Observer Street was not included in the sale. Mr. Stiles did not have $18,000 at the time, but he was able to obtain sufficient backing to enable him to borrow the money. With the issue of July 25, 1918, the South Side Observer and Nassau Post were merged. A statement by the publisher said the war had created problems, such as the difficulty of getting newsprint and creating a labor shortage, which made the merger necessary.

In quick succession after this, Mr. Stiles acquired the Nassau County Review, a Freeport weekly, and the century-old Hempstead Inquirer, along with their mechanical plants. After publishing them separately for a time he merged them all into a big weekly, printed at Rockville Centre, which he called the Nassau County Review. This paper boasted a circulation of 8,000 and carried heavy coverage of the Nassau County government as well as local news of Rockville Centre, Freeport, Hempstead and nearby villages.

On March 7, 1921, Stiles startled Nassau County by bringing out the first issue of The Daily Review. It was several years before it would be called Nassau Daily Review. In the meantime, Mr. Stiles had built a handsome building on Observer Street— the building now occupied by the Queens County Blood Bank— and accumulated debts exceeding $100,000.

Launched at a time when there were no large department stores in Nassau County and very little display advertising, the Daily Review prospered in a small way on real estate advertising and legal notices. The real estate boom that developed in the middle of the 'Twenties did much to enable the paper to get on its feet.

When it was built in 1920, the Daily Review Building on Observer street became the Rockville Centre Post Office. The post office had a 10-year contract and occupied half of the first floor. Office space also was rented on the second floor, as the paper had a small staff and did not require even half of the building.

James E. Stiles, center, Publisher of the Nassau Daily Review-Star, is honored by his executives at an anniversary celebration held in the mid 'Thirties. Daily Review was launched Monday, March 7, 1921, and anniversary was marked with some kind of party each year.

Starting with an initial daily circulation of about 3,500, by 1930 the Nassau Daily Review had about 20,000 circulation. It was gradually increasing its area of coverage and its staff was growing. In 1930 and 1931, Mr. Stiles having sold several hundred thousands dollars worth of stock in his enterprise, the building was remodeled into a model newspaper office at a cost of about $40,000.

By that time daily competition had developed in the area. In 1927, Col. Lloyd C. Griscom, a retired diplomat with an estate at Syosset, launched The Nassau Daily Star at Lynbrook. The Colonel had bought the Lynbrook New Era, one of the best South Shore weekly newspapers, several years before.

The Nassau Daily Star might have proved successful, operating in competition with the Nassau Daily Review, if it had not been for the depression. After operating as a daily for six years, with increasing deficits as the depression grew worse, Colonel Griscom was glad to sell out to Mr. Stiles. The Colonel, a Republican, subsequently bought the Tallahassee, Fla., Daily Democrat and letting his editors operate it as a Democratic paper, more than recouped his losses.

Mr. Stiles did not immediately merge the Nassau Daily Review and Nassau Daily Star. He published them as separate newspapers, with certain benefits from joint ownership, for four years. Finally in 1937, the two papers were merged into the Nassau Daily Review-Star, published out of the Rockville Centre plant.

During its best years the Nassau Daily Review-Star had an annual volume of business exceeding $1,000,000 a year. It had the largest payroll of any business in the village for years, exceeding $10,000 a week in the 'Forties when its staff included about 200 employees.

Besides benefiting from having a business of this size in the community, Rockville Centre always got better news coverage in the Review-Star than any other community by virtue of being so convenient to the residents. Although his business was located in Rockville Centre after 1918, Mr. Stiles continued to live in a modest home on West Dean Street, Freeport, until about 1931 when he purchased the home at 20 Oxford Road, Rockville Centre, at the corner of Plymouth Road, where he lived until a few weeks before his death in 1960.

In the late 'Forties the Nassau Daily Review-Star suffered keenly from the competition provided by Newsday, which had begun publication in September, 1940. The demise of the Review-Star was hastened by a long composing room strike in 1947 from which the paper never recovered. About 1949, Mr. Stiles sold the paper to S. I. Newhouse, publisher of the Long Island Press at Jamaica and many other newspapers. Stiles remained the publisher in name only, as management of the paper soon passed to Newhouse executives and in 1953, no longer being profitable as an independent newspaper, it was merged with the Long Island Press. The Review Building on Sunrise Highway was closed and stood vacant for years, closing one of the most exciting chapters in the history of the village. The older residents of the village had watched Stiles develop his enterprise with keen interest. They had seen him succeed when failure seemed certain in the early days. They had seen the paper become a center of bustling activity where the lights burned all night and men and women came and went at all hours of the day and night. They had seen various additions built and two residences on Merrick Road razed to provide The Review-Star with its own private parking field for its staff. They could not help but feel that Rockville Centre had lost something valuable to its life when the activity ceased, the building stood empty and the parking field was vacant until taken over and developed by the village as another municipal parking field.

Mr. Stiles, having acquired profitable interests in Roosevelt Raceway and various local banks—he served as a director of the Nassau County National Bank on Front Street until it was sold to the Franklin National Bank, and later was a member of the Board of Directors of the Lynbrook National Bank & Trust Company—suffered no personal financial distress by the decline of The Review-Star, but he finally sold it at a fraction of the millions he always confidently anticipated it would be worth in his lifetime.

James E. Stiles was a positive, and in some respects a picturesque character. As a young man he enjoyed robust health. He weighed upwards of 300 pounds and along with his great energy he had a facility for expressing himself in explosive language that might include quotations from the classic poets. He was able to generate a fine morale in his organization. When the paper was sold in 1949, he had on his staff executives and other employees who had been with the Review-Star as much as 25 years, even though the turnover in newspaper organizations is always higher than is usually found in other businesses.

After the Review Building was remodeled in 1931, Stiles operated from a suite of three offices on the second floor of the building. There was a kitchenette in the suite and high county officials and leading bankers and business men were often entertained there at executive luncheons. Developed in an era when most local offices were plain and modest, Mr. Stiles in the 'Thirties enjoyed the reputation of having the finest office in Nassau County. Typical of his status and inclination toward ostentation, he was able to have the state set-up a new series for Nassau County license plates and he was awarded 8R-1 which he used for many years. This identification became widely known and even at Belmont Park it was so familiar the guards stood aside and waved him to a reserved parking spot when it appeared.

When Mr. Stiles attended the semi-annual meetings of the New York States Publishers Association in Albany, Syracuse, Rochester or Lake George he always took most of his executives with him. He would take a large suite at the convention hotel and set up a bar, which soon made his suite the unofficial headquarters of the convention where all the leading members gathered. As a result of the wide acquaintanceship and prestige thus developed, Mr. Stiles became president of the New York State Associated Dailies, made up of the smaller dailies, in 1939 and in 1942 he served as president of the Publishers Association, which included all the daily newspapers in the State except those in Greater New York, which has its own publishers association. The Review-Star editor, this writer, served as president of the New York State Society of Editors from 1941 to 1943, which suggests the stature achieved by the Nassau Daily Review-Star among the daily newspapers of the State.

In 1938, Mr. Stiles sponsored the first Review-Star Distinguished Service Award dinner, the stated purpose of which was to honor each year the man who had given the most unusual and outstanding service to the County in the previous year.

The first Distinguished Award Dinner was held at the Lido Hotel and the first recipient of the award was Dr. Benjamin W. Seaman, leading surgeon of the County at the time and a native of Rockville Centre. During the dinner at the Lido Hotel, former Village President, David W. Longenecker, now living in retirement in Florida, asked permission to make an impromptu presentation to Dr. Seaman on behalf of his old Rockville Centre friends. Mr. Longenecker recalled that he and Dr. Seaman had both been members of Rockville Centre's crack baseball team in the days when all the South Shore villages had team and a sort of South

Shore League. The Longenecker-Seaman team he described walloped most of the other teams during its best season, according to Mr. Longenecker.

Mr. Stiles appointed a Review-Star Distinguished Award Committee to pick the recipient of the award each year. Earl J. Bennett of Rockville Centre served as chairman of this committee for many years. Its members included Dr. Paul Dawson Eddy, president of Adelphi College; Dr. John Cranford Adams, president of Hofstra College (it was not a university then); Surrogate Leone D. Howell, William F. Ploch, one of the leading Nassau County bankers; and Dr. John W. Dodd, superintendent of Freeport Schools. Mr. Stiles did not serve on the committee, delegating the editor of the paper, Arthur L. Hodges, to serve in his stead. In each instance, after suggesting several men or women he thought should be considered for the honor, Mr. Stiles accepted the decision of the committee and made the award accordingly.

After becoming acquainted with Mr. Stiles through the early meetings of this committee Dr. Eddy invited Mr. Stiles to become a member of the Board of Trustees of Adelphi College. The invitation was accepted and within two years Mr. Stiles became chairman of the board. He served for about 10 years in this capacity, during a period when the college actually was in bankruptcy for a while, and when he released his seat on the board it had become a growing, prosperous co-educational institution. Mr. Stiles made many gifts to the college and in 1956, several years after he had retired, the James E. Stiles Athletic Field at Adelphi was dedicated in his honor. Among the men Mr. Stiles picked to serve with him on the Adelphi Board was Supreme Court Justice Francis G. Hooley of Rockville Centre. Although Judge Hooley was a leading Democrat and Mr. Stiles was an ardent Republican there was always a warm friendship between the two men. In their years of retirement in the 'Fifties, they met frequently as fellow directors of the Nassau County National Bank before it was sold to the Franklin National Bank.

CHAPTER XVII

Rockville Centre in the 'Twenties

BY THE 1920's ROCKVILLE CENTRE had passed its 75th anniversary as an established community with a post office, but it was still extremely rural and countrified. The business district of Rockville Centre was largely centered along Village Avenue from Merrick Road to the railroad tracks. There were still residences on both sides of Merrick Road between Village and Park Avenues. Only a limited amount of business buildings had been erected on Park Avenue by the 'Twenties.

Two Davison homesteads stood at Park Avenue and Merrick Road. John T. Davison's home was at the Northeast corner of Park Avenue and Merrick Road, and after his death the old home was occupied for many years by Earl J. Bennett, father of Surrogate John D. Bennett, who was John T. Davison's son-in-law. Across Park Avenue at the Northwest corner of Merrick Road and Park Avenue stood the fine old residence of Alexander Davison, who died during this decade. Alexander Davison's back yard eventually became the site of the Fantasy Theatre, which was erected in the 'Thirties.

Dr. Robert Hutcheson's old home, then occupied by members of his family, stood where the Rockville Centre Post Office now stands.

There were no business buildings on South Park Avenue below the corner of Merrick Road. Dr. Frank T. Delano, president of the Bank of Rockville Centre Trust Company, lived in an old house about midway of the block between Merrick Road and Lenox Avenue. Edwin G. Wright, who had lived in many houses about the village, during that decade was living in a large house below Dr. Delano at the Northeast corner of South Park Avenue and Lenox Avenue. Frank P. Baylis, a vice-president of the Bank of Rockville Centre, lived on the South Side of Merrick Road just East of Park Avenue. Treadwell D. Carpenter, another vice-president of the Bank of Rockville Centre, lived in the old Robert A. Davison homestead on Merrick Road where the First National City Bank now stands. Most of the leading men of the village in the 'Twenties lived near enough to the business district to walk to work.

By the 1920's, Observer Street had been improved, to some extent, from about the intersection with Merrick Road all the way through the Village to Morris or Forest Avenue. There was a narrow, unkempt mall down the center of Observer Street. The monument to soldiers who served in World War I originally stood on this mall at the Village Avenue intersection. It was later moved to its present location on the grounds of the Rockville Centre Municipal Building.

The 'Twenties brought a great change to Rockville Centre, changing its character to a large extent. During the 1920's Nassau County more than doubled its population, from something over 100,000 in 1920 to about 300,000 in 1930. Many roads were widened throughout the county during this decade, including Long Beach Road. In the early 'Twenties traffic became so congested on Long Beach Road it could take as much as three hours to travel between Rockville Centre and Long Beach on a Summer Sunday. Much of this traffic later came through Lincoln Avenue to Merrick Road. North Village Avenue had not been paved all the way to Hempstead, so most of the travel between the two villages followed the Hempstead Avenue-Franklin Avenue route.

The population of Rockville Centre more than doubled during the 'Twenties, but there was still little building North of DeMott Avenue. The most popular new residential area of this decade was known as Canterbury, and roughly included the area between North Village and Hempstead Avenues, North of Lakeville Avenue and along Harvard Avenue to DeMott.

The Sunrise Highway was built through Rockville Centre during 1927. Originally called the Conduit Highway because it was built along the old Brooklyn conduit right-of-way, it owes its name to a Long Island booster named Frank G. Holly, who once conducted a famous restaurant called "Holly Arms" in Hewlett. Frank G. Holly had a pet promotion called Long Island in the Summer, Florida in the Winter. He is supposed to have originated the term Sunrise Homeland applied to Long Island by the Long Island Association, which was established in the 1920's. The Sunrise Highway was built out from the City and it was several years after it reached Rockville Centre before it was opened all the way East to the Suffolk County line.

Early in the 1920's the Rockville Country Club was established on an old farm lying along Oceanside Road North of DeMott Avenue. The old residence became the first clubhouse, to which many additions have been built in the last 45 years. Originally most of the leading citizens of Rockville Centre were members of the club, in an era when men wore knickers and long stockings on the golf course.

Presiding Supervisor Hiram R. Smith of the Town of Hempstead, a former President of the Bank of Rockville Centre, turned the first spadeful of earth when the Rockville Country Club was dedicated October 28, 1923. He was introduced by David R. Longenecker, a former village president and president of the new country club. Speaking on the same program were former Village Presidents Morley K. Dunn and Edwin W. Wallace. Mr. Wallace at the time was running for Assemblyman for the first time and was elected at the November election a few days later. In his address, Supervisor Smith urged the promoters of the new club to make it a civic and social center for the village in every way, not just a golf club.

The Rockville Country Club is given credit for attracting many high-salaried executives to the village and no doubt influenced developers to build a more expensive type of house in the late 'Twenties and during subsequent decades than had been built up to that time. The club was to have some lean years during the depression, but the owners of its stock tenaciously held on to the property when many clubs were being sold for real estate subdivisions.

In 1926 George D. A. Combes, who was then operating his

father's hardware store and lumber yard on North Park Avenue, spearheaded the campaign that resulted in the erection of South Nassau Communities Hospital two years later. There had been a small Rockville Centre Sanitarium at the Southwest corner of Lincoln Avenue and South Park Avenue for a number of years, operated by a registered nurse named Molly Pearson.

Mr. Combes conceived the idea, with other leaders of the community, of building a non-profit community hospital with better facilities to serve the South Shore villages. Up to that time residents had to go to Nassau Hospital in Mineola, St. Joseph's Hospital in Far Rockaway or to a hospital in the City.

The Rockville Centre hospital drive set a goal of $250,000 to build a 50-room hospital. In the 'Twenties there were certain well-known recognized leaders in all of the South Shore communities. Mr. Combes and his associates were able to enlist most of them in the drive. While small by today's standards, this drive was an outstanding success. The goal of $250,000 was reached in a few weeks after the campaign was officially launched.

The trustees of the hospital, after investigating many sites, chose the tract on Oceanside Road where the hospital was built. The land included several acres surrounding the home of Frederick M. DaCosta, a retired oil company executive, who was an officer and director of the Bank of Rockville Centre Trust Company. It had been understood from the outset that when the new hospital was opened the Rockville Centre Sanitarium would be closed and Miss Pearson would become administrator. A number of names for the hospital were considered before the trustees selected "South Nassau Communities Hospital" as best-suited to reflect the area the hospital was built to serve.

An important factor in the success of the hospital drive undoubtedly was the front page publicity it received from the Nassau Daily Review. As long as the Review was published as a local daily it always gave the hospital front page billing in all of its major programs and events.

A major improvement was added to Rockville Centre as the decade of the 'Twenties neared its close. After years of study and discussion Rockville Centre embarked upon its municipal sewer program about 1928. Most of the sewers probably were laid during 1929. Unlike the village of Freeport where the sewer program bogged down and years passed before it was resurrected and carried on to completion, Rockville Centre's program went through with comparatively no major delays, making the village one of the first in the County to complete its sanitary sewer system. For many years afterwards, however, many home owners were still using their old cesspools to postpone the cost of connecting their premises with the sewer in front of the house.

The Rockville Centre Sewer Commission consisted of Morley K. Dunn, chairman; Capt. James W. Carty and Harold E. Libby. A referendum on the proposal to build the Sewer System was held November 14, 1928, and was carried 1,149 to 961, with five blank votes and 15 votes being declared void.

Trustee Fred H. Doelle moved the resolution for the village to issue $1,800,000 in bonds to pay for the cost of the sewers and sewage disposal plant. The plan called for retirement of $40,000 of the debt each year for 18 years, starting five years after the bonds were issued, and $60,000 a year for another 18 years, so that the entire debt would be paid off in the 40th year. Under that schedule the last of the bonds would be paid off in 1969 or 1970, depending upon how soon they were sold.

The members of the Sewer Commission made a trip to New Jersey to inspect a sewer plant built by Clyde Potts, nationally-known sanitary engineer, and soon after Mr. Potts was engaged to plan and supervise the construction of the Rockville Centre system, at a fee of 7 per cent of the cost of the sewers, exclusive of any land purchased in connection with the program.

A hot issue developed when it was found that the site picked for the disposal plant was up where the new Senior South Side High School now stands, at the end of Shepherd Street East of Long Beach Road. As this was about the highest point in the village many asked the question, "Why pump sewage uphill?" It was also known that former Village President Edwin W. Wallace and members of his family owned the land. Mr. Wallace was then rated as the political leader of the village. Village Counsel Francis G. Hooley disqualified himself as acting for the village in the matter because of his close association with Mr. Wallace. The Board then employed Former District Attorney Charles R. Weeks, who lived in Great Neck, to handle the deal. It was emphatically stated that it was not practical to build a sewage disposal plant in the Mill River basin, which many thought the obvious site for it.

Morley K. Dunn, the chairman of the Sewer Commission and former Village President, was an attorney with offices in New York. He lived on Lakeside Drive. Mr. Dunn was a son-in-law of Capt. Tristam Cobrett, the old seafarer, and a brother-in-law of Willeby T. Corber. His personal popularity and prestige undoubtedly helped carry the sewer referendum, which was passed by less than 100 votes.

The year the sewers were laid—1929—is remembered as a year of great inconvenience to the residents. Many streets were torn up all the time. Sidewalks were destroyed and during the hot, dry weather there was much dust. If it rained there was mud all over the place.

In 1928 an unusual honor came to Rockville Centre when one of its residents was nominated for President of the United States. William F. Varney, a local insurance man and active member of St. Mark's Methodist Church, was nominated for President by the National Prohibition Party at its national convention. Mr. Varney had been active in the Prohibition Party for many years, but had not anticipated being nominated for the highest office in the nation when he went to the convention. Mr. Varney at the time was 47 years old. He was the son of a Methodist minister and the family had lived in Roosevelt at one time. He had several brothers and sisters living in various Nassau villages. He was the father of William F. Varney, Jr., Rockville Centre attorney.

The National Prohibition Party did not qualify to get its ticket on the ballot in all of the States, but it was an important minority party during the Prohibition era and Mr. Varney received thousands of votes. Subsequently he ran for Governor of New York State on the Prohibition Party and later was a candidate for Mayor Rockville Centre on an anti-administration ticket and made a strong race. Mr. Varney was a popular resident of the village and a successful business man although defeated in all the elections in which he sought high public offices. He lived to be about 80 years of age, dying in the late 'Fifties or early 'Sixties.

A significant development in the 'Twenties was the opening in

Rockville Centre and other Long Island villages of the first super-markets where shoppers took pushcarts and selected their own merchandise. The first two super-markets opened in the village were Big Ben and King Kullen and as they were highly competitive the Nassau Daily Review as the only local daily newspaper enjoyed one of its first sources of regular food advertising, which helped put it on a sound financial basis.

There was another important development which affected Rockville Centre in this decade. In 1927 the first large department store in the County was opened at Hempstead. A group of local capitalists formed a corporation that established the Franklin Shops on Fulton Avenue. This corporation built the first Nassau County "skyscraper," the six-story Central Nassau Building, and opened the first improved parking lot back of the building to serve its customers. Before the Franklin Shops were opened local residents had to go to New York, Jamaica or Brooklyn for much of their shopping. It inaugurated a new era of shopping by automobile. The Franklin Shops was the first big consistent retail advertiser of the Nassau Daily Review. James E. Stiles stated shortly after the store was opened that it was using about $1,000 a month in advertising. Long Island's first daily newspaper had never had a customer like this before.

Village President Joseph H. Monds, who had been elected in 1924 and apparently re-elected in 1925 became ill in March, 1925. Village Trustee Charles E. Richmond was Acting Village President during the early part of his illness, but later Mr. Monds became a patient at the Nassu County Tuberculosis Sanatorium in Plainview and resigned. Mr. Richmond was appointed Village President on June 10, 1925. Subsequently he was re-elected several times, serving until March 17, 1931. Mr. Richmond was the first Mayor of Rockville Centre, as the title of the office was changed in the late 'Twenties.

Mr. Monds spent several years at the Sanatorium without completely regaining his health. Eventually he was discharged and returned to his home in Rockville Centre but he never entered active business again. During the 'Twenties one of his sons conducted a garage on Washington Avenue before that area was developed as a municipal parking field.

Mayor Richmond was employed for many years by the New York Telephone Company, but while in office he resigned and entered the real estate business with Trustee Fred H. Doelle. When George Loft founded the South Shore Trust Company Mr. Richmond became its first president. In 1931 he became an officer of the First National Bank of Rockville Centre a few weeks before it closed its doors as one of the first victims of the depression among Nassau County banking institutions. Mr. Richmond then entered the real estate business in which he was engaged until his death many years later. In the 'Forties he served as chairman of a Rockville Centre Slum Clearance Committee, which was one of the forerunners of the Urban Renewal program.

The Congregational Church of Rockville Centre was organized in 1926. There had been a Congregational Church in Rockville Centre before 1900, but it finally disbanded and its building was taken over by Holy Trinity Lutheran Church when this congregation was organized. Rockville Centre was growing rapidly in the 'Twenties and many of those who formed the nucleus of the new congregation had been members of the Flatbush and Tompkins Avenue Congregational Churches in Brooklyn.

The first meeting to discuss establishing the church was held in November, 1925, in the Children's Room of the Rockville Centre Public Library at its old site on Clinton Avenue. On December 7, 1925, the group voted to organize a church to be called the Congregational Church of Rockville Centre. Help was sought from the New York City Association of Congregational Churches. Among members of the first Executive Committee were Fred C. Witte and Frank S. Disbrow, both of whom were still living in Rockville Centre in 1969.

It is interesting to note that Dr. Robert K. Atkinson served the new congregation as interim pastor for a time. Dr. Atkinson was a Methodist minister, who had spent many years with the Boys Clubs of America. More than a decade later he served for several years as a Village Trustee.

The church held its first annual meeting January 8, 1926, and later that year engaged the Rev. John B. Hanna as its first minister. Plans were also made to erect a church building on the present site of the church, which was purchased for $9,000 with funds provided by the Congregational Church Extension Society. When a building committee was organized Preston R. Bassett, one of the authors of this history, became its treasurer. A parish house was first built and was ready for use in the Spring of 1927. Dr. Hanna proved a popular minister and the new congregation grew rapidly. An intellectual with liberal leanings, Dr. Hanna used to conduct forums at the parish house to which distinguished speakers were invited to discuss national and international issues. This writer recalls attending a crowded meeting at the parish house on one occasion when Norman Thomas, the Socialist leader, was guest speaker.

Dr. Hanna remained pastor of the church until 1935 when he accepted a call to become pastor of the Congregational Church of Appleton, Wisconsin. When he left the congregation had grown to more than 500 members in less than a decade. Dr. Hanna was succeeded by the Rev. Frederick A. Meyer, who served the congregation effectively for many years. When it observed its 25th anniversary in 1951 there were about 1,200 members of the congregation and the present church plant had been built up to approximately its present status, at Princeton and Morris Avenues.

In June, 1951, the Reverend Meyer resigned to become Senior Minister of the Mayflower Congregation Church in Minneapolis, Minn. While the church was searching for a new pastor Dr. Ernest M. Halliday served as interim minister. Dr. Paul F. Battenhouse became pastor in September, 1952, and served until January, 1961, when he accepted a call from the First Congregational Church of Danbury, Conn. He was succeeded by the present pastor, the Rev. Ralph E. Ahlberg, who had been an associate pastor since 1959. At the time of his call to be pastor, Mr. Ahlberg requested and was granted a six-month leave of absence to study abroad. During this period the church was served by the Rev. Arthur S. Wheelock. In January, 1966, the church celebrated its 40th anniversary and the parish news gave a detailed history not only of the church, but of the prior Rockville Centre Congregational Church which had to disband about 1900.

CHAPTER XVIII

Rockville Centre in the Depression

Many rockville centre residents, as was the case all over the country, suffered acutely as a result of the depression starting with the stock market crash in 1929. Rockville Centre's population included a large percentage of white collar commuters, many of whom had the type of jobs that were among the first casualties of the hard times brought on by the depression.

In the late 'Twenties Rockville Centre was growing rapidly. Areas like the Canterbury section, North of Lakeview Avenue and along both sides of Harvard Avenue all the way to DeMott, were being developed with houses that were expensive for that time. The growing popularity of the Rockville Country Club was already being a factor in attracting executives to the village.

The depression grew worse during the 'Thirties. Residents began to lose their jobs and eventually they began to lose their homes. Many who had invested in stocks on the margin during the boom in the early part of 1929 lost all they had put into the market.

Early in 1931, typical of what was happening everywhere, James E. Stiles put into effect a 10 per cent across the board cut in pay at the Nassau Daily Review. There was a drop in home building, which threw many men out of work.

By the middle 'Thirties many men were happy to get $50 a week, less than half they had earned five years earlier. Mayor Charles E. Richmond reported receiving applications from former high-salaried white-collar workers who wanted to join the Rockville Centre Police Department where a patrolman was paid about $50 a week.

Soon there was an abnormal number of vacant homes in the village. There were more vacant stores than there had been and little business building in the community. Some of the automobile dealers went out of business as sales dropped to a fraction of previous years.

The Welfare system as we now know it had not been developed in the early 'Thirties. Local agencies were trying desperately to deal with the most acute cases of want caused by unemployment. A study of the Nassau Daily Review in the mid 'Thirties shows that almost all the benefit affairs were to raise money for relief.

In December, 1934, the Nassau Daily Review set a goal for $5,000 to help aid the "100 Neediest Cases" selected for it by the Nassau County Emergency Relief Bureau. The Review raised the money with wide-spread participation by its readers, church organizations, school children and policemen. Mr. and Mrs. George Loft finally put the drive over the top with a contribution of several hundred dollars, split up to represent gifts from Mr. Loft, Mrs. Loft and the South Shore Trust Company which Mr. Loft had organized in 1929.

In 1934 employees of Rockville Centre consented to a 5 per cent decrease in pay. This money was not a savings to the taxpayers, however, as the village kept it for a special relief fund to aid its needy residents. Funds were contributed from other sources, so that by the end of the year Village Clerk James Patten was able to report that over $20,000 had been distributed through his office.

One source of this money was a series of boxing bouts sponsored by the Rockville Centre Police Department. The proceeds, amounting to nearly $2,000, were turned over to the village's relief fund.

Nassau County, through Supervisor J. Russel Sprague, chairman of the Board of Supervisors, had named Lewis L. Delafield, Jr., a prominent attorney living in the Five Towns, as chairman of the Nassau County Emergency Relief Committee. This committee employed Dr. Edward T. Devine, a nationally known sociologist, to administer its relief funds. Dr. Devine served for about three years before he resigned after a disagreement over policy.

In an address at the annual dinner of the Nassau County Grand

Jurors Association on December 13, 1934, Mr. Delafield said there were 46,000 persons in Nassau County looking for help, or unemployed. As the population of the County in the 1930 Federal census had been 303,000 and growth had slowed drastically, this would suggest that about one-sixth of Nassau's population at that time was without visible means of support.

District Attorney Elvin N. Edwards, a dynamic, colorful man, said in an address before a Freeport organization that the village was slipping. He called for vigorous leadership to help it hold its vaunted position as "the largest incorporated village in New York State," its claim throughout the 'Twenties.

Village officials set out to refute Mr. Edwards, although he was a distinguished resident of the village. They brought forth building permit records to show that during 1934 permits for 35 new one-family houses had been issued for a total of $127,000, which suggests that there were all rather small houses. The village officials said, in fact, that total building permits in Freeport for the first 11 months of 1934 had been $159,151.

These figures simply proved that District Attorney Edwards had been right, although the depression probably was to blame. In the late 'Twenties building permit reports regularly published in the Nassau Daily Review showed that both Rockville Centre and Freeport were issuing permits for as much as $300,000 worth of new construction a month.

As the Rockville Country Club began to lose members it faced the prospect of losing its valuable property because it had difficulty paying interest on the mortgage and meeting operating charges. The club was thrown open to all respectable persons and organizations that wanted to use its facilities and help build up its volume of business. Ultimately the club installed a slot machine, known as a "one-armed bandit," in its locker room and a prominent member, now dead, reported that this produced $2,000 in revenue one year and helped save the old clubstead. Slot machines were illegal then as now, but the police were not raiding country clubs during the depression. Although there was less traffic, due to fewer cars on the streets, most villages also had reduced the personnel of their police departments as an economy measure.

During the depression many automobile owners got only six to nine months use out of their cars. Residents of Rockville Centre in some cases admitted they did not have enough money to get a new license at the first of the year, but hoped they could renew their license in March, or at least by Summer in order that they could take the children to the beach. It became a source of pride among Rockville Centre residents to boast of the age of their cars, as they had not been able to trade them in for several years. There was one newspaper man, marginally employed, whose shabby wardrobe and beat-up car led to him being described as representing "The Spirit of the Depression."

There was progress in Rockville Centre during the depression, nevertheless. The Fantasy Theatre, then one of the finest on Long Island, was built during the depression. While building slowed down, Nassau County increased its population by about $33\frac{1}{3}$ per cent during the 'Thirties, showing a total population of just over 400,000 in the 1940 Federal census.

As the depression intensified all agencies of local government had difficulty in collecting taxes. In time there were unemployed school teachers and unemployed college professors. As Federal Work Projects of various types were set up many former executives and professional persons were happy to get jobs with them.

One of the major make-work projects for white collar workers was financed largely by the Nassau County government and was called the Lot and Block Project, involving a massive change-over in the County's file of taxable property. During the years this program lasted scores of unemployed Rockville Centre men worked on it for varying periods of time. The men employed in this work ranged from former title searchers to printers.

Nassau County had an Art Project for unemployed artists, including commercial artists. This project, through the silk screen process, provided all the posters used for Nassau's participation in the Long Island Tercentenary in 1936. A Rockville Centre man, William F. Waltemath, widely known as a civic worker, eventually became head of the Art Project and ran it very satisfactorily. Mr. Waltemath, incidentally, was an artist only by avocation. Actually he was an unemployed printer.

A Nassau Collegiate Institute was set up as a relief college in the old Curtiss Building at Clinton and Stewart Avenues, Garden City. Among its students were many who later achieved prominence in the County and its faculty included numerous able educators who had been forced out of well known colleges and universities by the depression.

A crisis developed in the Nassau County public schools. Under the law Nassau County has to borrow money and advance it to the school districts if tax collections do not produce the money levied in their budgets. In 1932 Nassau County had difficulty borrowing money. A meeting of school trustees and administrators was called in Mineola, at which the County Attorney explained the situation and urged the schools to accept less money than they had budgeted for the year. He suggested the schools couldn't do anything about it, anyway. Thereupon John H. Scott, able president of the Rockville Centre Board of Education, as recalled by Former Superintendent Floyd B. Watson in his history of Rockville Centre schools, spoke for all the districts of the County in demanding the full amount of money to which they were entitled. Mr. Scott pointed out that most of the school districts had already cut their budgets "to the bone." He said that if the schools had to be closed or curtail their programs he would send home to every parent, by the pupils, a statement that the schools were closing or cutting back because County officials refused to live up to the law.

About this time Supervisor Sprague, as chairman of the Nassau County Board of Supervisors, made several trips to Washington and also appointed Winthrop W. Aldrich, a North Shore resident and president of the Chase National Bank in New York, an emergency financial advisor. It is believed, however, that Mr. Scott's strong stand helped avert a school slow down in Rockville Centre and elsewhere in the County.

The Mayor of Rockville Centre during the 'Thirties, from 1931 to 1941, was Horace L. Allen, a business executive employed in New York. As Rockville Centre had completed its sewer system in 1929 or 1930, it was under pressure to change its zoning laws to permit the erection of apartment houses. The residents generally strenuously opposed apartments and the zoning adopted about this time undoubtedly helped hold off apartment construction for many years and established Lakeview Avenue as the Northernmost point where apartments could be built.

The residents of Rockville Centre over the years had developed pride in their municipal electric lighting system, but in July, 1935, a proposition to expend $195,000 to improve and extend the system passed by only 11 votes, 157 to 146. Hard times had made the people wary of higher taxes, even though in this case the village appropriation was going to be matched in part with Federal funds. The Federal government was making money available for municipal projects as one way of combatting unemployment.

Mayor Allen had been urged to appoint a planning commission to help establish what could be built where in the village and accomplish other results. He compromised by appointing a Mayor's Advisory Committee on August 21, 1935. The personnel of this committee consisted of John W. Gewecke, Chairman; George R. Brennan, David W. Lellis, Jacob Wagner and Michael J. Madigan. These were all prominent men. Mr. Wagner and Mr. Madigan had served on the Board of Education. John W. Gewecke was the executive of a large company in New York, while George R. Brennan, an attorney, was chairman of the Nassau County Republican Committee. He later served briefly as Surrogate of Nassau County. When it was also proposed that the Mayor name a citizens committee to help prepare the annual village budget Mayor Allen named a committee that included most of these men and several others of equal prominence. Mr. Brennan resigned from the Mayor's Advisory Committee in March, 1936, and was replaced by Dr. Robert K. Atkinson, Dr. Atkinson during the 'Twenties and 'Thirties was one of Rockville Centre's best known residents. A Methodist minister, he had worked for years for the Boy's Clubs of America. He often preached at St. Mark's Methodist Church and other local churches. He conducted the Men's Bible Class at St. Mark's Church for a number of years, attracting many men of various faiths by his leadership and eloquence. Later Dr. Atkinson served as a member of the Rockville Centre Village Board.

A major Nassau accomplishment during the 'Thirties was the preparation and adoption of the Nassau County Charter, which modernized its government, created the district court system, put the County government under the direction of a County Executive. Prior to that time there had been no real head of the County government, only the Nassau County Board of Supervisors.

An honor came to Rockville Centre in this connection. When Supervisor J. Russel Sprague and the Board of Supervisors appointed a Nassau County Charter Commission Earle J. Bennett, Rockville Centre banker and attorney, was named to the commission and later became its chairman. Mr. Bennett had served briefly as County Comptroller many years before and was well versed in the laws pertaining to the County government. This Commission prepared the County charter that was adopted by a referendum in 1936, after being approved by the State Legislature, and went into effect January 1, 1938.

In the mid 'Thirties the death of veteran Village Trustee Ronald C. Daisley brought to the Village Board a young man with a distinguished name. Trustee Daisley's place on the Board was filled by the appointment of Sherman Moreland, Jr., an attorney who had been living in the village a number of years. He was the son of the New York State Senator for whom the Moreland Act was named. The elder Moreland often visited his son in Rockville Centre and also became well known here. While Sherman Moreland served only a short time as village trustee he later became Nassau County Commander of the American Legion and remained a prominent resident of the village until after World War II when he moved back Upstate to the town where his father had lived.

Evidence that the village was still growing despite adverse economic conditions was seen in March, 1936, when the Village Board authorized erection of a new water tank on the North Well Field near Mercy Hospital with a capacity of 1,000,000 gallons. The previous water tank, erected on the grounds of the Municipal Electric Light Plant, had a capacity of only 500,000 gallons.

The Central Synagogue of Nassau County was organized late in 1935. Representatives of 58 families met at the Milburn Country Club in Baldwin December 30, 1935, and started the organization with William Godnick of Rockville Centre as temporary president. Subsequently he became the first president of the synagogue. As this was a reform congregation serving a wider area than Rockville Centre some prominent men from other villages became charter members. Among them were Dr. Clarence Cohen of Hempstead, Dr. Rudolph Dery of Lynbrook and Samuel Gluck of Oceanside. Among Rockville Centre members were Samuel

Hornstein, later an active trustee of South Nassau Communities Hospital; John R. Pinover, well known Rockville Centre builder; Sydney Roos, long active in the Home Rule Party and in civic affairs; Mr. and Mrs. James J. Silvers, also active in the Home Rule Party and in many civic affairs; and Will N. Clurman, an original director of County Federal Savings and Loan Association.

The first service of the Central Synagogue was held February 13, 1936, at the McIntosh Music Studio of Hillside Avenue. Later services were held at the Masonic Temple. The property on DeMott Avenue, Rockville Centre, where the present temple and school now stands, was acquired October 29, 1941, and the cornerstone of the temple was laid January 12, 1947. Religious school classes were held in the Wilson School, adjacent to the temple grounds until 1953 when the new religious school building was completed.

The Central Synagogue has had only two rabbis. Rabbi Roland B. Gittelsohn was engaged in April, 1936, and served for about 15 years. Rabbi Gittelsohn was an Army Chaplain during World War II and was with the American troops when Iwo Jima was taken. When Rabbi Gittelsohn resigned to accept another charge Rabbi George B. Lieberman succeeded him and is still serving in 1969.

A national honor came to Rockville Centre in 1939 when Mrs. William H. (Doris) Corwith was elected National President of the American Legion Auxiliary. Mrs. Corwith had been active in the American Legion Auxiliary for many years, having served as Nassau County Chairman and in 1936 as State Chairman. In 1941, after she had retired as National President of the Auxiliary, Mrs. Corwith became associated with Radio Station NBC in New York. She remained a member of the NBC staff for 20 years, retiring January 1, 1961, after having been active for the station in the Nixon-Kennedy Presidential campaign. In the Spring of 1969 Mrs. Corwith received notice that she had been selected as one of the Distinguished Alumnae of the State University at Albany. She was honored at services in connection with the dedication of a portion of the new campus at the University on May 16, 1969.

Picture taken when Allan B. Wright was installed as President of the Rockville Centre Luncheon Club in September, 1949, at the Chef's, Center and Lincoln Avenues. Seated are Past President Edwin G. Wright, Allan B. Wright and Past President Floyd B. Watson. Standing, left to right, are Past President Raymond C. Alger, Dr. E. Kenneth Horton, Past President, and Retiring President Arthur L. Hodges.

The Rockville Centre Luncheon Club, originally the Rockville Centre Exchange Club, honored a veteran member when Village Counsel Francis G. Hooley became a Supreme Court Justice in 1936. Seated, left to right, are Mayor Horace L. Allen, Justice Hooley, Edwin G. Wright, who served as president of the Luncheon Club for 16 years, Mrs. Hooley and Jacob Wagner, president of the Rockville Centre Board of Education. Standing are James E. Stiles, Publisher of the Nassau Daily Review-Star, and Village Judge Maurice J. Moore.

CHAPTER XIX

World War II

WORLD WAR II HAD A MORE DESOLATING EFFECT on Rockville Centre than the depression, as far as outward appearances were concerned. The National Defense program that was started soon after the war began in Europe in 1939 reduced unemployment locally and throughout the nation, but when America entered the war it proved a great setback to local business.

The United States declared war on Germany, Italy and Japan immediately after the attack on Pearl Harbor Sunday, December 7, 1941. As of January 1, 1942, the sale of new cars was halted. Within a short time all of the automobile agencies in Rockville Centre were closed, or continued in business as service garages.

Automobile tires were the first commodity to be hit by rationing, which also went into effect at the first of the year. County Executive J. Russel Sprague appointed Earl J. Bennett of Rockville Centre chairman of the Nassau County Defense Council. Mr. Bennett had previously served as chairman of the Nassau County Charter Commission.

Probably the first major appointment of the Nassau County Defense Council was the selection of Augustus B. Weller as administrator of tire rationing. Mr. Weller was then president of the First National Bank of Merrick, one of the smaller banks of the County. It was not until after the war that Mr. Weller became widely known as organizer of the Meadow Brook National Bank through a series of bank mergers starting with his own institution and the First National Bank of Freeport. Mr. Weller served throughout the war as rationing administrator of

Nassau County when gasoline, food and many other articles were strictly rationed.

As the automobile distributing agencies closed their owners found employment in various occupations. W. Harry Lister, owner of the Buick agency in Rockville Centre, operated a farm in Connecticut during part of the war. Larry Harter of Harvard Avenue, Rockville Centre, who was associated with the Cadillac agency in Hempstead, became an insurance executive for Grumman Aircraft Engineering Corporation. The showroom of the Rupp Agency, Chevrolet distributor at Lynbrook, became South Shore headquarters for the Nassau County rationing administration.

As consumer items became scarcer many retail stores in Rockville Centre were closed and some of them deteriorated badly before the war was over. Gasoline rationing went into effect late in May or early in June 1942. Many owners found that they were entitled to only five gallons a week. Remsen B. Ostrander, well known Rockville Centre attorney who was then or later Village Counsel for a time, reported that he had laid his car up because five gallons was not enough to keep his battery charged. This was true of many automobile owners who did not have to use their cars for business. During the war there was less traffic on the streets and highways than there had been in the last 20 years. Motorists had the experience of driving up to traffic lights on County roads and waiting for them to change when there was not another automobile in sight.

There was a backlog of unsold houses in Rockville Centre when the war started and some may have been built during 1942 as many builders had had materials for additional houses on hand when war was declared. After the materials were used up, however, there was no more building. Oil burners and plumbing supplies were not available after rationing took effect, and this no doubt was true of all types of building materials which were needed for army cantonments, military hospitals and other buildings erected as part of the war effort.

The last major construction project in Rockville Centre prior to the war was Mercy Hospital, which was opened late in 1941 with 72 beds and 28 bassinets. Before Mercy Hospital moved to

North Village Avenue at Southern State Parkway in 1941, it had operated as a small hospital in an old residence on Long Beach Road, Hempstead, for a number of years.

Subsequent additions to Mercy Hospital, including the new $4,000,000 Kellenberg Pavilion opened in September, 1966, have increased its capacity to 386 beds and 64 bassinets.

The United States Army had been increased to approximately 1,600,000 by the time of Pearl Harbor, many of whom had been drafted. After Pearl Harbor draft calls increased rapidly and registration required all males from about 18 to 45 years of age to obtain draft cards showing their classification.

Willeby T. Corbett, who retired about this time from the United States Steel Export Corporation, became chairman of the local draft board. As the war continued, many professional men entered the service. Walter Halliday, Rockville Centre attorney, who had been elected Mayor of the Village in 1943, entered the service in 1944 and returned only shortly before his term expired in 1945. During his absence, Village Trustee George Storms was acting Mayor. The Rabbi of Central Synagogue of Rockville Centre became an Army Chaplain.

As war manpower needs increased many retired men entered the various local defense plants and many Rockville Centre women also took employment. Thousands of men throughout Nassau County, including many from the village, were in defense jobs during the latter part of the war because their own businesses were closed for the duration.

Evidence of the lack of accurate forecasting as to how long the war would last and how many men the armed services would require can be found in a proposal by Publisher James E. Stiles of the Nassau Daily Review-Star to send the paper free of charge to every Nassau County boy in the service. When he first suggested this to his executives there were only a few hundred men in the service from Nassau County. Before the war ended there tens of thousands and it would have bankrupted the paper to try to provide every one of them with a free subscription. The families of many service men did send them the paper or copies from time to time, with the result that Rockville Centre's daily paper was read in every theatre of the war as long as it lasted.

There was still a lot of vacant land in Rockville Centre during World War II and eventually the larger plots were parceled out to various citizens who wanted to plant Liberty Gardens, or Defense Gardens. Large quantities of beans, tomatoes and other vegetables were produced during that period on land that is now covered with apartment houses and single-family residences.

There was a great deal of unhappiness due to fuel oil rationing. Many homeowners insisted they could not keep their houses comfortable with their allotment. This produced a market for soft coal and coke to supplement oil supplies and many energetic householders drove to Long Beach and brought home large supplies of driftwood which they could burn in their fireplaces. During the Summer of 1942 and for a long time afterwards, German submarines were off the coast of Long Island. This resulted in the "blackout." All window shades had to be drawn at night, there were no street lights and motorists were urged to stay off the roads after dark or use their parking lights. Even the Long Island trains came through with all shades pulled down. A civil defense organization, with wardens responsible for every block, was set up to help enforce the blackout.

Roosevelt Raceway, which was just then becoming a profitable operation, in 1942 held its race meets late in the afternoon, trying to finish before dark. It called them the "Twilight Trots."

The fuel emergency became so serious that a special Nassau County bureau was set up to help home owners who could not get oil to heat their homes. On January 5, 1944, the Nassau Daily Review-Star reported that Rockville Centre village trucks were hauling coal from dealers to homes in the village which were still burning coal.

The Rockville Centre Volunteer Fire Department, on January 25, 1944, reported that 127 of its members were then in the armed services. It issued an appeal for temporary members to help maintain adequate fire protection until its regular force could be built up again.

Rockville Centre, as all other Nassau villages, had salvage committees collecting waste paper and old metal for the war effort. An especial plea was made for old automobile registration plates. It was during the war that the policy of using automobile registration plates for more than one year first came into use. By 1944 many motorists were driving without spare tires and the tires they were using would have been discarded altogether in normal times. Some relief from gasoline rationing developed late in the war when a type of fuel known as "naptha" came on the market. It could be purchased a gallon at a time from local hardware stores to supplement the small amount of gasoline to which most motorists were entitled under war rationing. While naptha produced a lot of carbon in engines it stretched the fuel supply and served best when mixed with what gasoline was available.

As no new houses were being built it became necessary to put rent control into effect as a housing shortage began to develop before the end of the war. It would reach critical proportions immediately after the war when service men returned home and got married, many without a place to set up housekeeping.

Millions of young men and women, and middle-aged men in fact, were in the service before World War II was over and while casualties were not high for the number involved they did touch every community and almost every family before the long conflict finally ended.

The extent to which Rockville Centre was affected was shown in part by the erection of a plaque in South Side High School shortly after the war, "Dedicated to the Alumni Who Gave Their Lives 1941–1945." There were 56 names on the plaque when it was erected, although some of these alumni probably were not living in Rockville Centre at the time they entered the service.

The organ pipe factory conducted by Walter V. Elliott, who is still living in Rockville Centre, on the West side of North Park Avenue between Front Street and College Place. The firm, George W. Badger Company, was operated by Mr. Elliott from 1921 to 1943 when the building was badly damaged by fire. Before organ pipes were made there the premises had been occupied by the Kayser Glove Company.

CHAPTER XX

Industry in Rockville Centre

As ROCKVILLE CENTRE STARTED as an agricultural community, it had, for many years, no industry other than the local mills along Mill River. These mills took care of the wants of the neighborhood, such as grinding grain, fulling wool, and sawing timber. It was not until about 1860 that the first manufacturing industry was started in the Village. The first issue of The Picket in June, 1865, carries the advertisement of Charles A. Losee, Carriage Maker. Losee manufactured carriages for about 20 years and in 1870 added a blacksmith shop to his enterprise.

By 1874, J. F. Cocks had established a tin shop in town and was making tin pails. In October of that year, Thomas Butt's house on Banks Avenue caught fire. The men of the town gathered quickly and by taking all of the pails from Mr. Cocks' shop they formed a bucket brigade to Smith's Pond and put the fire out. It was this episode that made them realize that they needed a fire department. So within two weeks a meeting was held and the Eureka Hook and Ladder Company was founded. The original name of the company, in fact, was Eureka Hook, Ladder and Bucket Company.

In 1877, A. V. S. Hicks established The Hicks Hammock Company. This was probably the first real manufacturing industry in the village. His first product was called the Centennial Hammock and he advertised it in small sizes for babies as "more convenient than a cradle." His company prospered and he added fish nets, fly nets for horses, and net school bags for children. In 1882, there were 15 employees and even J. F. Cocks carried

Hicks net products to sell along with his tinware on his traveling peddler's wagons.

By 1899 hammocks had become so popular that Hicks filled a single order from a New York Company for 14,500 hammocks. Some of these may have been sold to the government during the Spanish-American War.

In June, 1899, the Nassau Ice Company completed its plant and started on its 50-year career of manufacturing ice. The old ice plant, a forbidding looking bleak brick building, stood at the corner of North Park Village Avenue and the Long Island Rail Road, on the site now occupied by the new six-story building of the Catholic Diocese of Rockville Centre.

There was a legend that persisted for years that the late Frank H. Doubleday tried to establish the Doubleday, Page and Company publishing plant in Rockville Centre and that the village turned it down because it did not want any industry of that size in the village. Former Village President Edwin G. Wright says there is no truth to the story. He says Doubleday, Page and Company never sought permission to erect its plant in the village.

The late Leonard Barron of Rockville Centre, who was editor of the American Home when it was published by Doubleday-page and Company at its Garden City plant in the late 'Twenties and early 'Thirties, said Frank Doubleday looked over many sites on Long Island before deciding to locate in Garden City. He says it is quite likely that some site in Rockville Centre may have been inspected along with sites in other villages, but that Mr. Doubleday finally selected Garden City as the site for his plant. Mr. Barron, incidentally, wrote a souvenir history of the Garden City plant for Doubleday, Page and Company and gave the author of this history a copy of it.

In 1921, Walter V. Elliott, who is still living in Rockville Centre as this history is written in 1968, opened an organ pipe factory on North Park Avenue between Front Street and College Place. The firm name was the George W. Badger Company. Mr. Elliott, who had originally lived in Bridgeport, Conn., made organ pipes for the Midmer Organ Company of Merrick before opening the Rockville Centre plant. Mr. Elliott says the construction of organ pipes, as he made them, was little different from

the way they were made in the Middle Ages for the great cathe-
drals of Europe. This plant was in operation for more than 20
years when it burned down in 1943.

Mr. Elliott sold organ pipes all over America and even filled
orders for pipes that were sent to Europe. He employed about
15 workers, but stated that one of his problems in the latter years
was the difficulty of finding and keeping skilled labor.

Mr. Elliott's wife, the late Bessie M. Elliott, was an accomplished writer of original verse. Many of her poems were published by this writer on the editorial page of the Nassau Daily
Review-Star. In 1968 Mr. Elliott published a handsome pamphlet
containing many of the poems his wife had written, most of which
had appeared in print in the Review-Star and other publications.

Mr. Elliott recalls that the building he occupied on North Park
Avenue had been used as a manufacturing plant by the Kayser
Glove Company before he acquired it for his business.

The use of electricity for small industry has eliminated most
of the objections to industry that existed when they depended upon
steam power and needed tall stacks which belched forth columns
of black smoke from the coal they used for fuel.

There are areas in Rockville Centre which are now zoned for
light industry, chiefly along South Long Beach Road, Maple
Avenue, Ongley Street and other streets. There are now many
small industries in the village, employing a total of several hundred
workers and producing goods and services amounting to millions
of dollars a year, yet many residents of the village are hardly
aware of their existence.

The largest industry in Rockville Centre, of course, is the
Municipal Electric Light Plant at Morris and Maple Avenues,
where it has been located since it was established in 1895. This
plant produces all the electricity Rockville Centre requires for
street lighting, residential use and for local industrial plants.

Two of the largest industries in the village are adjacent to each
other on Maple Avenue, opposite Jefferson Street, just West of
Long Beach Road, both occupying multi-story buildings.

Belwin, Inc., a music publishing house, was established about
20 years ago on Maple Avenue by the late Max Winkler, who
had been a resident of Lynbrook for many years at that time.

About 1950, Mr. Winkler published a book which received considerable acclaim. It was called "Pennies from Heaven."

After Mr. Winkler's death, members of his family made substantial contributions to South Nassau Communities Hospital in his memory. They also erected the Max Winkler Building on Maple Avenue adjacent to Belwin, Inc., and a large part of the area in this building is leased to the Hampshire Press, which does much of the printing for Belwin, Inc. The Hampshire Press was started about the time of World War II as a very small job printing plant and has grown into one of the larger industries of Rockville Centre over the years.

CHAPTER XXI

The Lister Administration

Rockville Centre has been fortunate throughout most of its history in enjoying high-calibre municipal government. The most outstanding residents of the community participated in its incorporation in 1893. As a young village with a population of only a few hundred persons it was a pioneer in the establishment of a municipal electric light plant and a municipal water department. It has had its own police department, originally consisting of only one man, since the date of its incorporation. Early members of the Board of Trustees were concerned with street improvements and better fire protection, but they also helped built up an outstanding public library and establish the first bank and first high school on the South Shore.

All this contributed over the years to the development of Rockville Centre as an outstanding residential community, a financial center and the village that attracted the largest number of commuters—men employed in the City who desired to maintain their homes and bring up their families in an agreeable suburban atmosphere.

There was a period of approximately 15 years, however, which was not auspicious for village improvements. The Depression started in 1929 and lasted for approximately a decade, followed by World War II. During the Depression many residents of the village lost their homes or had to have them refinanced by the Home Owners Loan Corporation. It was desirable to hold taxes at the lowest practical level without embarking upon costly improvements. During the war priorities on materials for the war effort barred many types of improvements for this period.

It was, therefore, a happy circumstance for the Village of Rockville Centre that the end of the war in 1945 found it with a new administration—the Home Rule Party administration—whose leaders had the courage, enterprise and imagination to set to work to make up for the years the locusts had eaten. It was not a period for temporizing; the future was already pressing upon us.

The new administration was headed by W. Harry Lister, a native-born resident of the village whose father, William P. Lister, had been postmaster of the village during the Harding, Coolidge and Hoover administrations. Harry Lister, the young mayor, had achieved success as owner of the Buick automboile agency in Rockville Centre. He was a young man in his forties when first elected to office and he was destined to lead an administration whose accomplishments for the village enabled him to remain in office for 22 years.

The Home Rule Party that put Lister in office and maintained him in office until he voluntarily retired in 1967, was organized early in 1945 by a group of civic-minded citizens who thought the party then in power was leader dominated and too closely identified with a major political party. The organizers of the Home Rule Party said they visualized a village party that would attract forward-looking members of all major political parties and all groups irrespective of national origin and political and religious affiliations.

The nucleus of the Home Rule Party was the Auxiliary Police of the Civil Defense Organization set up during World War II. Some of its early meetings were held at the Woodland firehouse. Among the early members of the Home Rule Party were Chauncey Seedorf, Samuel Hornstein, Hobson Miller, Curtis Bowne, Robert B. Sasseen, John H. Glass and Edgar Senne. Some of these men no longer live in Rockville Centre and several have died in recent years.

The new Home Rule Party invited Harry Lister to become its candidate for Mayor largely because he had become prominent as Director of Civil Defense for Rockville Centre during the latter years of World War II. The men picked for his running mates were Julius Behnke and Arthur D. DeMott, who retired during

Former Mayor W. Harry Lister

1968 after many years of service as village clerk and treasurer, following his service as village trustee. In 1945 the Home Rule Party candidates were elected by only a narrow margin as there was much respect for the men in office who were seeking re-election. In subsequent election years the Home Rule Party candidates were to be returned to office by larger majorities and there were some years when no candidates in opposition to the administration were placed in the field.

The first dramatic accomplishments of the new administration were in the field of municipal parking. Rockville Centre already had a few lots set aside for parking, but the distribution was poor and the space inadequate. Years before James E. Stiles had purchased two old homes on Merrick Road, directly in back of the Nassau Daily Review-Star, and razed them to develop his own private parking field for employees. A number of such fields existed, but they were not part of a master plan for municipal parking. The Lister administration launched a comprehensive program for municipal parking that is still going forward nearly 25 years later as adequate parking space seems a goal impractical of achievement in a growing community.

There was no enthusiasm for the municipal parking program in some quarters. Just as the installation of the first parking meters on village streets had produced violent opposition in some quarters, many property owners objected to the Lister administration's plan of assessing a substantial portion of the cost of the new parking fields to business property that presumably would benefit from it.

The opposition, while quite noisy, does not appear to have held up the program to any great extent. The Lister administration began developing the interior of its business blocks as paved parking fields. Prior to this time the rear of most of the business establishments in the village was unsightly. The unpaved interiors of the blocks were overgrown with weeds and littered with junk. A few cars, entering by alleys, parked there, but the number was nominal compared to the potential space available. The new administration provided for the paving of these areas. Full width streets entrances to them were provided, with adequate curbs and markings to maintain orderly use.

As these fields were developed merchants began improving the appearance of the rear of their stores and providing direct entrance from the parking fields—a matter of great convenience to customers and bringing about a revolutionary change in the character of these former unsightly and unutilized areas.

The program of assessing part of the cost of these improvements to abutting property owners and other property in the retail district has been widely copied and many officials from other communities have visited Rockville Centre to study and admire what has been classed as one of the finest municipal parking systems in the country.

The first large project of this nature completed by the Lister administration (a few years after it took office) was the area bounded by Sunrise Highway, Park Avenue, Merrick Road and Morris Avenue. Since that time the program has been continuously expanded until in 1968, Rockville Centre has nearly 30 improved municipal parking fields with a net capacity of approximately 3,000 automobiles. There are more than 15 municipal parking lots in the central business district and over a dozen in outlying areas, some of which serve municipal playgrounds and parks, as well as neighborhood shopping centers.

Immediately after World War II a serious housing shortage developed in Rockville Centre and throughout the nation. Young married servicemen returning from the war could find no place to live. A massive home construction boom started in 1946, with the result that Rockville Centre was one of the first Nassau villages to run out of vacant land. There had been vacant individual lots on many streets throughout the village, but they were quickly bought up and built upon. The apartment house construction boom was to hit Rockville Centre in the 'Fifties and continue throughout the 'Sixties.

There was an improvement in the business district of the village after the War. Originally Rockville Centre's chief retail section was along Village Avenue between Merrick road and the Railroad. After World War II it tended to shift to Sunrise Highway between Park Avenue and Morris Avenue.

A few years after World War II Rockville Centre finally got its railroad grade crossings eliminated after being held up for nearly 20 years by the Depression and the war. The elimination of railroad grade crossings in Nassau County has been a long-drawn-out public improvement. Under legislation passed many years ago the greater part of grade crossing elimination costs is provided by the State, but incorporated villages must bear the cost of most of the incidental improvements which give purpose and full advantage to the elimination programs.

The first major grade crossing elimination in Nassau County took place in Valley Stream—the village nearest the City line—in the 'Twenties. About 10 years later Lynbrook's grade crossings were eliminated. Rockville Centre's program was not started until after World War II, or more than 20 years after the first project of this type was undertaken only a few miles away.

When World War II ended in the Summer of 1945 the Lister administration was immediately in contact with the State, urging all possible speed in the start of this program in Rockville Centre. The village succeeded in getting a favorable-appearing type of construction approved and the work actually began about 1948. It was finally completed, for actual use by the railroad, about 1950.

As the elimination program was nearing completion the worst wreck in the history of the Long Island Rail Road occurred near Banks Avenue, Rockville Centre about 10:30 o'clock on Friday night, February 17, 1950, when two trains met in a head-on collision. Twenty-nine persons were killed and more than 100 injured as the speeding trains plowed into each other, demolishing the first two cars on each train and throwing some of the others off the track. Within a week one other man died of injuries received in the wreck, making the death toll 30.

The collision was attributed to the failure of the Eastbound train to observe a stop signal. This train should have waited back on the double tracks until the Westbound train had passed. The wreck occurred on a section of gauntlet track where one track runs a few inches inside the other. The fact the trains did not meet completely head-on explained the way the front coaches were ripped apart.

When the accident occurred Preston R. Bassett, historian of the village at that time, was addressing a meeting of the Men's

Club at the Church of the Ascension nearby, and had just been giving the history of the railroad.

Within minutes after the collision, the Rockville Centre fire alarm blew its distress signal and many firemen, policemen and volunteers were at the scene. The Second Baptist Church, almost opposite the wreck, soon became a morgue where bodies of those killed in the collision were taken. Ambulances and improvised ambulances rushed the injured to South Nassau Communities Hospital and to Mercy Hospital. South Nassau Hospital then had only 98 beds capacity and was filled with regular patients beyond this number, but it managed to provide for 23 additional badly-injured victims. Others were taken to Mercy Hospital, some to be treated and released while others were hospitalized.

Within minutes after the wreck the Long Island Rail Road's headquarters in Jamaica ordered the Bee Bus Line, whose main office and garage was also nearby, to provide emergency buses to transport uninjured to Freeport and Valley Stream where special trains could take them on to their destinations. Rescue work continued through most of the night, with firemen and volunteers from Lynbrook and other villages aiding. Many local doctors came to the scene to administer to the injured. Of the 30 who died as a result of the wreck only one, Martin Steel, 55 Maple Avenue, was from Rockville Centre, although a number of Rockville Centre residents were among the injured.

This was a dark year in the history of the Long Island Rail Road as in the Fall another serious wreck occurred near Forest Hills when one train overtook another and the front car actually ended up on top of the rear car of the train ahead. The two wrecks resulted in a change of management for the railroad and extensive investigations as to the cause of each wreck. There were some deaths in the second wreck, but it was regarded as the lesser of the two.

Since Rockville Centre had at the time of the grade crossing elimination—and still has—more commuters than any other Long Island village outside of Greater New York, many inquiries were received by the Village Administration as to the possibility of providing an escalator at the station to provide easy access for the sick and elderly. Inquiries by the village showed the State had no funds for providing this improvement and no precedent for doing so.

The Village Administration, alert to the strong feeling in this matter and recognizing its desirability from many points of view, agreed to install the escalator if such an arrangement could be worked out with the railroad authorities and the State Department of Public Works. Such an agreement was favorably concluded with the result that Rockville Centre became the first community on Long Island to install an escalator in connection with its grade crossing elimination.

Completion of the grade crossing elimination resulted in Rockville Centre becoming a much more convenient community for motorists. Front Street was widened opposite the railroad plaza and extended from Village Avenue to Centre Avenue. A new road, running all the way from Village Avenue to Park Avenue, was provided at village expense on the opposite side of the elimination structure. Paved parking facilities were provided under the full length of the elimination structure from Centre Avenue to Morris Avenue. Facilities for a centralized bus terminal were provided under the elimination structure on the West side of Village Avenue at Front Street. It was decided not to build an enclosed waiting room at the terminal, but benches for bus patrons were provided and shields were fixed in place to afford protection from the wind during Winter months. Within a short time municipal parking fields were provided on both sides of the elimination structure through the heart of the business district. Some of the areas under the elimination structure and in the adjacent fields are metered for long period use and restricted to commuters who purchase an annual license to use them.

A striking improvement, actually incidental in cost but adding great comfort and increased safety to travel in Rockville Centre, was achieved through its efforts early in the days of the Lister Administration. North Village Avenue from the date of its origin had a sharp, dangerous curve just above Maine Avenue. Over the years it had contributed to many serious accidents. A member of the Village Administration termed this "dead man's curve" and raised the point that the County should eliminate it, since conferences revealed the County was agreeable to help relieve this hazard if some practical way could be found to do it.

The official pursued his project and found the owner of the property where the Rockville Centre Public Library now stands would be willing to deed some frontage so the County could construct a new section of road, easing the angle of the curve. All details involved were worked out satisfactorily and this improvement was put in effect in the Fall of 1950.

In the late 1930's Mayor Horace L. Allen of Rockville Centre appointed James E. Stiles, publisher of the Nassau Daily Review-Star, chairman of a Rockville Centre Improvement Committee to study what could be done "to improve the entrances to the Village."

Mr. Stiles did not trust his judgment or that of his committee with the task. He engaged W. Earle Andrews, a consulting engineer who was a close friend of Robert Moses and former assistant chief engineer of the Long Island State Park Commission, to make a complete survey of the village and report what could be done to improve its appearance and solve its traffic problems.

Some months later this engineer brought out what was called "The Andrews Report" for a fee that somewhat startled the village fathers and suggested improvements that seemed beyond the reach of a conservative regime. The high points of the report were a plan for elimination of the intersection of Merrick Road and Sunrise Highway at the Western entrance to the village and a program for the improvement of the Mill River basin.

The Andrews report aroused considerable interest at the time but action on all its suggestions was deferred. Within two years World War II had started and nothing could be done about its major provisions until the war was over.

The Andrews plan for separating the grades at the point where Sunrise Highway and Merrick Road crossed was approximately the same as the plan ultimately followed by the County and State in this epochal improvement. The intersection of these two major thoroughfares had always been a serious traffic problem and since it was within the village limits of Rockville Centre it was the principal headache of the Rockville Centre Police Department. As the volume of traffic increased delays at the intersection became longer and the frequency of accidents increased. More and more police hours were spent trying to keep traffic moving safely through this crossing.

A plan like the program for a separation of grades at the intersection of Merrick Road and Sunrise Highway can lay in State or County files for years unless the community involved shows interest and offers full cooperation if it is undertaken. The State and County Departments of Public Works soon found that Rockville Centre's Lister Administration not only was anxious to cooperate but insistent that the work must be started. In fact, it was almost contemporary with the grade crossing elimination, so that for the last 15 years, or thereabouts, this age-old headache has been a thing of the past, receding into memory as greatly increased traffic speeds through the village on these important routes without the necessity of any local policeman to assist or direct.

The Lister Administration also followed in broad terms the Andrews plan for developing the Mill River basin into a thing of beauty and utilizing its wasted space, previously a cattail swamp with some garbage thrown around. The Village Administration lost little time in embarking upon this program and vast improvements have been made over the years. In what is now called Lister Park, in the Mill River basin, there are now four fields for baseball and softball with parking facilities and lights for night games in the Summer season. Land along the Mill River has been filled in. The river has been re-channeled in some places and attractive landscaping and lawns make it an impressive asset to Rockville Centre. Purely aside from its recreational value, developed in a former wasted and unsightly area, its aesthetic value to the community is universally acknowledged.

The Lister Administration did not rely upon reclaimed land in the old Mill River swamp for all of its recreational facilities, however. Hickey Field, between Morris and Forest Avenues, on the North side of Sunrise Highway, undoubtedly was Rockville Centre's first park. This field was further developed and landscaped. A little League and softball field was developed, outdoor basketball and handball courts were provided and a children's playground at the Forest Avenue end was equipped.

In 1960 the village opened its $350,000 Recreation Center on

Oceanside Road, just North of the Long Island Rail Road. This is a showplace which few villages or cities of Rockville Centre's size can equal. It has won awards for its architecture and planning. Its facilities include 25,000 square feet of floor space that provides an auditorium, gymnasium, spacious lounge, game room and small rooms suitable for many purposes. All types of recreational and cultural activities emanate from this center. Business organizations and private social groups make extensive use of the various rooms by paying modest fees for their use when they are not required for the regular recreation program activities.

While most of the municipal utilities established in the Nineties and early 1900's have long since been abandoned or sold to private utility companies Rockville Centre's municipal utilities more than doubled their capacity in the two decades after World War II. Rockville Centre's electric rates are lower than those of private utilities in adjacent areas and the village generates all of its own electric power, except under unusual circumstances.

The Rockville Centre Municipal Utilities are now housed in modern buildings in area expanded from where they started, on the South Side of Maple Avenue between Morris and Forest Avenues. Despite the continuous necessity of adding new and larger generators as the population increases there is ample space for expansion.

Increased use of electricity was noticeable immediately after World War II. In 1950, in 1954 and in 1960 new engines were installed and in 1964 a super-charger was installed on Engine No. 11, bringing the plant's capacity to approximately double what it had been in 1945 when the war ended. With most of the available land in the village already built up, but with apartment houses replacing many single-family homes, another larger generator was installed in 1965.

A unique experience in 1965 demonstrated the value of their municipal lighting system to the residents of the village. When the famous "blackout" occurred through the Northeast on November 9, including most of New York City and virtually all of Long Island, Rockville Centre had no interruption of service except for a few minutes when its power plant helped the Long Island Lighting Company to start its engines at its Island Park generator.

The Rockville Centre Municipal Electric and Water Systems both operate at a profit, which has been greatly increased in the last 20 years. Both are able to make substantial annual payments to the village treasury, helping to hold down the tax rate.

The Rockville Centre Volunteer Fire Department has made its greatest gains in its history since World War II. As the various volunteer companies developed over the years most of them acquired their own firehouses in different sections of the village. These were old-fashioned frame buildings identified with a previous era. They were fire hazards themselves and one of them was destroyed by fire some years ago despite the fact it housed fire fighting equipment. Since the end of World War II two modern fireproof buildings have been erected to house four companies of the volunteer fire department. The first of these was the Fire Department Headquarters on Centre Avenue, opposite Washington Street, which houses Engine Company No. 2 and Floodlight and Rescue Company No. 1. This building also provides much better facilities for the firemen's recreation and social activities than the old buildings that were replaced. In 1966 the Eureka Hook and Ladder Company and the Live Oak Engine Company moved into a modern firehouse at Maple and Morris Avenues, opposite the Rockville Centre Municipal Power Plant. This new firehouse has a capacity for three pieces of apparatus. This building also has offices and recreational facilities for the members. The new firehouse is so attractive the Long Island Association awarded it first place in the category of Institutional Buildings in its 1966 Awards Program for outstanding new structures on Long Island. Rockville Centre, by recent purchases of new equipment, has one of the best-equipped fire departments in New York State, resulting in the New York State Fire Underwriters giving the village the lowest premium rate in its classification in the State.

Due to the rapid increase in population after World War II the Rockville Centre schools were soon congested. On October 17, 1950, School District No. 21, the Rockville Centre district, passed a series of resolution totalling $3,735,000 for additions to existing schools and construction of three new schools. The three new schools were a new Senior High School to be built on Allen Field and the site of the former Rockville Centre Sewage Disposal

Plant, to be built at a cost of $2,160,000, a new elementary school on Long Beach Road north of the Rockville Country Club and an elementary school to be built at Lakeview and Centre Avenues. The elementary school on Long Beach Road became the William S. Covert School and the Lakeview Avenue School became the Floyd B. Watson School, both named in honor of former Superintendents, both of whom had served for many years. The new high school became the South Side Senior High School, preserving the name that had marked the Rockville Centre High School as the first on the South Shore.

Before these new schools were completed, some years later, the district had to vote supplementary funds to meet the rise in building costs and some changes in the original plans. Meanwhile all of the old elementary schools had been enlarged.

In 1956 the old Brooklyn Diocese of the Roman Catholic Church was divided, due to the heavy increase in population in the four Long Island counties. The new Diocese was named the Diocese of Rockville Centre and St. Agnes Church became St. Agnes Cathedral. The Rev. Peter Quealy, affectionately known as "Father" Quealy, who had served St. Agnes most of his life as a priest, had been named a Monsignor a few years before. He was nearing, or over, 80 years of age. Close friends say that many years before Father Quealy could have been advanced and might have become a Bishop himself, but that he always preferred to remain a parish priest. They also say that when the handsome new St. Agnes Church was built about 1940 he knew that one day the Brooklyn diocese would be divided and Rockville Centre would become the seat of the new Diocese.

Bishop Walter P. Kellenberg of Ogdensburg was named the new Bishop of the Rockville Centre Diocese. A native of New York, Bishop Kellenberg had been Bishop of Ogdensburg since 1954. He took his new office in Rockville Centre early in 1957. Before that he had been an auxiliary Bishop in New York, secretary to Cardinal Spellman for three years, and had held many high positions in the Church. Bishop Kellenberg holds honorary degrees from Fordham University and several other colleges.

In setting up the new Diocesan headquarters the church acquired the old building of the First National Bank of Rockville

Centre at the corner of Sunrise Highway and North Park Avenue, Rockville Centre's first sykscraper, and in the early 'Sixties a six-story addition was built adjoining it on the site of the old Rockville Centre ice plant, replacing what had become an eyesore with a handsome modern office building.

The new Diocese also established a weekly newspaper, "The Long Island Catholic," which in a short time had a circulation in excess of 100,000. In 1956 Molloy College for Women was established to serve the new diocese. It was located on Hempstead Avenue at Southern State Park, contiguous to the land on which Mercy Hospital stands at North Village Avenue and Southern State Parkway. Thus within a decade Rockville Centre acquired a new public high school, a liberal arts college and both of the hospitals within its general area were more than doubled in capacity. While South Nassau Communities Hospital is over the line in Oceanside it has always been predominantly a Rockville Centre institution, having been promoted and largely administered by residents of the village for the first 30 years of its history.

During the 1950's the old Clinton Avenue School was sold by the Rockville Centre school district to St. Agnes, which remodeled it into a handsome elementary school to supplement the parochial school facilities of the parish. The old rectory where Father Quealy and other priests of the parish had lived also was replaced with a handsome new home for the Bishop and the additional priests creation of the new diocese brought to Rockville Centre.

The Lister Administration gave Rockville Centre the honor of being the first community of its size in the United States to launch an Urban Renewal Program that is now virtually completed and has upwards of 200 familes living in new housing. Work on the Urban Renewal Program was begun in the 'Fifties as a means of replacing sub-standard housing in Rockville Centre's Banks Avenue section, largely occupied by its Negro residents, with modern, sanitary apartments and providing profitable utilization of undeveloped land in that section.

As an Urban Renewal Program involves dealing with both the Federal and State governments progress was understandably slow. Mayor Lister and members of the Village Administration were forced to face disappointing delays, criticism and heckling at Village Board meetings, but they persevered in the program.

Seven town houses built under the Urban Renewal Program on North Centre Avenue were completed in 1964 and all were soon sold and occupied. Two of these were two-family houses, so that nine families were re-located by this initial project.

During 1967 nine multiple dwellings providing 164 apartments were completed in the area West of Centre Avenue and South of Maine Avenue, extending to Peninsula Boulevard. These apartments were made available to families that had been displaced by the Urban Renewal Program's demolition of sub-standard housing.

In early 1969 work was under way on a 152-room nursing home on the North side of Maine Avenue, West of Centre Avenue and across the street a Senior Citizens home with 96 units, for either elderly couples or single individuals, was scheduled to be built.

Work also was schedule to start during 1969 on 80 additional apartments adjoining the era where the nine multiple dwellings now stand. Approximately 36 acres of land was involved in the Urban Renewal Program, of which 16 was set apart for new housing. The remaining 20, it is hoped, will be developed for commerce and industry, providing new jobs in the area. Concerns using the 20 acres would be private enterprises and if plans are realized it would increase the tax yield of the 20 acres to 10 times the amount previously received from the entire 36 acres.

Early in 1969 plans were being developed for a citizens committee, incorporated as the Stable Inn Corporation and assisted with funds from the Small Business Administration, to erect three stores on Center Avenue North of Randall Avenue. The name was adopted because old-timers say there was once a stable and a blacksmith shop on the spot where the new stores would be built. The Village also hopes to erect a Community Center on North Center Avenue, with Urban Renewal Funds, which would be used during the day as a day care center where the Office of Economic Opportunity could care for children of working mothers. It also hopes that additional housing for senior citizens may be built in various appropriate places throughout the Village through the Housing and Urban Development program of the Federal government. This housing would take the form of a number of small apartment houses in areas zoned for this type of construction.

During the Lister administration another significant project in the village was carried forward to successful completion with the aid of many of the outstanding leaders of the community. This was the building of the new Shiloh Baptist Church, which has become recognized as the finest church erected by a Negro congregation in Nassau County and might be termed a monument to the perseverance and goodwill generated by its veteran pastor, the Rev. Morgan M. Days.

The Shiloh Baptist Church was organized in June, 1907. Mrs. Glendora Hawkins called a group together at that time and asked if they were interested in organizing a Baptist Church in Rockville Centre. A favorable response was received and the group held its first services, as a mission, in Mrs. Hawkins home at 9 Nassau Street. After spending some time at a building on Merrick Road the congregation purchased a lot of Banks Avenue in 1909 and acquired a small building which was moved to the property for use as a church. There had been several pastors before the Reverend Days accepted a call to the church in 1937. He celebrated his 30th anniversary as pastor in 1967 and is still making plans for expansion of the church in 1969 as this story goes to press.

Shiloh Baptist Church grew rapidly under the Reverend Days' leadership. The mortgage on the little church was burned in his second year with the congregation. In 1945 a new site was acquired at the corner of North Centre Avenue and Willoughby Street and the Rev. Days launched his campaign for funds to erect a modern church. During the early years of his drive and throughout the time the church was under construction he received strong support from local business men and bankers and virtually all of the other congregations in the village.

The Reverend Days recalls important support from George W. Loft of the South Shore Trust Company, James E. Stiles of the Nassau Daily Review-Star, John D. Bennett, then a State Senator, Mayor W. Harry Lister and Harry B. Carter, owner of the Bee Bus Company. "He was our guiding angel all through the building of the church, until his death," the Reverend Days recalls. Started in the late 'Forties the congregation moved to the new church in June, 1954. In 1951 a village-wide drive was conducted and receipts from the Jewish congregations, Protestant congregations

The Rev. Morgan M. Days.
Below, *the Shiloh Baptist Church at North Centre and Willoughby Street, started in 1949, received support from many prominent citizens, other congregations and leading organizations in the village. When completed and furnished it represented an investment of approximately $300,000.*

and Catholic congregation—St. Agnes—totaled $33,000. Men from the congregation contributed their services in laying the floors and building the steps.

A list of special gifts compiled by the Reverend Days shows that Monsignor Peter Quealy of St. Agnes Church contributed the furnace, Mayor Lister a public address system installed at his expense, D. Herbert Kastner, a local automobile dealer, shrubs for the grounds, Temple B'nai Sholom the pews, the Episcopal Church of the Ascension a baby grand piano and the Congregational Church School a communion table and cross. Members of the congregation also made notable gifts to the building program. Mrs. Matilda Robinson gave the steel steps that lead from the basement to the social hall, Deacon Eli Washington the bronze fixtures on the exterior of the church, Deaconess Mamie Jones had a telephone installed, Trustee Edward Stephenson contributed the bell in the tower, Mrs. Rosa Young a puplit in memory of her husband and Mrs. Evelyn McTootle a refrigerator for the kitchen. The contracting firm, Dominic Milone and Sons, was generous and patient in its relationship with the congregation throughout, as various delays occurred when funds ran short.

When it was finally completed and fully equipped the church property and furnishings had an estimated worth of $300,000. Within a few years it was entirely free of debt and early in 1969 the Reverend Days announced that there was a large sum in the treasury to acquire some adjoining property needed for expansion, and for parking space for members pending a new construction program.

The Reverend Days has received many honors in recognition of his leadership in building the new Shiloh Baptist Church with community-wide assistance. President Harry S. Truman, while in office, gave him a citation for making the most notable contribution to race relations in Nassau County. On May 27, 1957, Dr. M. C. Allen of Virginia Seminary and College of Lynchburg, Va., conferred an Honorary Degree of Doctor of Divinity upon the Rev. Days. He has also held many offices in ministerial associations on Long Island, including that of Vice-President of the Nassau County Council of Churches.

CHAPTER XXII

Rockville Centre's Diamond Anniversary

IN SEPTEMBER, 1966, Mayor W. Harry Lister announced that he would not be a candidate for re-election when his term expired in March, 1967. By then he would have been Mayor of Rockville Centre 22 years, the longest period any Village President or Mayor of the village had spent in office.

Mayor Lister's administration undoubtedly had been the most productive in the history of the village, modernizing it in many respects and still retaining the character that has always made it the most attractive residential community on the South Shore. In the period following World War II and in the boom years of the 1950's as Nassau County's population passed 1,000,000 Rockville Centre suffered less in comparison than almost any Long Island village. In the 1960 Federal Census Rockville Centre had a population of 26,335 and by 1968 it was estimated to have grown to 28,000. While Rockville Centre's business district had expanded, principally along Sunrise Highway East of Park Avenue, it had suffered no marked decline from the major shopping centers and by its failure to become a major shopping center itself it was able to retain much of its previous character with antiquated buildings gradually being replaced by modern ones.

In the 'Fifties and 'Sixties there was a great boom in apartment house construction, but good zoning laws enacted years before restricted the apartment area and this growth had the effect of replacing many of the older homes of the village near its business center with modern apartment buildings, while the newer, modern residential districts were not invaded.

When Mayor Lister announced his forthcoming retirement the Home Rule Party which had originally sponsored his election and sustained him in office for more than two decades began planning a continuation of its rule. Early in 1967 the Home Rule Party nominated Village Judge John A. Anderson to succeed Mayor Lister. Judge Anderson had served on the Village Board for many years prior to the retirement of Judge Maurice J. Moore. Judge Moore retired in the early 'Sixties after having served for approximately 30 years and Trustee Anderson was appointed to succeed him.

Village Trustee Charles V. Day also had announced he would not be a candidate for re-election, so the Home Rule Party nominated two of its leading members—Philip J. Eisenhauer and Leonard Sandel—as running mates for Judge Anderson. Village Trustee Albert A. Rubin was nominated for Village Judge to succeed Judge Anderson. Both Mr. Eisenhauer and Mr. Sandel at the time were members of the Board of Zoning Appeals.

While an opposition ticket was placed in the field the Home Rule Party candidates won the election by approximately three to one, Judge Anderson being elected Mayor by a vote of 4317 to 1266 for his opponent.

The first two years of Judge Anderson's administration, just completed as this history goes to press, proved very productive. The Urban Renewal buildings under construction when he took office were completed and occupied and additional work, described in the preceding chapter, was started.

The village also was able to complete its long-deferred plan of widening Front Street at the Village Avenue end, of paving the parking space gained by acquiring and demolishing the old Strand Theatre on Sunrise Highway and constructing a street one block long extending from opposite the Rockville Centre station to Sunrise Highway. The road on the South Side of the elimination structure also was widened at the Park Avenue end, at the spot where the old Knickerbocker ice plant once stood. These improvements have had the effect of opening up the area adjacent to the Rockville Centre railroad station, of improving the movement of traffic in the area and providing many additional parking places. No other Long Island village can claim such an attractive environ-

Mayor John A. Anderson

ment for its railroad station as Rockville Centre since these final improvements were completed.

Mayor Anderson also was able to announce in his talk at the annual dinner of the Home Rule Party in the Fall of 1968 that extensive additions were proposed for Rockville Centre's Recreation Center and that a new firehouse would be built on Forest Avenue to replace the venerable home of the Reliance Hose Company. The new building, he stated, will compare favorably with the new firehouses already built on Center Avenue and Morris Avenue.

A multi-use court area is to be developed on the grounds adjoining the Recreation Center. There will be tennis courts, a basketball and handball court, a shuffle board and various facilities for use by Senior Citizens, who have enjoyed the Recreation Center along with the youth of the village. In 1968 Pedal Boating was introduced on Mill River adjacent to Lister Park.

A swimming pool provided by the County was opened in the playground at the end of Randall Avenue, now a part of the Urban Renewal Area, in 1968 and the Village re-dedicated the park as the Rev. Morgan M. Days Park in recognition of the Reverend Days' accomplishments and leadership in the community.

The park and ball field on Mill River below South Park Avenue, on land filled in by the village over a period of years and then developed, was named the Edward J. Bligh Field in honor of the man who is credited with being the father of Little League baseball in the village. The field just North of South Park Avenue had previously been named the Barasch Field in honor of the late Samuel Barasch, who also was a leader in the development of recreation in the Village.

During 1968 the Village improved the first of a series of vest pocket parks it hopes to establish on vacant plots throughout the community. Treccasi Park, named in honor of the present owner of the land who granted the Village use of it until it is needed for other purposes, was established on the site of the old Village Inn at the corner of Front Street and North Park Avenue. The old basement was filled in, the plot sodded and landscaped and park benches placed there for the use of the residents.

The Village also acquired title to the Southwest segment of

Former Trustee Charles V. Day, Chairman of Rockville Centre's 75th Anniversary Committee.

Morris Avenue at Morris Avenue and Sunrise Highway for the purpose of widening the street and making it of equal width with the remainder of the avenue, eliminating what has proved a bottleneck in periods of heavy traffic.

In 1968 the Village of Rockville Centre celebrated the 75th anniversary of its incorporation. Mayor Anderson appointed Former Village Trustee Charles V. Day chairman of a large committee that planned several events to mark this important milestone. There were 51 members of the 75th Anniversary Committee, including the chairman, representing every phase of life in the community.

The members of the committee, in addition to Chairman Day, were as follows: Surrogate John D. Bennett, Associate Judge Irving Levin, Harry J. McCann, LeRoy Millard, active in the Rockville Centre Chamber of Commerce; Salvatore A. Milone, Republican Leader of Rockville Centre; Morris Schneider, Democratic Leader of Rockville Centre; Robert E. Scholly, Supreme Court Justice William J. Sullivan, Assemblyman John S. Thorp, Jr., William P. Gordon, Former Village Trustee and Village-Clerk Treasurer Arthur D. DeMott, Daniel G. Buckley; Former Village Clerk Robert T. Eichmann, Former Mayor W. Harry Lister, Robert Ledlie, Herbert May, Mrs. Jean Finfer of the Rockville Centre Public Library Board, Former Village Judge Maurice J. Moore, Dr. Richard Byers, Superintendent of Schools; Arthur L. Hodges, Village Historian; Former Village Clerk Frank A. Ernst, Former Village President Edwin G. Wright, Mrs. Robert Greene, Former Village President David R. Longenecker, now living in Florida; Edward J. Walsh, Jr., Former Village President Edwin W. Wallace, Mrs. Rose Hart, Mrs. George McLean, Mrs. Fannie Atkins, the Rev. Morgan M. Days, pastor of Shiloh Baptist Church; Mrs. Joseph Thompson, Ed Dyroff, former Superintendent of Recreation; Former Mayor Walter J. Halliday, Floyd B. Watson, former Superintendent of Schools; Simeon E. Holland, Robert Stahl, president of the Rockville Centre Chamber of Commerce; Ed Glaser, Peter Moran, Mrs. Walter Wood, the Rev. Frank Robinson, Mrs. Oscar del Guidice, Karl Wegner, Former Police Chief Lloyd C. Slade, Frank Kondla, Mrs. August Kalb, Ray Heatherton, well known

James F. Conway, Rockville Centre attorney who became President of Rotary International on July 1, 1969.

radio and television star; Wallace Payne, a retired 50-year employee of the Rockville Centre Electric Light Department, Jules Martell, president of the Rockville Centre Luncheon Club; Fire Chief N. W. Palmeri and Donald Horn.

The Committee as appointed included five former Village Presidents and Mayors—Edwin G. Wright, Edwin W. Wallace, David R. Longenecker, Walter J. Halliday and W. Harry Lister— but during the Summer Former Village President Edwin W. Wallace died. A grandson of Capt. Edwin Wallace, an original officer of the village, Mr. Wallace also had served as Assemblyman and Nassau County Commissioner of Public Welfare.

One of the first jobs of the 75th Anniversary Committee was to prepare a list of organizations and businesses that had been active in the village for at least 50 years. A list of 36 was made up after publicity in The News-Owl aided the work and on July 8, 1968, the 75th anniversary of the Date of Incorporation, Mayor Anderson awarded scrolls to each at a special meeting of the Village Board. The list of firms and organizations, with the date of their inception, was as follows:

St. Mark's Methodist Church, June 21, 1870; First Baptist Church, October, 1870; Eureka Hook & Ladder & Bucket Co. No. 1, 1875; Church of the Ascension, February, 1885; St. Agnes Cathedral Parish, 1887; Independent Order of Odd Fellows, February 15, 1888; Nassau Savings and Loan Association, April, 1889; Live Oak Engine Co. No. 1, February 12, 1890; Chemical Bank New York Trust Co., originally Bank of Rockville Centre, January 2, 1891; Defender Hose Co. No. 1, October 1895; Alert Engine Co. No. 2, November, 1895; Forbell Funeral Home, 1895; Massapequa Lodge No. 822, F. & AM., June 26, 1897; Fortnightly Club, 1898; Holy Trinity Lutheran Church, January 4, 1899; Dominick Milone, Inc., 1899; The Arbor Inn, 1900; Pettit-Clayton, Inc., 1901; Charles Becker & Sons, January, 1907; Temple B'nai Sholom, 1907; Shiloh Baptist Church, 1907; Jones Window Shade Shop, 1907; Reliance Hose Company, 1907; Charles V. Day Agency, July, 1908; Grabau's, Inc., May, 1909; United Presbyterian Church, June, 1909; Harold Brindley Agency, 1909; Joseph T. Froehlich Co., Inc., February, 1910; Acorn Publishing Co., Inc., 1910; Woodland Engine Company,

Dedicating the plaque placed on the grave of Mordecai Smith during celebration of Rockville Centre's 75th Anniversary. Kneeling from left to right are Charles V. Day, chairman of the 75th Anniversary Committee, Assemblyman John S. Thorp, Jr., Village Trustee Philip Eisenhauer, Village Trustee Gerald F. Digan, Postmaster Joseph A. Huber and Village Trustee Leonard Sandel. Standing in costumes of the 1850 period are Mrs. John K. Henesy of the Rockville Centre Historical and Landmark Society, at the left, and her daughter at the right. (Photograph by James Bove, Jr.)

Mayor John A. Anderson, left, presents, a 50-year certificate to Ex-Captain Jerry Chiusano of Defender Hose Co. No. 1. Charles V. Day, chairman of the 75th Anniversary Committee, stands at right. Defender Hose Company was established in October, 1895, when Rockville Centre Fire Department was being established. Some of the volunteer fire companies had been established many years earlier.

Mayor John A. Anderson presents Proclamation calling for observance of Martin Luther King Day to Miss Lucille Smith, chairman of the Rockville Centre Chapter of the Poor People's Campaign, one of the organizers of the Rockville Centre Economic Opportunity Council and a member of the Tenants' Association.

1912; Sterling's Pharmacy, 1913; Troop 40, Boy Scouts of America of United Presbyterian Church, 1914; Arthur Brindley & Co., Inc., October 14, 1914; the Kloski store, March 10, 1915; Macken Mortuary, March, 1918; Mrs. Harold Bucken, June 2, 1918; Littlefield-Alger Signal Co., Inc., 1918.

During 1968 a number of successful events were held in connection with the village's 75th anniversary. The Kiwanis Club saluted the opening of the anniversary with an evening of entertainment at the South Side High School Auditorium Saturday night, April 27, which it called a "Gay 90's Revue."

A 75th Anniversary Pancake Breakfast at the Recreation Center Sunday, May 19, from 9 to 11 a.m. attracted several hundred persons. Members of the Rotary, Kiwanis and Lions Club were present to assist serving the guests. Later members of the Village Board arrived to re-dedicate the Recreation Center as the "John A. Anderson Recreation Center."

While Village Trustee Mayor Anderson served as chairman of the Recreation Committee of the Rockville Centre Village Board and played an important part in the establishment and early organization of the center and the creation of a Village Recreation Department.

An exhibition, "Only Yesterday in Rockville Centre," sponsored by the Rockville Centre Historical and Landmark Association, was held at the public library Monday and Tuesday, May 27 and May 28. This exhibition assembled many pictures of the early homes, churches, schools and businesses in the village, as well as many historical items associated with its past. This exhibition was well attended. During the time the exhibition was open ladies in costumes of an earlier period served as hostesses and guides.

The major event of the celebration was a march from Village Avenue and Sunrise Highway to the Rockville Cemetery at Merrick Road and Ocean Avenue, Lynbrook, on June 15 to dedicate a new bronze plaque at the grave of the Rev. Mordecai "Rock" Smith, the old pastor and miller, for whom the village was named. This event also attracted a large attendance. Originally planned for Saturday, June 8, it was postponed on account of the funeral of Senator Robert Kennedy, which took place on this date, following his assassination several days earlier in Los Angeles.

A table at the dinner given by Chemical Bank New York Trust Company in honor of Oscar Gast, who retired in the early 'Sixties after serving as President of the Bank of Rockville Centre Trust Company for many years prior to its merger with Chemical. Several hundred attended the event at the Rockville Country Club. In this picture, seated, left to right, are William A. Kennedy of Kennedy Associates, Arthur L. Hodges, Former Village Clerk-Treasurer Arthur D. DeMott and Arthur Brindley, Rockville Centre insurance broker. Standing, left to right, are Aaron Schneider of the Sunrise Furniture Co., Glenn Tracy, one of the founders of the GAP Instrument Corp., Joseph Puerling, owner of business property in Rockville Centre, and the late Lewis A. Abrams, hardware merchant and former director of the Bank of Rockville Centre.

In September a costume ball, which attracted several hundred guests, was held at the Recreation Center by a special sub-committee of the 75th Anniversary Committee.

The wide participation in the 75th Anniversary events produced considerable revenue in addition to an appropriation of $1,000 from the Village Board. Writing to members of the committee in December, 1968, Chairman Day reported that all bills had been paid and that a balance of several hundred dollars remained, once again reflecting the fine community spirit that has long prevailed in Rockville Centre.

During the anniversary year a number of associated events also were held, inspired by the observance but not actually planned and arranged by the 75th Anniversary Committee. All of the public schools held fairs or tree plantings in recognition of the anniversary. A 75th anniversary band concert was held at St. Agnes school and the Garden Club donated a magnolia tree for the village hall grounds. The magnolia tree standing on the grounds of the old home of Dr. Bulson at the Southwest corner of South Park and Lincoln Avenues inspired the adoption of the magnolia tree as the official tree of Rockville Centre.

Several dozen students from South Side High School and St. Agnes High School participated in a contest to design an official Village Flag containing a magnolia blossom. After studying all designs submitted the Village Board adopted the flag designed by Gerald Pelc, son of Mr. and Mrs. John Pelc of 341 Beech Street, South Hempstead, a Senior at South Side High School. Gerald was awarded a $50 prize offered by Karl Wegner, proprietor of the Arbor Inn.

In the Spring of 1969, following a public hearing on the proposal, the Village Board decided to erect a new municipal building on the East bank of Mill River at Merrick Road and Windsor Avenue where the village has a tract of several acres, now part of the park along both sides of the river at this point.

Some years ago, during the Lister Administration, the Village acquired the old Wright homestead and adjacent property at Hempstead and Randall Avenues for additional municipal parking and a possible site for a new municipal building. Mayor Anderson stated at the hearing that the Village believes it can sell this property for enough to erect the new municipal building on the Mill River site without an increase in the Village tax rate for this purpose. He noted that mandatory salary increases and other costs tend to increase the Village tax rate almost every year, anyway, but that the new municipal building should not be a factor in this increase.

Walter Spellman, Rockville Centre architect, was engaged to draw plans for a new Village Hall. The plans call for a one-story building with full basement 72 by 217 feet, having about 25,000 square feet of office space. Hope has been expressed that work on the new structure can begin during the Summer of 1969. Because of the large amount of space available at the Mill River site ample parking can be provided for village employees and taxpayers who have to visit the Municipal Building on business.

The Village plans to keep the Police Department at its present location in the old Municipal Building. The Village Police Court also will be kept there, while a portion of the old building will be made available to the Rockville Centre Historical and Landmark Society. Estimates place the cost of the new building at approximately $750,000.

Mayor Anderson stated that the Village has acquired an old home adjacent to the park where the new Municipal Building will be erected and that this land will be added to the park along Mill River. Mayor Anderson said the Village Board is committed to preserving and improving the beauty of the Mill River basin, which he regards as one of the major assets of the Village.

SIGNIFICANT DATES
IN THE EVOLUTION OF ROCKVILLE CENTRE

January 27, 1849	Rockville Centre Post Office Established.
September 23, 1867	Long Island Rail Road Service Began.
January, 1872	Union Free School District Established.
1882	Rockville Centre Public Library Founded.
July 15, 1893	Rockville Centre Village Board Holds First Meeting.
1895	Municipal Water Department Established.
1898	Municipal Electric Light Department Established.
1906	New York Telephone Company Opened Service.

Rockville Centre Presidents
of Nassau County Bar Association

Rockville Centre has furnished more presidents of the Nassau County Bar Association than any other village in the County. In addition to being the financial center of Nassau County for many years Rockville Centre for almost a century has had outstanding members of the bar among its residents or maintaining offices in the village.

George Wallace, who bought the South Side Observer in 1870 also had a law office in the same building and for decades was recognized as one of the leaders of the Queens County and subsequently Nassau County bar. Robert A. Davison, founder of the Bank of Rockville Centre and an attorney, was regarded as the leading resident of Rockville Centre in his time. John Lyon, first village president, had a law office that served as a training ground for such prominent Rockville Centre attorneys as Earl J. Bennett, Francis G. Hooley and Edwin G. Wright, and Sidney H. Swezey of Freeport and Charles E. Schweitzer of Lynbrook.

The Nassau County Bar Association was founded in 1899 when Nassau County was formed out of the three Western towns of Queens County. Since that time 10 residents, natives or attorneys practicing in Rockville Centre have been president of the association. The order of their service was as follows:

ALFRED T. DAVISON	1910
EDWIN G. WRIGHT	1914
EARL J. BENNETT	1921
FRANCIS G. HOOLEY	1923
SANFORD A. DAVISON	1927–1929

REMSEN B. OSTRANDER	1952
ALLAN B. WRIGHT	1953
JAMES F. CONWAY	1957
W. RUDOLPH PREUSS	1962
ARTHUR A. KAYE	1965

Edwin G. Wright and Allan B. Wright represent the only instance in the history of the association where both a father and son have served as president.

Rockville Centre Village Trustees 1893-1969

Trustee	First Elected or Appointed
Capt. Edwin Wallace	August, 1893
Glentworth D. Combes	August, 1893
Edwin Seabury	August, 1893
Capt. Marcus H. Tracy	August, 1896
John T. Davison	August, 1896
Cornelius E. Gritman	March, 1898
Frederick W. Fielding	March, 1898
Robert J. Halgin, Jr.	March, 1898
Alfred J. Lamb	March, 1899
Edwin G. Wright	March, 1899
Winfield Davison	March, 1899
Dr. J. Ensor Hutcheson	March, 1900
Nelson L. Seaman	April, 1900
Christ an L. Grim	September, 1901
Joseph McDougall	March, 1903
George J. Quinn	March, 1904
Will am Richensteen	March, 1905
Thomas J. Murphy	March, 1905
Robert H. Taylor	March, 1907
Tredwell D. Carpenter	June, 1908
Alonzo W. Fisk	March, 1909
Alvin T. Powell	March, 1909
Frederick H. Doelle	March, 1911
Joseph H. Russ	March, 1911
Capt. James W. Carty	March, 1912
John Weldon	March, 1912
Edwin W. Wallace	APRIL, 1912
John W. Cross	September, 1912
George E. Sammis	March, 1916
Joseph W. Richardson	March, 1916

241

Frank P. Baylis	March, 1917
William F. Phillips	March, 1917
Lee G. Greiner	March, 1917
Henry M. Dodge	March, 1918
Arthur G. Ackist	July, 1918
Frank B. Gardner	March, 1919
David R. Longenecker	March, 1920
Joseph H. Monds	March, 1920
Frank J. Reynolds	March, 1921
Frank H. Erisman	March, 1921
Charles E. Richmond	March, 1922
Fred H. Doelle, Jr.	August, 1922
Horace L. Allen	March, 1923
Ronald C. Daisley	March, 1924
Henry W. MacVicar	June, 1925
Charles C. Martin	October, 1927
J. Bennem Hopkins	March, 1931
Francis J. Klaess	March, 1933
Sherman Moreland, Jr.	May, 1935
Chester P. Farrington	April, 1936
Edgar T. Beamish	April, 1936
Frank A. Ernst	April, 1937
Howard M. Snell	April, 1939
Dr. Robert K. Atkinson	April, 1940
Andrew J. Fox	March, 1941
Walter J. Halliday	April, 1941
John J. Hayes	January, 1942
George S. Storms, Jr.	April, 1942
Charles G. Schultheis	April, 1943
Joseph Huber	April, 1943
Carl A. Espach	April, 1944
Henry S. DeMott	April, 1944
Arthur D. DeMott	April, 1945
Julius C. Behnke	April, 1945
Leon J. morgan	March, 1946
Ellis B. Baker iii	Apilr, 1947
John A. anderson	April, 1950
Raymond C. Williams	April, 1952

MILTON H. CASH	October, 1954
ROBERT M. STEWART	April, 1955
ALBERT A. RUBIN	April, 1959
CHARLES V. DAY	October, 1962
FRED A. OTT	May, 1963
LEONARD SANDEL	March, 1967
PHILIP J. EISENHAUER	March, 1967
GERARD F. DIGAN	April, 1968
FREDERICK P. COLE	March, 1969

VILLAGE OF ROCKVILLE CENTRE

Presidents and Mayors

1	John Lyons	July 15, 1893
2	Charles W. Hayes	August 16, 1894
3	Edwin D. Seabury	March 21, 1898
4	George W. Smith	March 27, 1899
5	William Richensteen	March 22, 1909
6	Thomas L. Murphy	March 21, 1911
7	D. N. Bulson	March 22, 1912
8	Edwin W. Wallace	March 21, 1916
9	Edwin G. Wright	March 20, 1917
10	Edwin W. Wallace	March 25, 1918
11	Joseph F. Russ (in absence of Wallace)	July 24, 1918
12	Joseph F. Russ	March 18, 1919
13	Morley K. Dunn	March 16, 1920
14	Edwin W. Wallace	March 21, 1921
15	David R. Longenecker	March 27, 1922
16	G. B. Latimer	March 26, 1923
17	Joseph Monds	March 24, 1924
18	Charles Richmond (acting)	March 7, 1925
19	Charles Richmond (appointed)	June 10, 1925
20	Horace Allen	March 17, 1931
21	Edgar Beamish	March 18, 1941
22	Walter Halliday	March 16, 1943
23	George E. Storms (acting)	March 22, 1944
24	Walter Halliday (returned)	January 10, 1945
25	W. Harry Lister	March 20, 1945
26	John A. Anderson	March 21, 1967